Traits of a Happy Couple

Larry L. Halter, Ph.D.

Illustrations by James Bradrick

WORD BOOKS
PUBLISHER
WACO, TEXAS

A DIVISION OF
WORD, INCORPORATED

DEDICATION

To Linda—
If we'd only known.

TRAITS OF A HAPPY COUPLE

Copyright © 1988 by Larry L. Halter. All rights reserved. No
portion of this book may be reproduced in any form, except for brief
quotations in reviews or as instructed in the text, without written
permission from the publisher.

Library of Congress Cataloging-in-Publication Data:

Halter, Larry L. (Larry Lee), 1936–
    Traits of a happy couple / Larry L. Halter.
        p.   cm.
    Bibliography: p.
    ISBN 0-8499-3117-7 (pbk.)
    1. Marriage—United States.   2. Communication in marriage.
3. Marriage counseling—United States.   4. Interpersonal relations.
I. Title.
HQ734.H256   1988   88-5716
646.7′8—dc19   CIP

Printed in the United States of America

8 9 8 0 1 2 3 9 RRD 9 8 7 6 5 4 3 2 1

CONTENTS

LIST OF FIGURES

ACKNOWLEDGMENTS

This book is based on some landmark research that happened between 1975 and 1985. During that time, 130 family scholars completed seventy-five studies on the cause and cure for marriage breakdown. Thanks to their research, we now know what makes marriage work. Without the work of these behavior scientists, *TRAITS OF A HAPPY COUPLE* could not have been written.

Thanks to the many people who took an interest in this book. Special recognition goes to Mr. Bill Perry and his fine staff at Hamburger Patti's: Jennifer Busse, Kathy Corbin, Julie Corbus, Jennifer Corbus, Karen Dixon, Barbara Hearn, Debbie Hulscher, Timothy Jensen, Taffy Johnson, Julie McEntee, Marceen Miller and Jamie, Angie Navarra, Lisa Opoka, Emily Perry, Dagny Regan, Wendy Shelton, Richard Venable, and Laura Walker. Their concern boosted me as I wrote the book. Their constant question, "When's it going to be finished?" gave me energy and helped me realize that maybe there was an audience who really wanted to know how to have a happy marriage.

I also want to thank the people at Acacia, especially Mr. Ken Kallmeyer, who gave me a place to write, and his staff, who took an interest in the project: Noel Allen, Jean Borde, Dan Croy, Ken Gates, Scott Hastings, Brent Hamilton, Tim Haveman, Earl Hinds, Stuart Jorge, Linda Murphy, Larry Pember, and Dan Walters. A very special note of thanks to Wendy Jean Mitchell, who gave me words; Pat Wood, who helped me learn to use the computer; and Robert Taylor, who advised.

Friends played an important role in completing this book. Special thanks to my good friend Don Sass, who believed in me and shared my vision; to Donna Scarth, who gave me a valuable book at just the right time; to Elaine Grannis and Don Fivecoat for their enthusiasm. Thanks to Dick and Kathy Hurley, Mac and Marlene Soderquist, Carolyn Ballard, Sharon Templeman, Carla Land, and Rev. John Denney, who read chapters and gave me important feedback. Special mention also goes to Jim Campbell, who kept reminding me that conclusions and thinking habits play a critical role in marital success. I am also grateful to Barbara Woolensack, who helped design the BEST graphics.

And thanks to the members of my family: To my sister, Linda Hancock, who advised me about the manuscript. I owe much to Mom and Dad, who put up with my presence, especially Mom, who proofread the manuscript and cooked the best meals ever. To my children— Heidi, Hugh, and Hayley—thanks for your interest and support.

Thanks to my colleagues who helped on the book. To James Bradrick for his excellent art work and ability to draw concepts. My thanks to Sally Stuart, who contributed much to this project by helping make the scientific research friendly and readable.

Finally, I thank Word Publishing for giving me a chance to tell a story with a happy ending—with special thanks to Beverly Phillips for her useful ideas and effective editing, and Jim Nelson Black for guiding this challenging project through some unforeseen hazards.

INTRODUCTION

All of us believe we know how to be married, but sad statistics tell us otherwise: One out of two marriages fail, and of the couples who remain together, 75 percent report unhappiness (these are the "emotionally divorced"). And when one considers that half of all first-time admissions to psychiatric hospitals are caused by the stress of a bad marriage, it's clear we are not playing the marriage game very well.

No one gets divorced alone. Each year, 2 million children watch their parents divorce. These young people become "high risk" kids—the ones most likely to suffer learning problems or turn to delinquency and crime. When we count up all the adults and children touched by marital breakdown, there are a lot of hurting people in our land.

The end of a marriage is an awful thing—a devastating experience that affects body, mind, and soul. Emotionally, it brings the pain of rejection, loneliness, guilt, shame, and failure. Death has been called the ultimate stress, but divorce is a close second. A major assault on the human system, divorce is the psychological equivalent of a triple coronary bypass. It can take years for the ripping and tearing caused by a broken relationship to heal. I know; I still carry the scars of a broken marriage.

During my own tragedy, I was especially tormented by confusion and the sense of failure. How could this have happened to me? I had three college degrees and loads of knowledge about human relationships. Yet, I still failed. Why? What went wrong? Whose fault was it? Did I pick the wrong mate? Then came the bigger questions: What is it that allows some couples to get along so well? What are their secrets? What behaviors set them apart from the rest of us? Does anybody really know?

At first, I tried to unravel this riddle myself. But looking for answers in my own mind only tempted me to explain my failure by casting

7

blame. I soon realized that marriage is too complicated for self-analysis and began to look elsewhere. Because of my background in research it seemed to me that the place for the most objective answers might be the university library. It was here I finally learned what makes marriage work.

For a year, I buried myself in a world of exciting, new knowledge. Since 1949, scientists had been searching for the secrets to marital happiness, but the most useful discoveries occurred from 1975 to 1985. In that period, seventy-five research projects were conducted by many teams of family scholars.

Their stories fascinated me. Like expert detectives looking for clues to an unsolved crime, these behavior scientists had explored couples from every conceivable angle. They studied both good and bad marriages to pinpoint key differences. They investigated small groups of couples as well as groups of several hundred. They looked at new marriages and those of couples in retirement. They focused on how couples solve fights, negotiate conflicts, and change one another. They videotaped couples and analyzed their behavior with sophisticated computers. And they carefully observed couples in both home settings and experimental laboratories. As I reviewed these revelations, I was convinced that it was priceless knowledge—these scientists had discovered why some marriages succeed and others fail. The great mystery of how to have a happy marriage was solved. This was exciting news!

As I read the research, three things leaped out at me. First, since many of the studies had compared both happy and unhappy couples, vital differences had been spotted—five key traits distinguished these couples. This discovery is an extremely important find. No longer do we have to wonder about what causes marital happiness—the "happy couple" has been defined; now we have a successful model to follow.

The second thing that came to my attention was that these researchers had also developed effective treatment programs for distressed couples. The five traits that lead to a happy marriage could be learned by others. This was also heartening news—unhappy couples can be changed! I have since confirmed this good news with couples in my own counseling practice.

The third fact that caught my attention was that the new marriage science was like a well-kept secret. While it had been communicated to professionals in psychology, counseling, and sociology, this much-needed knowledge had been hidden from public view.

So after reading the research, teaching the key traits to other couples, and recognizing that these truths had not been openly shared, it was only natural to take the next step and write a book of hope telling about these remarkable advances in human relationships.

Among marriage books, this one is unique. While most of us

struggle with marriage, few ever seek out trained counselors for help during the stress times. And since "Mohammed" rarely comes to the "mountain," the mountain will come to you. Using my background in clinical counseling, I have decided to tell a story of a troubled couple who bring their sick marriage to a counselor for treatment. It's a case study, and you are invited to tag along and learn with them.

The book has two purposes: One, it will explain the five traits—the conditions, behaviors, skills, characteristics, components, factors, and determiners—which make marriage run smoothly. Two, it will show step-by-step how to add these essential traits to your marriage.

As you read this story, please keep this in mind: Marriage is the most difficult and demanding of all human relationships. It's too important for wild guesses, uneducated opinions, or half-baked theories. What we need to do is apply some solid, common-sense science. That's the most positive way of helping enrich and renew a marriage.

Larry L. Halter

HOW TO USE THIS BOOK

You are about to read a story of an unhappy couple—Tom and Jean—as they are successfully guided through a series of counseling sessions by a knowledgeable marital therapist—Dr. Martin. You will be able to watch their progress as they move from the edge of despair and divorce to hope, reconciliation, and renewal of their marriage.

Because this story is a case study—not a textbook on science—you can read it quickly and easily. It will probably take only a few days to read the book cover-to-cover. But completing all the homework assignments or "Enrichment Activities" will take several weeks. These useful activities are found at the end of each counseling session and are aimed at helping you practice the traits and marriage skills necessary for relationship happiness. To gain the most from this book, it is vital that you do these activities in the time frame given.

Here are some specific guidelines to follow as you read the book:

1. If possible, find a competent counselor to supervise you as you learn the traits and skills presented in this book.

2. Take the Happiness Test (see Appendix A) two times. Take it as you begin the story and again after you have read the book and carried out all Enrichment Activities. This before-and-after testing will allow you to see how much progress or growth has happened in your marriage. Session One and Appendix A will tell you how to self-administer the test and how to send it for scoring.

3. Read the counseling sessions in order—do not skip around. This way, you will learn the "happy-couple traits" in a logical sequence: First, you will learn attitude skills, then caring skills, behavior change skills, problem-solving skills, self-esteem skills, and companionship skills. Follow this sequence in order!

4. Remember to do all Enrichment Activities at the end of each session. Be especially diligent to complete the "Partner-Pleasing"

skills found in Session Four—this is the heart of the book and uses a checklist called the BEST.* It will take fourteen days to finish.

5. Do not attempt to solve major relationship problems immediately. For most couples, it is tempting to jump right into tackling big problems—such as poor communication. But while communication is essential, it is not the starting point for rebuilding or enriching a marriage. Attitude skills and partner-pleasing skills must be learned first.

6. Please keep this in mind: While the book can be read in just a short time, it will take about four to five weeks to complete all Enrichment Activities. Be patient and the rewards of a happier marriage will result.

Now we are ready for a little "couch time" in the counselor's office.

---

* A companion book, *Traits of a Happy Couple Study Guide* also by Larry Halter, offers the Happiness Test and BEST Checklist in a larger format with perforations for easy removal, along with a Christian readers' guide to *Traits of a Happy Couple*.

Rebuilding a Marriage

THE UNHAPPY COUPLE

Tom and Jean entered the counselor's waiting room in silence and sat on opposite ends of the couch. The fact that they did not sit close together said a lot about the mood of their marriage. It was one of separateness, discord, and a growing dissatisfaction with each other. The small waiting room filled with the tension of unspoken words.

Most Saturdays found Tom on the golf course. But not today. Instead of chasing golf balls, Tom sat chasing answers to some tough questions: *Why was their marriage failing? What had caused their relationship to deteriorate so badly that they both saw divorce as the only way out? Who was at fault?*

This wasn't the first time Tom had asked these questions. Even though he considered himself a fair and objective person, his conclusions were always the same—Jean was mostly to blame. She was a nagging, critical, disapproving wife. Her sharp tongue and you-never-do-anything-right attitude toward him were the cause. Deep down Tom wondered if this marriage counselor could change her into the gentle, nurturing, affirming spouse he wanted. Tom caught a glimpse of Jean over the top of the magazine he pretended to read. She was still an attractive lady—but not a friend.

Jean sat biting her lip. She was close to tears as she thought about the unhappiness in their marriage, but she was determined not to cry in the counselor's office. Jean was also thinking about what had caused their marriage to collapse. She knew exactly who the villain was. Tom! He had never given their marriage top priority. For eighteen years,

other events and people had come first—work, golf, the kids, and TV were more important to Tom than their relationship. More than anything, Jean wanted to be valued and made to feel that she was in first place. But over the years, she had been at the bottom of Tom's totem pole. The painful recognition that she was last in his life left her with feelings of inferiority and low self-esteem. Tears filled her eyes. A few splashed on the magazine that lay on her lap.

In spite of the tears, Jean did feel a small sense of victory. She had finally pulled Tom off the golf course long enough to come to counseling with her. Maybe now this counselor could make Tom see that it was *his* fault they were on the edge of divorce. Maybe this Dr. Martin, whom she had only spoken with briefly on the phone, could change Tom into the loving, affectionate husband she had always longed for. He *had* to make Tom see that their marriage deserved top priority.

Both Tom and Jean looked up self-consciously as the door to the inner office opened. The man standing in the doorway was short, pudgy, and fiftyish. He smiled broadly and extended his hand to greet them. "Hello," he said. "I'm John Martin. And you must be the

Andersons. Feel free to call me John or Dr. Martin—whatever you are comfortable with. Please come in and sit down."

LEARNING THE TRAITS OF HAPPY COUPLES

Tom and Jean were ill at ease, but began to relax a little as they sat down, accepted a cup of coffee, and made small talk with Dr. Martin about the collection of World War II airplane pictures that covered his office walls.

Dr. Martin then turned the conversation to the reason for their visit. "I understand this is your first time in marriage counseling, so I want you to know it's normal to feel a little uptight. I'm sure you're wondering just what we will be doing in these sessions and, most of all, if it's going to make a difference in your marriage. It's important to know where you are going, so to help you understand what's ahead, I'll explain how I approach marital therapy. Then you can tell me why you came for counseling—what your goals are, what you expect to get out of it, and the specific problems you'd like to solve."

When Tom and Jean heard Dr. Martin mention goals, they both had the same thought: *Goals? You bet I have goals! I want you to change my mate into the kind of partner I need. Then I'll be happy.* But they kept their silence and continued to listen.

"Before I share my counseling philosophy, there are a couple of things I want to say. First, I want to affirm your decision to come into counseling. I know it's embarrassing and awkward to admit something's wrong, and that your relationship is in trouble. There are so many miserable couples with mediocre marriages who won't take the important step you are taking. Tom, I especially want to applaud you. Husbands are usually reluctant to let someone help them with marriage problems. Wives are generally more willing to accept counseling. But for both of you, I'm glad that you've had the courage to admit your unhappiness and begin to do something about it."

"Well, it's nice to know someone sees I'm trying," said Tom, throwing a barb at Jean.

"Second," continued Dr. Martin, "you need to realize that marriage is the most demanding human relationship that adults face."

"Boy, that's an understatement if I ever heard one!"

"Tom, will you stop interrupting?" scolded Jean. "We're never going to get anywhere if you keep butting in!"

"As I was saying, marriage is a terribly hard relationship. Of all the relationships we form in life the husband-wife relationship is the most difficult to make successful. Let me show you what I mean." Dr. Martin walked over to a flip-chart where he began writing. "Marriage is hard because you must continually work through these thirteen major conflict areas."

"I've never seen anyone put all the problems down on a list like that before. It looks like a pretty impossible list—you have to be 'Super Couple' to get through those."

"Yes, Tom, it is a difficult list. And to complicate matters, we have to cope with these thirteen problem areas without having the necessary knowledge or insight about what makes marriage work. The point is this: We all thought we knew how to be married—but we really didn't. No one ever showed us the special traits, skills, and behaviors which make a happy marriage. No one educated us about relationships. So naturally, we've got some learning gaps that need to be filled. It certainly would have helped if we could have all attended some kind of 'marriage school' to learn how to be perfect partners, but unfortunately, none of us did. So it's no wonder that most of us struggle with marriage."

"Well, I'll enroll Tom if it'll help. He could certainly use some lessons in being a better husband."

AREAS OF CONFLICT
1. Care
2. Communication
3. Empathy
4. Sex
5. Parenting
6. Friendship
7. Independence
8. Self-Esteem
9. Household Tasks
10. Money
11. Personal Habits
12. Job/School
13. Problem-Solving

"Just ignore her, Dr. Martin. She's not happy unless she's on my case about something."

Dr. Martin was keenly aware of the negative exchanges between the couple. In the few minutes they had been in his office, he had seen them both aim critical darts and put-downs at each other. He knew that this kind of behavior was normal for most couples who enter counseling, and that a good counselor must thwart this sniping tendency early in the therapy process. But Dr. Martin decided this wasn't the right time to confront them about their hostile attitudes. He continued.

"Tom, I understand that you're a golfer."

"I sure am."

"Well, a good marriage is like a good golf game. You must play with a full set of clubs if you're ever going to maneuver that little white ball into the hole. It would be pretty frustrating to try to play the whole game with only a putter. It's the same with marriage—you must have all the right traits and a full set of skills to help work through those thirteen relationship problems. We can't be expected to play the marriage game successfully without key traits, skills, and knowledge."

"Dr. Martin, I wish you hadn't mentioned golfing," said Jean; "that's a sore spot around our house, but I do understand about the need for the right tools. I attended a course on marriage at my church, and I've read all kinds of books on the subject. I know more about marriage already than I know what to do with."

"I like to hear you talk about golf and marriage," rebutted Tom. "It makes sense that marriage requires some skills. But what skills and traits are you talking about? Do you mean things like flying off the handle, being bossy, and having a sharp tongue?"

"No, Tom. When I use the word *trait*, I'm not talking about personality traits like anger, dominance, or being critical. I use the words *trait, skill,* and *behavior* to mean the same thing. Traits are unique characteristics, and we now know there is a special group of factors that make marriage easier."

"You mean marriage really can be easier?"

"Absolutely, Tom. Thanks to recent research, we know what skills make a good marriage. Most people don't realize it, but during 1975 to 1985, behavioral scientists conducted seventy-five research studies. The subjects were both happy and unhappy couples, and some dramatic discoveries were made. By comparing the behaviors of these two groups, they found out what relationship traits help couples succeed and which ones lead to failure. The most important finding of these landmark studies was that these couples differ in five distinct ways. I'll show you what I mean." Dr. Martin then stepped to the flip chart and listed the five key traits that distinguish good and bad marriages.

"The type of counseling I'll use with you is based on these five traits. If you choose to stay with me in counseling, it will be my job to teach you how to add them to your marriage. I feel optimistic that when you learn the traits and practice them daily, it will help you have an above-average marriage. I hope this helps you to understand my approach to marital counseling."

"Sounds okay to me," responded Tom.

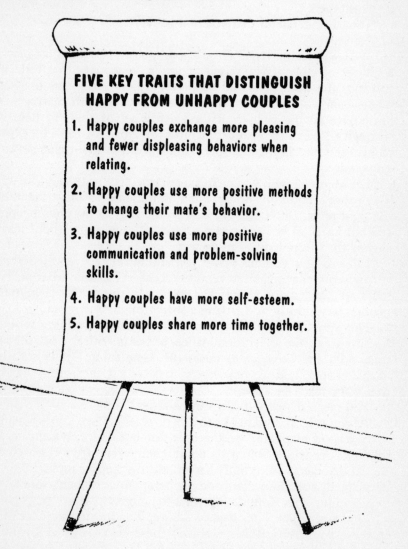

FIVE KEY TRAITS THAT DISTINGUISH HAPPY FROM UNHAPPY COUPLES

1. Happy couples exchange more pleasing and fewer displeasing behaviors when relating.

2. Happy couples use more positive methods to change their mate's behavior.

3. Happy couples use more positive communication and problem-solving skills.

4. Happy couples have more self-esteem.

5. Happy couples share more time together.

"I don't know, Dr. Martin. In some ways I'm glad to hear that you're using the latest research, but at the same time, I get turned off by being told I have to do something just because some so-called marriage experts say so. How do we know any of this will work with us? I'm not in the mood to be someone's guinea pig. I'm just not sure about all this science."

"I understand your concern, Jean, but the reason I put a lot of stock in this approach is because this kind of counseling is the best supported of any approach to marital therapy. This method of counseling has shown extremely positive results—three out of four couples who are trained in these skills substantially improve their marriage. Not all couples get better, but most do. You see, the reason we get such good results is that we now have successful models to follow—the happy couples.

"Most of us never have the chance to peek into the relationships of happy couples to see what makes their marriage work so well. But with this new research we know what successful couples have in common. We have a profile. We know how they communicate and solve problems. We know their unique way of interacting that makes them happy. With this scientific knowledge to guide us, we don't have to guess about the best way to help couples improve their marriage. We know that the attributes of the well-adjusted couple can be copied by others. So Jean, that's why I'm confident that whatever is troubling you and Tom can be helped by applying this science to your marriage."

RESISTANCE

An interesting thing had happened to the couple since they came into Dr. Martin's office. Tom had come reluctantly, not sure this was anything but a waste of time. Jean, however, had been excited about the chance for counseling, feeling sure it would be the answer to all her problems with Tom. But now, Tom was responding to the logic of the counselor's words. He enjoyed hearing Dr. Martin talk about golf, and being asked to learn some new skills was okay with him. Tom had gone from reluctant to ready.

In contrast, Jean had flip-flopped. Each time the word *golf* was used, sirens and red lights went off in her head—she almost felt that Dr. Martin and Tom were in collusion against her. And the very thought of learning more skills was a turn-off for her. In her mind, she was already well-schooled in marriage skills. Furthermore, she was especially suspicious about bringing science into marriage. In a matter of a few minutes, Jean had gone from ready to resistant.

THE BLAME GAME

"Well, I've been doing all the talking. Now, let's talk about you. Tell me why you came into counseling."

Tom began, "We just can't get along. We've both been unhappy for a long time. It's gotten so bad that we think separation and divorce might be the only answer. We can't talk without fighting, and we never agree on anything—big problems or small. There's a long list of things that aren't settled—sex problems, how to discipline the kids, how to manage our money. Instead of finding solutions, we just argue and dredge up new things to fight about. Problems are piled up all over the house, and we keep bumping into them. We can't even get along two days in a row before another fight breaks out. I feel so defeated about our bad communication that I have no motivation to try to work things out. I'd rather stay at work late or go golfing where I can at least find some success."

When Tom mentioned the word *golf*, it triggered an explosion inside Jean's mind. With hurt and anger in her voice she said, "Dr. Martin, *that's* the reason our marriage is a failure. Tom's dumb golf game is more important to him than our relationship. His golfing buddies mean more to him than I do. He should have married a golf ball." And with a wagging finger at Tom, she raised her voice and poured out more anger, "It's all Tom's fault! He just doesn't care about me or . . ."

Before Jean could finish, Tom interrupted with a counterattack. "How come you see everyone else's faults and are blind to your own? I'll tell you why I play so much golf—it's better than staying home and listening to all your nagging and yelling. I'm fed up with it! It doesn't matter what I do; I can't please you. You've never once told me I was a good provider or thanked me for the things I've given you and the boys. I work long hours to give you all the things you want, but you never show any gratitude for it. If you weren't always tearing me down with your ripping tongue, maybe I'd feel more like being around you. I'm sick of your critical attitude and the way you put me down in front of the kids. You've got a lot of changes to make, Jean. This marriage is falling apart because of you!"

THE GREAT DISTORTION

Dr. Martin listened to the negative talk between Tom and Jean—angry voices, attacks and counterattacks, interruptions, hostile gestures, and blaming. It was obvious that one of his therapy goals would be to help them change this destructive communication pattern by

showing them how happy couples communicate. It was clear why a
mountain of unresolved problems had accumulated—Tom and Jean's
poor communication skills and inability to fight fair stood in the way
of any problem-solving. But before Dr. Martin could teach them how
to be better problem-solvers, he had a more important task: He must
get them to deal with the crucial mental factors of distortion and
blame. This meant that the couple would have to accept a realistic
perspective of how their marriage had failed, and they would have to
stop blaming. A change in their thinking would be the first step in
rebuilding this marriage.

The correction of faulty thinking plays a big role in determining
whether or not couples will improve their marriage. If there are irrational conclusions, faultfinding, or thinking distortions, it is doubtful
that a marriage can be healed. Such thinking problems are common in
unhappy couples. Troubled couples who have spent months, even
years, in conflict and the pain of unmet needs usually enter counseling hurling blame and accusations at each other. Tom and Jean were
no exception—they each felt their suffering was caused by the other
spouse. They saw themselves as blameless and their spouse at fault.
They believed their marriage would improve only if their mate made
all the changes.

Dr. Martin knew better. Tom and Jean had each contributed to the
problem. Thus, the prescription for their happiness required that they
both make changes. This approach to marriage interaction is what psychologists call "mutual-cause-mutual-change." Teaching this concept
to couples is usually the first goal in counseling.

CHANGING A BLAMING ATTITUDE:
THE CONFRONTATION

With this goal in mind, Dr. Martin confronted the couple, who
were locked in heated battle. "Hold it, both of you. Blaming is not
going to help—it won't bring happiness into your marriage. As long
as you are in counseling with me, there's one unbreakable, relationship rule I'm asking you to obey: No blaming!

"Each of you believes your partner is responsible for the problems
in your marriage. Jean, you think it's because Tom has put you last
over all these years. Tom, you think it's because Jean nags and criticizes. You each see yourself as faultless and not needing to change.
You think that if the other person would only change, you'd instantly
be a happy couple."

"You said it, Dr. Martin. If Jean would just stop her constant nagging,
I'd be a lot happier, and our marriage would be a whole lot better."

"Sure, Tom, blame it all on me—that's what you've been doing for years," said Jean as she fought back the tears.

"Whoa!" called Dr. Martin. "You're both breaking the rule already. Now, I need you to listen carefully so I can explain two reasons why blaming is wrong—why it's counterproductive." Dr. Martin then walked to the flip chart to show what he meant.

"First, blaming assumes that one person wrecked the marriage. But the real perspective is this: Marriage is a dance done by two and seldom is one spouse at fault.* You've both contributed to the crisis in your marriage. Unfortunately, you haven't had the opportunity to learn the

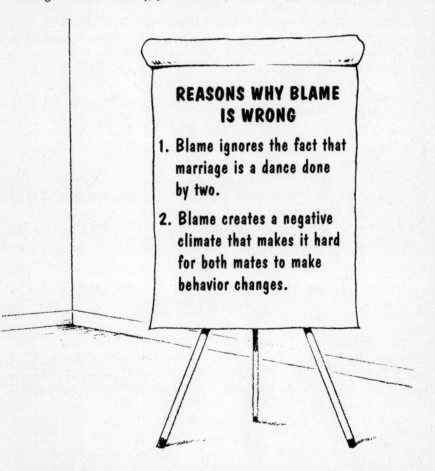

REASONS WHY BLAME IS WRONG

1. Blame ignores the fact that marriage is a dance done by two.

2. Blame creates a negative climate that makes it hard for both mates to make behavior changes.

* In *Helping Couples Change: A Social Learning Approach to Marriage Therapy* (Guilford Press, 1980, p. 192), R. B. Stuart describes marriage as a "dance done by two people" to express the idea that marriage difficulties are seldom the fault of the husband or wife alone—there is always some measure of shared blame for a failure.

positive ways to problem-solve or change each other. And as a result, problems have heaped up around you.

"Besides these skill deficiencies, you also lack some vital insights about what factors build a happy relationship. Without these skills and insights, a lot of pain has come into your marriage—hurt, anger, resentment, mistrust, and frustrated needs. You've been in this pain for so long that your mind is mixed up. Distortions happen. You lose your objectivity. Right now, you're hurting so much that you're blind to your own behavior. The belief that your mate is the fault is a distortion—it's not real.

"There's a second reason why you can't cast blame: It creates a negative atmosphere for change. A blaming position puts the whole responsibility for change on your mate. And when you shift the task for improving the marriage to your spouse, you become passive while you wait for your partner to do all the work. The act of blame takes away your energy, initiative, and motivation. When you blame, you stop making effort. The worst thing about blame is that it makes marriage rebuilding a one-person process, but the truth is it takes two people to bring about relationship change. You can easily see what happens when you both blame and abandon your responsibilities for behavior change—nothing gets done. There's no progress. It's an impasse. If your marriage isn't going anywhere, it may be a matter of blame and distorted thinking about your mate. That's why you have to keep the 'No Blaming' rule. A different approach is to take a cooperative attitude of 'we caused it together; now, let's change it together.' You've got to get in the same boat, grab an oar, and pull with all your might—together."

Dr. Martin was working hard to give Tom and Jean a new perspective of why their marriage had failed. He was trying to convince them to re-examine the cause of their unhappiness. He was hoping they would re-attribute the source of their problems to "bad relationship skills"—not to "bad people" in the relationship.

But Jean hardly heard what Dr. Martin had said about burying blame. "Dr. Martin, I just can't buy your idea that we're both equally to blame for our poor marriage. You haven't seen Tom over the years like I have—his job and sports always come first. Can't you see how wrong he's been in not taking time to be with me? He never talks to me or takes me anywhere. I feel so lonely and rejected—like such a nothing. You've got to set him straight about how he's ruined this marriage."

Dr. Martin could see Jean's pain of low self-esteem. He acknowledged her suffering but also reminded her about the blame problem. "Jean, I can sense your hurt, but until you are ready to stop hugging those old grudges and pointing a blaming finger at Tom, I won't be able to help you. I'm sure Tom has made some errors in not fitting you into his life, but I doubt they were intentional. I'm guessing he didn't maliciously plan to put you last. Maybe Tom does put his job first, but his whole self-esteem is built on his ability to make money, achieve career goals, and become a success at work. He's only doing what his male subculture has programmed him to do. Unfortunately, Jean, you got left out of the picture. Without knowing it, Tom has deeply affected your feelings of self-worth.

"Nevertheless, here's what I'm asking you to do: You must put the brakes on blaming. You must not fault Tom for your unhappiness. As I've said, blaming makes it hard for both of you to change. When you think *Tom is at fault, he's got to make the changes* or *I'm okay, but he's not okay*, Tom gets defensive and you stop trying. If you convince yourself that he's responsible and has to make all the changes, you are naturally going to sit back and do nothing. When disaster strikes—and marriage collapse is a disaster—it's only human to look for someone to blame. But if you're looking at Tom as the reason for your marriage difficulty, then you are looking in the wrong direction—you must also look at yourself and be open to change. It's vital that you shift your attention away from blaming Tom and focus on the need for both of you to make changes.

"Jean, there's something else I'm asking you to do: You must face up to your distortion of seeing Tom as the cause. I know it's hard to believe what I'm saying, but marriages don't decay because of just one spouse—you both caused the failure. It's critical, Jean, that you accept this new belief about the cause and cure for your problems. I am confident that if you can stop blaming and start cooperating with Tom, it will help him make the kind of behavior changes you want."

Dr. Martin then shifted his attention toward Tom to confront him with the mutual-cause–mutual-change idea. "Tom, I want to also stress to you what I've been telling Jean about marital conflict: *Marriage unhappiness does not result from the behavior of one mate but from the negative interaction of both mates.* I want to say this without criticism—you're both responsible for the problems in your marriage. So you must both make changes. The best way to improve a marriage is to replace blaming behavior with cooperative behavior. My whole counseling program is based on this rationale.

"I know it's hard to see yourself as being responsible for any of the problems when all you see are Jean's negative communication habits. I can understand how her nagging, criticism, and harshness would drive you away and keep you from wanting to talk with her or spend time with her. But when you work long hours or escape to TV and golf, Jean misinterprets that to mean you don't love her or want to be with her. There's something you must learn about your wife, Tom—a relationship with you is her key source of self-esteem. When you put other things ahead of her, she's not sure of her personal value. She feels hurt, discarded, and insignificant. Before long, the hurt and rejection turn to anger, and she jumps on you with even more criticism and hostility. Both of you will have to work hard to break this negative reactionary cycle—Jean needs to be gentle, and you need to pay more attention to her."

"Dr. Martin, it sounds like if we're going to put our marriage back together, we'll have to make it a 'team sport' where we get on the same side and pull on the same end of the rope—not against each other."

"I like the way you put it, Tom. And to have a winning team, you have to admit that each of you has weaknesses that are affecting the team—and then learn to work together to change those things that are causing problems. It does no good if half the team sits on the bench and lets the other half do all the work."

"Dr. Martin, you've spent a lot of time talking to us about blame— and I can see the logic in what you're saying. But that still doesn't change the fact that Tom's made me miserable. I still believe he's more to blame than I am. I want to do my part, but it's really hard to accept what you're saying."

"Acceptance of new ideas comes slowly, Jean. Remember, your attitude of blame did not happen overnight; the truth is both of you lost touch with reality a long time ago. Now I realize my speech-making won't change your mind immediately. As I've said, when you're in pain and your need to be cared for is not being satisfied, it's hard to be objective. Right now, Jean, you only see one side of the problem— your own. Naturally, it's easier for me to be a neutral observer and see both sides of it, and I hope that is why you are here—to get an objective analysis of why your marriage is failing. Yes, it's normal to resist the idea of mutual blame, but I still want you to be open to that fresh, new perspective. It will release you from the destructive blame game so that you can redirect your energy into the work of rebuilding your marriage."

DECISION AND COMMITMENT

"Most couples think counseling is where you come in and talk about your partner's faults. But it's more than that—it's a place to get perspective. Each of you came in today believing that your partner was the problem, but the real problem was an incorrect perception, a blaming attitude, and distorted thinking. You thought your bad marriage was caused by your mate. But in these last few minutes, I've asked you to disagree with that distortion. I've encouraged you to replace it with a new point of view that says you both unknowingly caused the discord and that you both need to change behavior—an idea called 'mutual-cause–mutual-change.'

"Mutual-cause–mutual-change is the starting point for improving a marriage. It means you look for solutions, not blame. It means you can't abdicate your duty to change behavior. It means you will have to restructure your thinking and put your failings into perspective. Perspective is everything!

"It sounds like I'm up on my soapbox again, doesn't it? But I want you to see how important thinking is to your happiness. I've got to be very frank with you about your thinking and attitudes. It is doubtful we can remedy your situation if you hold stubbornly to distortions, blame, and wrong explanations. It's normal to want to make sense of a distressing experience like a failing marriage. But when your thinking is wrong, you end up explaining your unhappiness by pointing an accusing finger at your mate. Blame is a dangerous thinking pattern that blocks change. To be quite blunt, it will be difficult to make progress if you hang on to your old thinking.

"So, at this point, I have some key questions for you. Can you think differently? Can you see that you have contributed to the problem? Can you accept the idea that you are partly to blame? Can you join forces and work as a team instead of spending your energy being angry and fault-finding? Can you build new conclusions about what caused your marriage to fail? Are you ready to see your marriage problems from a new perspective? If you can say yes to most of these questions, we can move ahead and learn the five key traits that characterize happy couples."

Tom and Jean sat quietly for a moment. Tom was the first to speak. "I don't know how Jean feels about it, but I can't take much more of the way things are. What you're saying makes sense. I don't know if we can do it—we're both feeling worn out with this marriage—but I'm willing to try."

"All right, Dr. Martin, I'll give it a try, too. This isn't what I expected to happen today. I was so sure of what the problem was when I came in—now I'm confused. But something's got to change—Tom's right about that. I just hope we have enough emotional energy left to make the changes you're talking about."

"You've both made a wise decision—one I'm sure you won't regret. I hope you don't think I've been too hard on you today or that I'm unsympathetic to your individual concerns. I've listened, and I think I understand where each of you is coming from. In time, you will come to realize that I had to confront your faulty conclusions and cause you to rethink the blame problem—that's the starting point for helping couples rebuild a shaky marriage. Treating your marriage begins with changes in thinking. Well, we have a lot of work ahead of us, and our time is nearly up for today."

HOMEWORK ASSIGNMENTS

The Happiness Test

"Before you go, I have a homework assignment for you." Dr. Martin handed them each a form. "You need to independently complete these forms—it will only take about fifteen minutes—and then mail them back to me. This is called the 'Dyadic Adjustment Scale,' which was developed by Graham B. Spanier,* but don't let the big name scare you. It is simply a happiness test to show how satisfied or dissatisfied you are with your marriage. It measures the degree of happiness, adjustment, or distress in your relationship."

"I thought by now you'd know how unhappy we are, Dr. Martin. I wouldn't think you'd need a test to prove that?" questioned Jean.

"I know how unhappy you think you are right now, but this test will give us an objective measure of just how unhappy you *really* are. It's a pre-test—it gives us a starting point or a benchmark; we can't get anywhere unless we know where we're starting from. Our job, then, will be to work hard to raise that level of happiness by learning the happy-couple traits. When our counseling sessions are over, you will take the test again. That way, you can see how much growth and change have occurred. Do you have any questions about what to do?"

The No-Fight Rule

"My question is not about the happiness test," responded Jean. "When are we going to start talking about some of our really big problems? I'm very upset about Tom's horrible relationship with our oldest son, Chris. And we are always arguing about money and sex. I think these are the real reasons why our marriage is so bad. These unsettled things put so much tension in our marriage. This is why we came to see you in the first place."

"I was going to ask the same question," said Tom. "What are we going to do with all our conflicts? We haven't learned anything yet that will help us deal with them. We need answers fast—I don't want another week of fighting with Jean."

---

* See pages 175-177 in this book and pages 11-12 in the separate *Traits of a Happy Couple Study Guide.*

"I understand your concerns. I realize that you came in with some long-standing problems and complaints about each other. Yes, you need to get rid of these irritations because when problems stockpile, it only prompts the conclusion that your marriage is hopeless. I promise that we will eventually deal with these issues. In fact, we are going to spend a considerable amount of time learning some communication skills that you can apply to these conflicts. One of my counseling goals is to help you become effective problem-solvers. There's no doubt that you need to learn to communicate successfully in conflict situations, but now is not the time to learn these essential skills.

"There are two reasons why we need to postpone your problem-solving. First, we need to shift your attention from negatives to the positives in your marriage. At this early phase of rebuilding a marriage, it's not good for you to attack problems. You see, that's been your concentration for a long time—problems, problems, problems. No wonder you're burned-out! You've spent so much negative energy focusing on problems that you've reached a point where you don't like each other, don't trust each other, and you doubt your relationship will ever improve.

"So we need to set the problems aside and look at the positives. To do that, I'm going to give you some activities where you can achieve some immediate happiness, experience success, and discover that relationship improvement is possible. These activities will help you see good things in each other, build trust, bring changes, and help you feel cared for. If we can infuse your marriage with a quick dose of hope and happiness, it will prepare you to tackle the weighty problems that led you into counseling. But if we pay attention to problems, it steals the time that should be spent increasing those positive relationship behaviors.

"There's another reason for putting off problem-solving. As I said, our counseling goal now is to improve attitudes—not confront unsolved problems. Like most couples, you're very aware of your communication problems, but you don't see your attitude problems. It's normal to want to start right out working on conflicts. But first things must come first—changes in thinking must come before changes in communication. As you realize, I've spent a lot of time today talking about the importance of attitude, thinking, and perspective. I hope you are coming to see how they play a powerful role in determining whether or not your marriage will improve. Because thinking influences marital adjustment, happiness, and change, we still need to center our attention on the mental parts of marriage. We'll get into problem-solving discussions later, but for now, we must continue to help you build positive attitudes.

"I hope these two reasons help you see why we must temporarily put your unsolved problems on 'hold.' Now, I'm going to ask you to do a hard thing: For the next three weeks, I don't want you to deal with any problems at home. During that time, we will work on other things—dropping blaming attitudes, getting proper perspective, seeing strengths in your relationship, getting some small changes, putting care back into your marriage, and learning to be positive partners. So I want you to promise that you won't try to grapple with problems until you have the talk skills to deal with them. To problem-solve now would be like climbing a mountain without a safety rope—you'd be likely to fall and hurt yourselves. Do both of you understand this no-fighting rule?"

Tom and Jean exchanged glances of both frustration and relief. What a challenge! Could they really honor such a truce? It would be a real trick to avoid stumbling over the debris of unresolved conflicts that littered their home. It wouldn't be easy to hold their tongues and keep the peace. On the other hand, what a sense of relief—Dr. Martin had just given them permission to ignore the "monsters." He was right—they had been knocking heads for a long time. They certainly needed a rest from the fighting. Inwardly, they both endorsed the no-fight rule.

After a second counseling session was scheduled, Dr. Martin showed the couple to the door. Handshakes and goodbyes were exchanged. Tom and Jean had taken their first step toward becoming a happy couple.

ENRICHMENT ACTIVITIES FOR READERS

1. Complete the Happiness Test (the Dyadic Adjustment Scale) and return to the author for scoring. A copy of the test and directions are found on pages 175–177 in this book and on pages 11–12 of the *Traits of a Happy Couple Study Guide*. You may make four photocopies—a pre-test and a post-test for you and for your mate.
2. Make an agreement with your mate to keep the no-fight rule for the next three weeks.
3. Keep the no-blame rule.
4. Begin reading Session 2.

Changing Attitudes

As Tom and Jean settled into their chairs to begin their second session, Dr. Martin asked how things were going at home.

Tom began, "Well, we didn't get into any arguments. We had to tiptoe around each other all week—afraid we'd do something wrong before we got back here to get things straightened out. Your advice to stay away from trouble made sense, but it's been hard."

"That's understandable, Tom. I know it's like walking on egg shells, but I'm happy to hear that you avoided conflict. That showed cooperation—good for you! Jean, how did the week go for you?"

"Well, I'm glad you gave us the no-fight rule. That was the best part of my week—not getting into a new fight with Tom. It was easy to keep that rule, but I had a hard time keeping the no-blaming rule. I mean, inspite of all the time you spent telling us to stop blaming, my mind still holds Tom responsible for most of our problems. He's got more changes to make than me. I know that's not a good attitude, but that's honestly how I feel."

TURNING THE CORNER FROM BLAME
TO COOPERATION

Dr. Martin listened to Jean admit that she was still wrestling with distortion and blame. Up to this point, he had tried to convince the couple to value mutual-cause–mutual-change by using "talk therapy." He knew, however, that persuasion alone often fails to budge a couple away from blame and toward a cooperative, we've-got-to-work-together attitude. This is especially true when a distressed couple has been in conflict for a long period of time.

Since his little speeches on mutual blame, mutual change, and teamwork had not been completely effective, Dr. Martin decided to use a different method to help the couple endorse a nonblaming philosophy. Instead of just talking about the importance of becoming a team, he would have them *experience* what it means to work together as a team. Dr. Martin decided to use two procedures to help Tom and Jean change their attitudes toward cooperation: recalling the romance history and identifying partner positives.*

"Jean, I appreciate your honesty about struggling with the blame attitude. You know by now how strongly I feel about blaming behaviors— they will stop your marriage from moving forward. As I've said, your relationship is best helped by cooperative behaviors.

"But I'm also realistic; I realize that blame can hang on like a bad cold. When you came to counseling last week, it was obvious that you didn't come in as a team ready to work together. You came as adversaries busy blaming each other for the mess your marriage was in. Your bad feelings about each other had built up over a long period of time. So it's naive to believe that you can change thinking, conclusions, mind-sets, thoughts, and perspectives at the snap of your fingers. Instant attitude changes are hard to make."

"But, Dr. Martin, it's not just my attitude about Tom. I'm worried about the relationship in general—I wonder if our marriage is beyond repair. Can we put new love into an old, worn-out marriage? I'm trying to keep my hope that our marriage can be better."

"Jean, it sounds like you're dealing with both distortion and depression," analyzed Dr. Martin.

"That's it exactly," responded Jean with tears in her eyes.

"Well, I've got some good news, then! Because today, I'm going to have you work on two activities that are aimed at helping you deal with those problems. They are designed to help you overcome some negative thoughts about your partner, and I believe that they will give you hope and optimism that your marriage is worth working on. I told you last week we'd do some activities that would put some happiness and success back into your marriage, so now is a good time to begin. These are collaborative activities—you're going to work together as a team. I think you will enjoy doing them. We'll spend the rest of our counseling time today on these exercises.

* A concept to add positives to marital relationships. See P. H. Bornstein and M. T. Bornstein, *Marital Therapy: A Behavioral Communications Approach* (New York: Pergamon Press, 1986). Also see N. S. Jacobson and G. Margolin, *Marital Therapy: Strategies Based on Social Learning and Behavior Exchange Principles* (New York: Brunner/Mazel, 1979).

Strategy 1: Recalling Tom and Jean's Romance History

"The first activity is called 'The Romance History.' To get started, I need to know something about your early years together. How did the two of you meet?"

"We met in high school," answered Tom. "Jean and I were in the same Junior English class. I sat right behind her."

"What made you ask her out for your first date? I mean, what was it that attracted you to Jean?"

"Well, I was kind of shy with girls, but Jean was so friendly. We always found something to talk about after class. She was easy to talk to, but what really attracted me was her looks. She had the biggest brown eyes—they really turned me on! One night, Jean and her boyfriend double-dated with me and my date. We went bowling, but I practically ignored the girl I was with; I couldn't keep my eyes off Jean. I thought she was the most beautiful girl at Franklin High."

"You did? You never told me that," blushed Jean. Dr. Martin noticed Jean blush, and he thought he saw some of her glacial look melt just a little at Tom's last comment.

"Okay, Jean, what about you? What attracted you to Tom?"

"Well, I was impressed with the way he took charge. He was a good leader. We worked together on the Homecoming Committee—he was the chairman—and I loved the way he was able to organize things and charm everyone into doing just what he wanted.

"And he was good in sports—he played on the Junior Varsity baseball team. I can still remember how handsome he looked in that old uniform."

Tom smiled as he heard Jean recall these positive memories. He was especially delighted to hear her use the word "handsome." She had never told him he was handsome in their eighteen years of marriage. It felt good to be praised. Dr. Martin saw the smile on Tom's face. It made him feel optimistic to see Tom happy.

"How long did you date before you got married?" asked Dr. Martin.

"Well, we went steady the last year of high school, and then I started college while Tom worked. We got married during the summer after my freshman year at the university," answered Jean.

"What kind of things did you do together back then?"

"We did a lot of fun things during high school," said Jean. "We were both involved in school and church activities, so we kept busy with ball games, retreats, school dances, club projects—things like that. After I went away to college, we only saw each other on weekends, but when I came home Tom would take me bowling, to movies, or to concerts. And then there was the Dairy Queen a few blocks from my house. Tom and I went there all the time for their specialty—square hamburgers and 7-Up floats."

"We enjoyed athletic things together, too," Tom recalled. "We'd play ping-pong at my folks' house or hit tennis balls against the wall behind the school. We didn't care that the balls were flat—we just enjoyed being together. We were always laughing about something."

Jean began to wiggle in her chair. "There was one more thing I remember us doing. Remember the time we rode our bikes to the zoo? You'd brought that whole bag of red-hot candies, and we fed them to the monkeys. I've never seen anything so funny—I thought we'd die laughing."

"How could I forget! They were all over that cage like something was after them, taking nose dives into the water bucket." Tom and Jean started to laugh uncontrollably. The laughter was contagious. Dr. Martin began to chuckle, too.

Dr. Martin felt good about the changes he had seen in Tom and Jean during the last few minutes. What a turn-around! They had come into his office the week before with nasty, angry, blaming attitudes—ready to give up on their relationship—and now they were laughing over good times.

Dr. Martin knew that unhappy couples focus on the negatives; they are problem-oriented, and due to the pain-distortion phenomenon, they see nothing good in each other or their marriage. It is, therefore, essential that in the relationship rebuilding process, couples take time to consciously resurrect positive events and good memories. They need to look at some of the reasons why they appreciated each other in the first place and notice what brought them

together. They need to re-experience the happy times that have been
buried for so long. When positive histories are brought to the surface, current gloom dissipates and a successful working relationship
in the present is begun. Dr. Martin felt confident that if Tom and
Jean would stay in counseling to learn the happy-couple traits, that
the laughter, fun, and love of those early years could be recaptured
and become a real part of their current relationship. They could get
back to enjoying each other again.

Strategy 2: Identifying Partner Positives

While Tom and Jean were still in a good mood, Dr. Martin intro-
duced the second activity. "Now we're going to do an activity called
'Tell Me What You Like.' This activity is an about-face from what you
have been doing. Last week, you came in citing one complaint after
another about each other, but now we are going to talk about what
you like about your partner."

"This ought to be interesting," laughed Tom. Jean smiled half-
heartedly.

"This activity is based on some important marriage research that
happened at the University of South Carolina in 1976. The purpose of
that study was to determine if happy and unhappy couples are accurate
in observing their mate's pleasing behaviors. When the accuracy of the
two groups was compared, two big differences were found. I'll summarize the differences here on the flip chart.

"The first discovery was that happy couples see their partner's pleasing behaviors—they accurately notice when their mate acts in a positive
manner. They catch their spouse doing good. The second discovery was
just the opposite—unhappy couples do not see their mate's good behavior. They are inaccurate observers of their partner's positive actions.
They seem to be blind to many of the good things their spouse might
do; pleasing behaviors fly right past them. In fact, unhappy couples
underestimate 50 percent of their spouse's good behaviors.

"This research matches my experience in counseling couples,"
continued Dr. Martin. "Most couples enter counseling by listing
grievances against each other which only does more damage to their
relationship. They not only criticize their mate's unpleasing behaviors, but they also overlook their mate's desirable behaviors. So it is
vital that we do an activity which allows you to spotlight what is good
and pleasing. I think you'll both have to agree that you've been paying attention mostly to the problems. Now it's time to be reminded
of the positive dimensions of your relationship. In fact, one of the
best ways to rebuild your marriage is by using positives."

Dr. Martin then handed Tom and Jean a blank sheet of paper with

these instructions: "In the next five minutes, I want you to complete this activity independently; that is, don't show it to your partner. At the top write *What I Like about My Partner.* Then I want you to write down everything you can think of that you appreciate about your spouse. The items can be as simple as 'I like it when you compliment my cooking' or 'I like the way you're able to keep the checkbook balanced without mistakes.' Just number the items as you write them down on the paper. Don't worry about the actual number you end up with—it's not a contest to see which of you can get more items. When you finish, I'll have you share your lists with each other.

"As you think about what you like in your spouse, try to be very specific. For example, if you said, 'I like the way you discipline the children appropriately,' your mate may not understand what you mean by the word *appropriately.* It would be better to say, 'I like it when you discipline the children without anger.' See what I mean?"

Sarcastically, Jean blurted out, "What if Tom can't come up with any?"

"Don't worry about what your partner's doing," cautioned Dr. Martin. "Just concentrate on your own list. Do you both understand what to do?"

"Sounds okay to me," said Tom.

"This should be very interesting," replied Jean suspiciously.

At the end of five minutes, Dr. Martin announced, "Okay, let's see what you have on your lists. Just exchange them." Dr. Martin gave Tom and Jean a few seconds to read what their spouse had written about them.

"Tom, let's look at your list first. Read what Jean likes about you, and I'll write the items here on the flip chart." There were six items on Tom's list: intelligent; good father; willing to help around the house; neat, clean, and well-dressed; good humor and joking attitude; nice to me on bad days.

"Tom, how do you feel about your list?" asked Dr. Martin.

"Well, it's really nice to know that Jean thinks I'm intelligent. I don't remember her ever telling me that she thought I was smart. I've never thought about it before, but hearing Jean say I'm bright would really make me feel good. It's a little embarrassing to admit, but I'm always looking for a pat on the back from Jean."

"Anything else about your list, Tom?"

WHAT I LIKE ABOUT TOM

1. Intelligent
2. Good father
3. Willing to help around the house
4. Neat, clean, and well-dressed
5. Good humor and joking attitude
6. Nice to me on bad days

"I'm surprised that she likes my sense of humor. She never laughs at my jokes, and to be honest, I start feeling like a real dope sometimes. I know they're pretty corny, but it sure would raise my self-confidence if Jean would laugh at my jokes more. I'm glad she really does like my sense of humor. Just knowing that frees me up to be more humorous."

"Good. Now, Tom, as you look at your list, do you have any questions you would like to ask Jean about what she's written? Do you understand everything on her list?"

"Well, we often disagree about how to discipline the boys, so I'm not sure what she meant by my being a good father."

"Jean, can you clarify that for Tom?"

"He's right—we don't always agree about how to handle our two teenage sons. But Tom is a good dad when he takes time with the boys, like when he plays catch with them or takes them swimming. And he's a good dad when he doesn't raise his voice while scolding them. I also like it when he goes with me to visit the boys' teachers on report-card conference day. That's what I mean about Tom's being a good father."

"Does that help, Tom?"

"Yes. Now I know exactly what she means by those words. I'm glad to know that she feels that I'm okay as a dad. I sometimes worry about how I do as a father, especially when we argue so much about discipline."

"Any other items on Jean's list that are confusing?"

"Maybe the third one—willing to help around the house. I never feel like I'm doing enough to please her. Now that she's working part-time, I know Jean needs more help around the house. But I guess I'm a typical male chauvinist—when you're raised to believe housework is women's work, it's hard to change. What did you mean, Jean?"

"Well, I'll admit there are plenty of times when I wish you'd help more, but since I've gone back to work, I've noticed your help—vacuuming, cleaning the bathroom, and even cooking some of the meals. I'm really grateful for that. And your example has encouraged the boys to help more, too."

"Any other questions for Jean?"

"Just one—about being nice to her on bad days. What exactly do you mean by that?"

"I was talking about when it's that time of the month and I'm cranky and miserable. You get the boys off to school so I can sleep a little later. And you've even brought me breakfast in bed. I do appreciate that—thanks."

"You've never told me how important that was to you. I'm glad to hear that you like that behavior." Tom made a mental note that in the future, he would be sure to bring Jean breakfast in bed on her bad days and help the boys get ready for school.

"Now, Jean, it's your turn. Read what Tom appreciates about you, and I'll copy them here on the chart." There were seven items on Jean's list: friendly, excellent musician, organized, good cook, strong moral character, good mother, keeps house clean and running smoothly.

After Dr. Martin had written the list, he asked, "Jean, how do you feel about what Tom wrote about you?"

"Well, I was very surprised that he said anything about my musical ability. I had no idea that he considered it important. I didn't even think he cared—he's never said anything positive to me when I play the piano at church. Maybe that's why I don't play much at home anymore."

"When I think about her music talents I feel like a real jerk," said Tom. "Early in our marriage we should have arranged for Jean to continue her music training. She could really have done something with her music. Instead, we kept putting our extra money into my projects—like working on old cars and buying new golf clubs every year."

Jean sat looking at her hands and realized that it was too late in life to accomplish anything special with her music skills. She quickly wiped away a tear that rolled down her cheek.

"Jean, are there any items you want Tom to explain?"

Jean composed herself and said, "Number 3 is a little confusing. Tom says he appreciates my being organized, but he always complains that I spend too much time setting up files and working on household records. I thought he resented it." Jean looked at Tom with a puzzling glance.

"Jean's right; I do get on her case about it. She drives me crazy sometimes with all that filing and organizing—she's got a box for everything. Sometimes I think if she would give me half as much tender loving care as she gives to all that stuff, we could work out some of our problems. But I have to admit that I do appreciate it when she can put her hand on car titles, receipts, or guarantees for appliances as soon as I ask. And the income tax records are right there waiting when we need them."

"That's nice to hear, Tom. I didn't know you valued my ability to organize things."

"Is there anything else that's unclear to you, Jean?"

"Yes, number 4. Tom, you never compliment me about my cooking, but here on the list you say I'm a good cook. I've been so discouraged about never being able to please you that I have lost all interest in cooking lately."

Tom felt a little guilty as he said, "I guess I haven't told you often enough that I appreciate your cooking—I thought you knew how I felt. I brag about your cooking all the time to the guys down at work. Nobody beats your apple pie, not even my mother. You know, if you'd enter your apple pie in the State Fair, it would be a sure blue-ribbon winner!" As Jean listened to Tom's praise, she was motivated to go home and peel apples.

"Does that take care of your list, Jean?"

Jean glanced again at the list in her hand and nodded yes.

"Well, I've enjoyed going through the Like List Activity with you. You both did a good job identifying your partner's positives and then explaining what you meant. Like Lists are extremely helpful when renewing a marriage. There are five benefits to completing a tell-me-what-you-like list.

"*First,* when you focus on the positive behaviors in your partner, it helps you break the bad habit of *negative tracking.* Without realizing it, the two of you have developed a destructive habit of searching for your spouse's bad behaviors. It's like you've had your antennae and radar screen tuned in to see only your partner's mistakes or displeasing actions. A troublesome phenomenon in the unhappy couple is

that they focus upon the wrong aspect of each other's behavior—they only see the negative. But the Like List is a way to help you stop computing the bad and start counting the good."

"Like my appreciating Jean's organizational skills instead of resenting the time she spends at it?" questioned Tom.

"Exactly. Now let's look at the *second* benefit of the Like List. When you turn your attention to the good behaviors in your mate, you break another bad habit—the one of *underestimating*. It's like those happy and unhappy couples I talked about earlier—the happy ones see the good, but the unhappy ones miss half the positive things their partners do. The Like List is one way to help you pay attention to the positives, and in a later counseling session, I'll show you another technique which helps you tune in to strengths of your mate. You see, when partners fail to realize the good behaviors that are currently being given but not observed, they mistakenly conclude they have a bad partner or a bad relationship. But the Like List helps you see the good. Really, there are so many wonderful things that are going on between you, but you never tell each other about them."

Dr. Martin continued, "The *third* benefit is that the Like List helps you build a *realistic perspective* of your relationship. All the negative tracking and underestimating that's been going on over the years have clouded your thinking. These two habits only serve to convince you that your marriage is hopeless and that your mate is doing nothing right. But the list of positives can show you that your relationship and your mate have strengths that please you; this results in a more balanced perspective. This new outlook will help you fight those ugly distortions of blame and despair, and it will supply the energy you need to work hard on your marriage.

"The *fourth* benefit of the Like List is that it helps you practice an important communication and problem-solving skill called *pinpointing*. Pinpointing is the ability to discuss a behavior in a precise, exact, or specific way. Happy couples are able to specify what behaviors they like or dislike in their mate, while unhappy couples are so vague and unclear in communicating those things that it results in confusion, frustration, and poor problem-solving."

"I see now why you had us explain exactly what we meant by the items we put on our lists," said Jean. "That helped a lot."

"Good," said Dr. Martin. "Now, the *fifth* value of the Like List is that it has let you experience *cooperation and teamwork*. Like the Romance History, this activity has given you another chance to cooperate on a mutual task instead of blaming. Building a working relationship is so vital at this point. A team approach on these kinds of tasks is a good way to fight your tendency to blame and distort the truth. And the more you work together, the less you'll blame."

"I'm starting to see what you mean, Dr. Martin. It was kind of fun working with Jean on these two activities. At least it got our minds off all the problems we've been battling. I just hope we can keep our energy up to tackle all the problems we have to deal with. We're both still feeling angry and drained over the whole mess right now. Do you really think we have enough left to hang on to?"

"Yes, Tom, I do. I know that you still have some major problems to solve, and I realize that you are both unhappy and angry at each other. And because you've been preoccupied with the negatives in your relationship, it's hard to immediately overcome pessimism about the possibility of improving your marriage. But I want to emphasize that in some ways you have a very strong relationship. It may not seem that way to you now because you are paying attention mostly to the problems. But your Like Lists prove that you've been able to find some good traits and behaviors in each other. Jean, you were able to list six things that Tom does which please you, and Tom, you listed seven behaviors that please you about Jean. That's great! Coming up with thirteen things is no easy task even for happy couples. That's a real strength—you do like things about each other. You need to recognize that and build on that good foundation. Let's not lose sight of the number and importance of those positives that still exist between you. From my perspective, you can feel optimistic about creating a thriving, happy marriage that you will both enjoy."

After Dr. Martin had finished explaining the reasons for using the Like List he said, "Well, our time is up for today, so I want you to go home and continue to observe the no-fight rule during the coming week. Is Saturday at ten o'clock all right for your next appointment?"

Tom and Jean nodded an agreement.

"Okay, then start focusing on those positives you've identified, and next session we'll discuss the crucial factors that make a marriage work."

ENRICHMENT ACTIVITIES FOR READERS

1. Keep the no-fight rule for another week.

2. With your mate, spend some time recalling your Romance History. Separately make a list of the traits, behaviors, or qualities that attracted you to your mate. Then exchange lists.

3. Focus on your partner's positive behaviors. Make a list of five things he or she does that pleases you and exchange lists. Discuss any items you don't understand.

SESSION THREE

Why Marriages
Succeed or Fail

Dr. Martin met Tom and Jean at the door and welcomed them to another session.

"Well, folks, how did your week go? Are you still having problems with the no-fight rule?"

"I don't know if we could say we're having trouble," answered Jean, "but it's still pretty strange. In some ways it's a relief not fighting about things, but at times it's frustrating knowing that all the problems are still right there under the surface waiting to spring out on us."

"You can say that again," agreed Tom.

Jean continued, "This week Tom lost his temper with Chris, our oldest boy, and I felt like I really needed to step in and defend my son, but I just bit my tongue and let Tom handle it. It was hard, but I didn't want to trigger another argument."

"Your ambivalent feelings are perfectly normal, Jean. This is a very hard time for both of you. The issues are still there, but we'll get to them when you're ready, that is, when you've developed skills in problem-solving.

"Now, we need to get into our session. Today, I want to explain why marriages fail, or to look at it more positively, why they succeed. The successful marriage was once a mystery—we didn't know why some couples got along so well and others failed. But thanks to the family scholars who have studied good and bad marriages, we now have some specific answers.

THE HAPPINESS DECLINE IN MARRIAGE

"To begin, let's look at a graph that shows what often happens to marital happiness over seven stages of the family life cycle." As Dr. Martin handed them each a copy, he asked, "What do you notice about this graph?"

"What jumps out at me," answered Tom, "is that marriage happiness doesn't last—the longer couples are married the more unhappy they seem to become. They are happiest on their wedding day, but it's mostly downhill from there. That's not very encouraging!"

"You're right. When scientists study the life cycle of a marriage, they usually find a progressive deterioration over most of the seven stages. It's a sad but true fact that the quality of the marital relationship erodes throughout most of a couple's life. It's an erosion that is subtle, gradual, and often fatal. Fifty percent of all marriages now end in divorce. Frequently, couples are unaware that their relationship is suffering this slow death until it is too late."

"The graph shows me that couples start happy, soon become unhappy, and then get happy again as children leave the home," said Jean.

"Right. We could describe the happiness erosion in marriage as a U-curve. That is, marital satisfaction is the highest in young couples, declines after the birth of their first child, and continues to slide through the Launching Stage. Then there is a sharp spurt in the happiness curve as the children leave home."

"That must mean that children cause unhappy marriages," theorized Jean.

"That's an easy conclusion to make, but it's much more complex than that," cautioned Dr. Martin. "Even though they put stress on the relationship, children don't cause the marriage to fail. While this study shows a sudden rise in happiness in the post-parental stages, other studies on the family life cycle show a continued decline through all seven stages. For many couples, a rebound in happiness never takes place even after the children are gone. So we can't blame children."

"Well, if children aren't the reason, what is?" asked Jean. "Why do some marriages make it and others don't? What happened in our marriage? How did the problems begin? I knew all along that something bad was happening, and looking at this graph only confirms the inner tension I've felt. It wasn't just my imagination—our marriage *really has been* coming apart. Why did our happiness fade? Can we ever get it back, or are we past hope?"

"I'm wondering the same thing, Dr. Martin. Can we ever be happy again? Maybe we'll be like those couples you've just mentioned who never get their happiness back even after the kids are gone. How does unhappiness creep into marriages over time?"

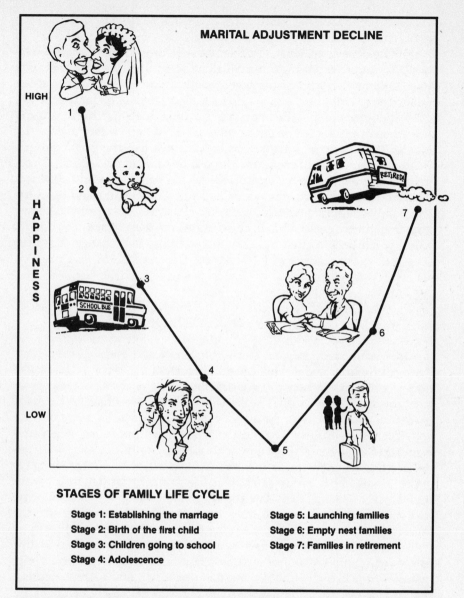

Figure 3. Happiness in marriage often declines over the family life cycle especially through Stage 4 or Stage 5. Based on G. B. Spanier, R. A. Lewis, and C. L. Cole, "Marital Adjustment Over the Family Life Cycle: The Issue of Curvilinearity," *Journal of Marriage and The Family* (May 1975): 263–275.

"You're both asking some good questions, and I understand your concerns. It's easy to be pessimistic about your chances to regain happiness. But I can sense that you both want a good marriage—you want to improve it but don't know how. I'm pleased that you have taken this step to admit your failure and then to learn about relationship-building. The world is full of mediocre marriages because people aren't willing to get the help they need. All around us, we see the facades of perfect marriages, when in fact, most couples are experiencing a happiness erosion just like the graph shows.

"But I want to assure you that there is hope. A marriage can disintegrate but it can also be reconstructed—it can be reborn and revitalized. You can reverse the downward spiral if you stop blaming and learn the five happy-couple traits. Adding these traits to your marriage will boost your happiness greatly. We'll be working on these traits later, and I think you'll be surprised at how quickly things will change. But first, let's look at the reasons why marriages succeed or fail."

THE HEART OF A HAPPY MARRIAGE: THE LAW OF RECIPROCITY

Dr. Martin then stepped to the flip chart and said, "Many people have pet theories about what causes marriages to go wrong, but they're mostly opinions. When you are dealing with a relationship as complicated as marriage, you can't make wild guesses—you have to be exact. A better approach is to base our explanation on solid research. For example, let's consider what 130 marriage scientists found when they compared the lives of the happy and unhappy couples.

"First of all, their research shows that marriages don't just suddenly go to pieces. They erode as couples fail to understand a basic law of human relationships. The law that I'm talking about is the law of reciprocity. This law best explains success or failure in marriage. It's the heart of what makes a marriage work. By definition, reciprocity is when you trade pleasing behaviors equally with your mate. I know that the word *reciprocity* sounds awfully scientific. For that reason, I prefer to use words like *give-and-get, behavior exchange,* and *partner-pleasing.* I'll write these words here on the flip chart to help us remember.

"When a psychologist looks at reciprocity between a husband and wife, he asks these specific questions: Are partner-pleasing behaviors exchanged? How often? Do the exchanges go both ways or in one direction only? For example, if a wife does twenty things to please her husband during the day while he does only three pleasing behaviors in return, she's going to be unhappy, especially if this inequity continues over a long period of time. But if the exchange of partner-pleasing is equal, there is happiness.

"At Stage 1 of your marriage, you exchanged partner-pleasing behaviors at a high rate. In fact, we would describe your marriage then as a give-get relationship because you spent so much time giving pleasing behaviors to each other. Not only was the number of positive experiences high, but the number of negative exchanges was low. In a relationship, the positive events we call *benefits* and the negatives are called *costs*, so at Stage 1 it was almost all benefits and no costs. It's no wonder you were happy—there were many positives and almost zero negative outputs toward one another."

"Dr. Martin, is there any special reason why couples at Stage 1 find it so easy to exchange nice behaviors?" asked Jean.

"Yes. The big reason is that you were so attracted to each other then. Because of this attraction, you consciously did things to please your partner. Remember, that was the honeymoon stage of your relationship, so your goal was to make your mate happy. During that time, you were very attentive to each other's needs. Each day, you'd ask yourself, 'How can I please my partner?' Naturally, because of these feelings of mutual concern and love, you consistently exchanged pleasurable behaviors. This daily frequency of positives was the key reason for your early happiness. Let's stop here and see if you can recall any of those pleasing behaviors."

"I remember some," said Jean. "It used to please me when Tom would take me out for Sunday dinner so I wouldn't have to cook. It also pleased me when he would help me knead and bake bread—we talked a lot then. And I loved it when Tom would ask me how my day was when he got home from work. But he never does those things now."

"Thanks, Jean. And what about you, Tom? Do you remember any partner-pleasing behaviors from those early days?"

"I'm trying to shake the cobwebs off my memory of that first year of marriage. I do remember that Jean often pleased me by fixing my favorite meal—spaghetti and meat balls with lemon meringue pie for dessert. And it was great when she would come watch me play softball on the church team or go bowling with me on Friday nights. I also liked it when Jean would do exercises and fitness stuff with me—we spent a lot of time together then."

Dr. Martin continued, "Those are good examples of behaviors that were exchanged at Stage 1, and it helps me illustrate this important law of human interaction: *Individuals enter and stay in a marriage as long as the relationship positives are greater than the relationship negatives.* You may not have consciously realized it then, but the powerful force that motivated you to choose each other were the positives—what attracted you to each other and moved you together were the positives. The drama of attraction in the first place was because you were pleasing each other. Simply, couples connect and bond because they share more good experiences than bad ones. Here's another way of saying it: *Your positive actions encouraged positive reactions, first in your partner's attitude and then in your partner's behavior.* It's vital that you understand the important role of positives because it is this principle that will guide us as we rebuild your marriage. In short, it was the flow of positives between you that caused your happiness then, and it's what will make your marriage happy now.

"There's one more dimension of reciprocity I need to explain. Not only was your positive behavior exchange at a high rate at Stage 1, but just as important, it was a perfect form of give-and-get. It was unconditional—you pleased your mate without thinking of whether or not your mate was returning the favor. You didn't worry if the exchange of pleasing behavior was balanced or reciprocated by your spouse. You didn't say, 'I'll give *if* you give back.' In a loving, caring, and unselfish way, you suspended the requirement that give-and-get be balanced. But the beautiful thing was that since you were both giving, you were also getting; so there was balance and equity. Give-and-get was perfect, and you were happy."

"But what happened to that perfect relationship?" asked Tom. "It sure skidded off the rails somewhere along the way."

"Well, early in your marriage some critical events happened which seriously disrupted the give-get balance. So now, in your present state of unhappiness, it's hard to give pleasing behaviors to each other. There's an unwritten law between you that says give-and-get has to be balanced. Your care for one another is conditional. You're both playing the waiting game—waiting for the other person to give first. I'm sure you can see how this I'll-move-*if*-you-move-first mentality is destructive to your relationship."

"I know you're right about that conditional thinking, Dr. Martin," responded Jean. "I have to admit that I don't feel much like giving anymore nice behaviors to Tom unless he starts giving back. I feel as if I've been giving and he's been taking for eighteen years. It's always been one-sided and unfair."

Tom was quick to react. "It's been one-sided all right, but I was the one doing most of the giving. But no more! I'm just not motivated to please Jean anymore because when I did try to please her, she found fault with it or didn't even notice. So I finally gave up."

"Be careful! You're both getting back into the distortions and blame game again. It may seem one-sided, but in reality you've both stopped giving good behaviors. That's why one of our major goals is to help you resume a give-get relationship where you are both giving equally, often, and unconditionally. That's the best way to give your marriage a quick happiness boost."

"Dr. Martin, I think I'm getting a handle on the reciprocity and partner-pleasing idea. But I still don't understand what caused our give-get to be out of sync. What were those 'critical events' you just mentioned?"

"The critical events are a combination of conditions that caused your marriage failure, and they all relate to the reciprocity concept. Keep in mind, reciprocity is the heart of a marriage—it's the key to understanding marriage happiness. Let's spend the rest of our session discussing the five reasons marriages collapse and how these factors contributed to your unhappiness. I'll list them here on the flip chart. As I explain each factor, I'll show how it disturbed the give-get relationship. I'll also show how each cause relates to the traits found in happy couples."

WHY MARRIAGES FAIL

Cause 1: The Breakdown of Pleasing Behaviors

"The first cause of your unhappiness has to do with the fact that dating and courtship was a time of delusion and nonreality. You were both on your best behavior, and there was little or no conflict. But that

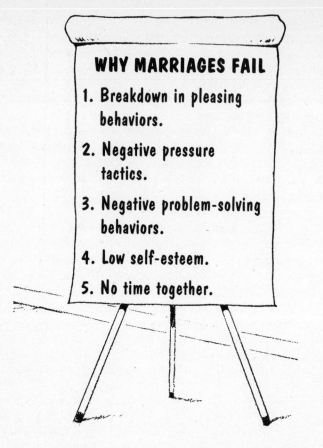

WHY MARRIAGES FAIL

1. Breakdown in pleasing behaviors.

2. Negative pressure tactics.

3. Negative problem-solving behaviors.

4. Low self-esteem.

5. No time together.

only lasted so long. Eventually, because you are both imperfect human beings, your 'other side' became visible to your partner. As you finally came into contact with the 'real person' behind the veneer, you began to notice irritations and frustrating behaviors that you didn't like. During courtship and honeymoon, you either ignored or did not discover differences between you. But then, these annoying behaviors became sources of displeasure. Simply put, you started to get on each other's nerves. The important point I want to make is this: The pattern of exchanges changed—what had been a constant flow of positive behaviors now became punctuated with these annoyances. Your happiness curve began to plunge as the pleasing behaviors decreased and the displeasurable aspects of the relationship increased.

"These new, displeasing behaviors were a major turning point in your marriage. The give-get relationship changed dramatically—instead of giving only good behaviors, you unconsciously began to displease your mate. Now there were more costs and fewer benefits. As the level of positive behaviors went down and the level of negatives went up, you naturally began to experience distress and unhappiness. This restructuring of exchanges brought new problems that you were not trained to handle. I'm wondering if you can recall some of those hidden flaws that became sources of conflict?"

"I sure remember some!" responded Jean. "During courtship, Tom was so neat and tidy, but after we got married, he suddenly became a sloppy person. He left his dirty clothes and towels on the bathroom floor for me to pick up, and he always left newspapers or dirty dishes in the living room. I felt like a maid—or his mother."

"Uh, huh, I understand," nodded Dr. Martin. "Any other annoyance you can think of, Jean, that caught you unaware?"

"Well, as long as we're getting everything out on the table, yes. To be honest, Tom's sexual behavior also frustrated me. I knew the sexual drive of a man is greater than a woman's, and I had read that the male's sexual alarm-clock goes off three times more often than a female's. But Tom's buzzer was ringing twenty-five hours a day. At first, I thought it was my wifely duty to be available to him, but I could only take that for so long. Then, when I would say no, he would pout like a child. It got so I even hated to go to bed at night. I'd make up excuses by saying I wanted to watch the late TV show."

"Okay, those are examples of what I'm talking about. And, Tom, what shocking revelations or disappointing behaviors did you suddenly see in Jean which were hidden from you in courtship?"

"Well, before we were married, Jean was a good listener—she was always so interested in what I had to say. But after we were married, all that changed—all she wanted to do was talk. Almost overnight, it was like she caught a bad case of open mouth. She dominated every conversation and hardly heard a word I said."

"Anything else, Tom?"

"The other behavior that upset me had to do with Jean's accepting me. Before marriage, when we'd discuss current events, politics, and sports, she seemed open to my ideas. But afterwards, she started to challenge me about everything I'd say. Suddenly, I was the dummy, and she was always right. I didn't expect her to agree with everything; it's just that I wanted more agreement and less disagreement from her. Even to this day, I feel that she resists me most of the time."

"All right. You've both been able to think back on some real examples of behavior that caused you to feel angry and dissatisfied with one another, and it illustrates the point I'm trying to make: The honeymoon magic began to disappear as you each came face-to-face with some disappointing behaviors that you never knew existed. Now, instead of being on the receiving end of a lot of warm fuzzies, there were more and more barbs. Jean, you were annoyed by Tom's sexual demands and sloppy personal habits. Tom, you were frustrated by Jean's communication habits of over-talk and resistance.

"But that was only the beginning of facing new problems about each other. Eventually, there would be other aggravating traits and needling behaviors which would surface as you moved through the stages of your family life cycle and dealt with problems in parenting, companionship, communications, managing money, affection, individuality, and employment.

"I'll summarize cause number one briefly. Discovering troublesome behaviors in your partner was the first pivotal event that caused your marriage to begin unraveling—the appearance of these negatives triggered the decline in your happiness curve. As I explained before, your early marriage was marked by a high number of positive events and a low number of negatives exchanged between you. But that's changed now—the pleasing rates have gone down and the displeases have gone up. This shift in the kinds of exchanges has dissolved much of the happiness in your marriage. This breakdown in pleasing behavior was the first great danger to your marriage.

"There's just one more thing I want to say about this breakdown in positives. When scientists compare the profile of couples, they find that the happiest partners are those who exchange high rates of pleasing and low rates of displeasing behaviors. But the exchange pattern is just the opposite for unhappy mates—they trade fewer positives and more negatives. So obviously, we're going to work hard to make your exchange pattern similar to that of happy couples. Okay, let's move on to discuss the next cause."

Cause 2: Skill Deficits and Negative Pressure Tactics

"Skill deficiencies are the second factors that have contributed to your marriage problems. You were hurt and angered by your mate's irritating behaviors, but you didn't know how to change those behaviors constructively. Neither of you had been trained in the three positive skills to help you cope with each other's faults: The skills of *partner-pleasing, behavior change, and problem-solving*. Without them, problems accumulated, tensions built up, hurts festered, resentments lingered, and anger mounted. The seeds of discontent, which had been sown by the emergence of displeasing behaviors, now began to grow rapidly because of these skill deficits. Without these relationship skills, your marriage began to collapse."

"What you're saying makes sense so far, Dr. Martin. Our list of complaints did grow—we were an awful pain in the neck to each other. But we had no idea about how to make the other one change. We've tried to talk each other into changing, but we can't seem to work through a problem without tearing each other up. I sure wish I knew an easier way to get Jean to be different."

"I understand, Tom. Of the three skill deficits, your inability to change your partner has severely damaged your marriage. In fact, it created a whole new set of problems. Because you've never been taught positive change tactics, you responded negatively—you resorted to *negative pressure tactics or coercion*. Coercion includes behaviors like humiliating comments, demands, angry words, nagging, threats, criticism, yelling, the silent treatment, accusations, deprivations, penalties, and withdrawal. Not knowing what else to do, you tried to change your mate with these negative change tactics.

"Did coercion work? Well, yes and no. Sometimes it worked temporarily as a way to get change or compliance from your spouse. But in the long run, these abrasive approaches backfired—they intensified the conflict, alienated you, and drove you further apart. Coercion was a tragic tactic that speeded up the happiness erosion in your relationship. These tactics were new forms of displeasing behavior that only destroyed the positive behavior exchange that once flourished in your marriage—you were now punishing each other more and rewarding less. Yes, you were right in wanting to restore the old give-get relationship but wrong in the tactics you used. Trying to reverse your unhappiness by resorting to negative pressure tactics only added to your misery.

"There's something else you should understand about this second factor. Research has shown there's a strong link between marital happiness and change tactics. When unhappy couples were studied to see how they changed one another, they were found to over-rely on negative control methods—they would bully, become aggressive, use force, and verbally abuse each other to get behavior changes. But happy couples were just the opposite; they controlled their mate's behavior by using positive reinforcement—things like rewards, praise, approval, affection, sex, a special meal, or a night out. This research helped us see that negative change methods are a crucial factor in the breakdown of marital happiness. One of our chief goals will be to learn new behavior change methods based on positive control instead of punishment. This is another way couples differ: Happy partners use positive control to change their mates, whereas unhappy spouses use negative pressure tactics."

Cause 3: Negative Communication Behaviors

"The other skill weakness that harmed your relationship was in the area of communication and problem-solving. During your marriage, you've been confronted with issues that all couples have to work through—money, sex, children, career, personal freedom, and so on.

Sadly, no one ever explained to you the set of twenty-five communication skills for solving these problems. They are called 'Helpers' because they help couples resolve fights and negotiate conflicts so that both partners come out feeling like winners. Without this knowledge, you fell into the trap of relying on a group of negative communication behaviors—they are called 'Killer' messages because they stop the process of problem-solving. And when you can't solve problems, they pile up and cause tension. It's like storing dynamite. All of a sudden, you can be in a hot or cold war that can last for days, months, or years. By studying happy and unhappy couples, we know that marriage success and communication success go hand-in-hand. So another goal will be to help you become effective problem-solvers."

"Dr. Martin, I'm glad you're explaining what went wrong in our marriage, but I'm also angry to think that there were answers to our problems, and we waited so long to find them. Why didn't someone teach us these skills?"

"I understand your frustration, Jean. It's an unfortunate oversight that we live in a culture that allows young people to enter a difficult relationship like marriage without requiring that they learn some essential marriage skills. The irony is that we educate people to drive cars and do their jobs right, but we don't educate people about relationships. It puts heavy pressure on any marriage when the partners enter without skills in partner-pleasing, behavior change, and problem-solving.

"The staggering divorce rate makes a powerful statement about couples' skills in resolving conflict—they don't have any! We simply don't teach each other the skills for solving relationship problems. If we sent you off rafting over the rapids of a dangerous, white-water river without proper training and life jackets, you'd almost certainly get hurt. But this is exactly what we do in marriage—we send you off to live through seven stages of a family life cycle where you have to problem-solve through thirteen conflict areas, and you're expected to do it without first mastering some vital skills. It's no wonder people get hurt in marriage. With skill shortcomings, you were programmed to fail, not succeed."

Cause 4: Low Self-Esteem

"It's obvious we've done very little right so far. What else went wrong in our marriage?" asked Tom.

"The fourth factor that threatened your marriage has to do with self-esteem. Since our time is getting short, I'll talk about it briefly now, but we will devote an entire session to self-esteem in marriage later on.

"Self-esteem plays a big role in marriage, and the best way to see that is by understanding how people with high self-esteem differ from people with low self-esteem. People with high self-regard generally feel good about themselves. They feel self-confident, significant, competent, able, and worthwhile. Because they have positive self-concepts, they are flexible, adaptable, open to change, and they can accept feedback from others. However, people with low self-esteem have just the opposite characteristics: They suffer feelings of inferiority and self-doubt, and they tend to be selfish and resistant to change.

"With these two descriptions, I'll show you how self-esteem affects marital happiness. In all marriages, it's inevitable that the need arises for a change in spouse behavior. But what happens when a high self-esteem mate requests change from a low self-esteem partner? The spouse who already fears being inadequate reads into this request that something else is wrong with him. Thus, to agree to a behavior change would only be an admission that something about him really is bad. This partner's self-esteem isn't strong enough to deal with negative feedback—he just can't handle being wrong. So that person digs in his heels, defies his mate, and resists.

"The requesting mate, who finds it easy to change, doesn't understand this stubbornness. This mate gets frustrated and resorts to negative pressure tactics. A vicious cycle begins: Request for change, resistance, frustration, coercion, escalation of conflict, pile-up of unsolved problems, and unhappiness. Just picture what the behavior change process looks like in a marriage where *both* mates suffer low self-esteem. It's an explosive environment!

"As you can imagine, the behavior change interaction in a marriage where both mates enjoy high self-esteem is much less a hassle. Requests for change are met with agreement and compliance. Problems get solved quickly and marital happiness is strengthened. Marital research shows that self-esteem and happiness are found together—couples who report high self-esteem also report happiness in their marriage, but low self-esteem couples usually have a troubled relationship. In another session, I'll show you how to build each other's self-esteem."

Cause 5: No Time Together

"Now, there's just one more factor that contributes to marital breakdown—lack of time together. At Stage 1 of your marriage, it was easy to please your partner because there were only two of you—there were no children yet to interfere with your freedom and intimacy. Without child-rearing responsibilities to worry about, you spent much time sharing pleasurable activities. Since you were free to concentrate on pleasing one another, there was a high output of positive exchanges. But when your first child was born, your time together changed dramatically. Do you remember?"

"I sure do," responded Jean. "We had complete togetherness for two years, and then Chris was born. All of a sudden, I became a full-time mother in addition to working as a part-time secretary. From that point, my life was filled with crying babies, sleepless nights, diaper folding, spilled milk, colic, and tantrums. Chris was a handful—a strong-willed child with a mind of his own. I was exhausted all the time."

"Right. The fatigue of being a working mother set in and robbed you of time for yourself and your husband. But here's what I want to emphasize: You began to shift your attention away from Tom. And, Tom, you were shifting your focus, too. Like most men in our culture, your job became your priority. It was your badge of respectibility and self-worth. Unknowingly, you were more concerned about being a success at work than in relationship-building with Jean. Correct me if I'm wrong, but that's probably what happened."

"You're right on that. Being good at my job was a strong goal, but money was so important. I had to work a lot of overtime to make ends meet and to get the better jobs at the plant. Then when I became shop steward, there were the Union meetings and all that. It was almost like another part-time job—I felt like a workaholic. I hardly had enough energy to get through the day; there wasn't much left for Jean and the boys by the time I got home.

"But I did all that to give Jean and the boys a good home and a secure future," defended Tom. "I didn't have any choice."

"Tom's right, Dr. Martin. We needed the extra money he made on overtime, and my first priority was to be a good mother. We were tired, but we were just doing what we had to," added Jean.

"Yes, you were both responsible, dedicated people who wanted to succeed in your own separate worlds. But here's the problem: That kind of dedication is very hard on a marriage. The devotion to children and careers looks innocent enough, but the truth is it stole time from your relationship. You spent less and less time with each other in fun ways. Instead of nurturing your relationship by giving good behaviors to one another, you gave your best time and energy to child-rearing and career-climbing. You were preoccupied with kids and job when you should have been concentrating on giving care and support to each other. This focus shift away from each other toward other people and projects naturally decreased the number of pleasing behaviors being exchanged between you. And this weakened your marriage."

"I can see how we shifted our priorities, but I think the reason we don't do things together is because we don't enjoy each other's company anymore. If we go out to dinner alone, we can't even carry on a conversation. After we've said, 'pass the butter' and 'looks like rain,' what's left to talk about? It gets embarrassing when after five minutes you've said everything you can think of about the house or kids, and you can't come up with another thing to talk about. We just sit in silence until Jean makes some crack about me, and then the evening is ruined."

"That brings me to another point, Tom. The children and career focus aren't the only reason you don't spend more time together—coercion is a factor, too. Because you are exchanging more and more negative behaviors, you don't like being together. Remember, you are still trying to get change from each other, so when you get together there's a tendency to coerce, criticize, interrupt, or nag one another. You now look at each other as punishers rather than rewarders. So it's only natural that when your coercion tactics are high the number of companionship activities will be low. You simply don't like to be together because you're afraid you are going to get punished for something. I'm sure that you would choose to spend more time together if you could anticipate experiencing positive satisfactions during that shared time. But now, you expect only more punishment—so you avoid each other. The coercion factor, plus the children and career focus, have all caused your shared time to dwindle.

"I predict that as you learn to stop using the old, abrasive change tactics, you will start to enjoy each other again—you'll then look forward to spending time together. As you start setting aside time for yourself as a couple, it will help your happiness to return. I say this with confidence because the research shows that companionship and happiness are strongly related—more time together is linked to happiness while a lack of shared recreational activities is linked to unhappiness. This is another important trait of happy couples: They enjoy a higher number of shared times together than do unhappy couples. More time together is another goal for your relationship."

"Let me get this straight, Dr. Martin. Are you saying that we'll be happier automatically just by planning to do more things together?"

"Just spending time together isn't the single answer to a happy marriage, Tom. Simply doing that one thing and forgetting the other traits and skills won't make much difference in your happiness level. Time together is only one trait found in happy couples—our goal is to learn all five happy-couple traits."

DR. MARTIN'S SUMMARY

"As we finish up this session, I think it would be a good idea to summarize what we have talked about. We spent a lot of time today learning about why marriages fail, and we covered some complicated concepts. What strikes you most about our discussion?"

"I'm still bothered by the fact that our marriage was almost destined to go downhill," responded Jean. "Why didn't someone warn us before we got married so we could have avoided all the misery and happiness fallout?"

"For the most part, Jean, the information I've shared with you— family life cycles, happiness deterioration, the profile of the happy couple, and the cause of marriage failure—is new knowledge that has not been shared with couples. This practical knowledge hasn't been mainstreamed yet because those of us in the counseling and mental health profession have not done a good job communicating the research findings. We've just barely started to educate the public about why marriages fail or succeed and how happy couples can be distinguished from unhappy ones.

"It's vital that couples learn about the family life cycle and realize that marriage happiness does not naturally endure—we get married with the idea that life will get better all by itself, but it doesn't. Without knowing it, your marriage was on a banana peel even at Stage 1, and it began to run its natural course of decline. But it's even more important to learn about reciprocity and how the lack of it caused the deterioration in your marriage. By understanding the powerful role of reciprocity, you can reverse the decline. Reciprocity was the root of your problem. It was the key to the happiness erosion. I hope I've explained this concept well enough."

"I understand it," said Jean. "Reciprocity is when we trade positive behaviors. I can see now that it was the positives that brought Tom and me together in the first place."

"Right. Two people marry because of the law of reciprocity. It's the emotional glue that holds a marriage together—the giving and receiving of positives is the essence of a healthy, happy marriage. Positives are the binding, bonding force of all human relationships, especially marriage. But gradually over time, you switched your exchange pattern—you decreased the positives and increased the negatives. Keep in mind that the deterioration in pleases happened without your noticing it. This change has been a near-fatal consequence for your relationship. Tom, how do you understand the reciprocity idea?"

"To me, reciprocity is when we give and receive good behaviors. That means that Jean and I are most likely to get into conflict when we're not receiving much care from each other."

"Right. Conflict and unhappiness in marriage result when there is a scarcity of positive outcomes for each person. So, the best way to improve your marriage is to get the positives back fast. Remember, positives are linked to happiness. In fact, what separates happy from unhappy couples the most is the exchange of positive behaviors."

"But I heard you say that it's more than just a lack of positives—it's the negatives, too," interjected Jean. "We've been irritating each other a lot. Didn't you say we've got to change the negative exchanges also?"

"Exactly, Jean. Reciprocity means we have to look at both positive and negative exchanges—marriage unhappiness results when you receive few pleases and/or many displeases from your mate. We're going to put the law of reciprocity to work right away. That's going to be the first trait to work on—it's our agenda for the next session. Is there anything else you'd like to bring up as we close this session?"

"I'm glad you explained the five reasons why our marriage went down the tube. I think we've been struggling with all of these and didn't even know it. I can see how deadly it can be for a marriage when all five come together at once."

"Correct, Tom. When these contributing forces join up, look out! It's like setting a match to a bonfire. When you stop pleasing and start displeasing, when you use negative pressure tactics instead of positive behavior-changing skills, when you communicate poorly, suffer low self-esteem, and spend little time together, it's a dangerous mixture that means big trouble for any couple. A marriage just can't survive that negative series of events."

"Dr. Martin, I'm still amazed that you've been able to diagnose our marriage problems so accurately. I have to agree with Tom; the five failure factors fit us exactly. I'm also glad you explained what happened to us. I just wish we had known about these pitfalls when we got married and about the happiness traits."

"I appreciate how you feel, Jean. There are two reasons why I give an analysis of what went wrong to the couples I counsel. First, when couples learn about the law of reciprocity and the five factors that led to their marriage failure, they can more easily see what needs to be done and commit themselves to working on their marriage. Second, I want you to understand that you didn't fail because you were bad people with abnormal personalities. It happened because you and Tom—like most couples—are 'information poor'; you've lacked relevant insights, knowledge, and skills. You were especially unaware of the five traits that produce marital happiness. Knowledge is power, and without the trait knowledge, you've been powerless to shape or change your relationship. But if you will learn these key traits, you can regain happiness. I'm looking forward to our next session so we can work on that first trait.

"In the meantime, your homework assignment is to keep the no-fighting rule. Don't go looking for trouble. I know you've got some

problems stacked up at home, but they'll have to wait until you have
learned the skills needed for effective conflict resolution. I'll see you
next time."

ENRICHMENT ACTIVITIES FOR READERS

1. Agree with your mate to continue observing the no-fight rule
until you have learned the necessary skills to resolve conflicts. These
skills will soon be discussed.

2. With your mate, list the five causes of marriage failure. Then,
opposite each of the failure factors, write the success factors.

SESSION FOUR

Partner-Pleasing Skills

Tom and Jean came to their weekly counseling session with eager anticipation—Dr. Martin had promised that today they would learn the first trait of happy couples.

"As we begin our session, I want to summarize where I've taken you this far. In our first session, we dealt with the problem of blame and distortion. In the second session, I wanted to help you rebuild your image about each other and your relationship. When you came in, you were both battle weary, burned out, and paying more attention to the negative exchanges. You'd lost sight of the positives that still existed between you. That's why we did the Romance History and the Like Lists—to let you see the worth in your mate that you haven't been looking for.

"Then in our last session, we discussed the happiness erosion in marriage, and I explained the five causes of marital breakdown. Now that you've had some time to digest all that information, does it make sense to you?"

"I've thought a lot about what you taught us last week, Dr. Martin, and it seems like positives are the key to a happy marriage. You told us that we have to give more positive behaviors to each other, be positive in how we change each other, use positive communication, have positive self-esteem, and spend more time together. I like the idea of putting more positives into our relationship, but which one comes first?"

"Excellent question, Jean. The starting point is to increase your positive exchanges. They have to dominate the scene in your home. In fact, that's the best description of a good marriage—a relationship with a reciprocity of positive exchanges. As I explained last session, the best way to understand marital happiness is to look at the rewarding and punishing behaviors that are daily traded between spouses. For example, in your case the beginning of your unhappiness was because you didn't please each other much and/or you displeased one another often in your day-to-day interaction. We've got to reverse that destructive pattern. And we'll do it by learning the skills of partner-pleasing. Relearning to please each other will be enormously helpful to your marriage."

THE STORY OF THE P's AND D's

"Now, before we learn the partner-pleasing skills, let me show you how powerful positives are in making a marriage happy." Dr. Martin then handed the couple a graph and explained, "This graph shows the results of a study that was conducted in 1975 at the University of Oregon by psychologists Birchler, Weiss, and Vincent. This study helped us solve one of the mysteries of marital happiness by pinpointing a set of behaviors which are found more frequently in happy couples but less often in the lives of unhappy couples. Happy couples have more *pleasing* (P's) behaviors, and unhappy couples have more *displeasing* (D's) behaviors.

"The purpose of the study by these three psychologists was to learn if behavior exchange patterns differed in good and bad marriages. To find out, they asked twelve happy and twelve unhappy couples to keep a record at home for five days of the number of pleasing and displeasing behaviors they noticed in their mate. The graph shows what they discovered. There are a number of lessons we can learn from it. Tom, what strikes you about the graph?"

"From our discussion in the last session, I'd have expected the happy couples to be higher on the pleasing side, but I didn't think there would be such a big difference."

"Right, Tom. Behavior exchange is dramatically different between the two groups. In fact, on any given day, the happy couples delivered 100 percent more pleasing behaviors as compared to the unhappy ones. Jean, what do you notice most about the graph?"

"Well, I'm not surprised to see that happy couples do more nice things for each other than do the unhappy couples, but I'm amazed at how often the spouses in the other group make one another unhappy. They gave 200 percent more displeases than did the happy group. No wonder they were unhappy."

"That's a good point, Jean. The happy group not only exchanged more pleases, but they also traded fewer displeases when interacting.

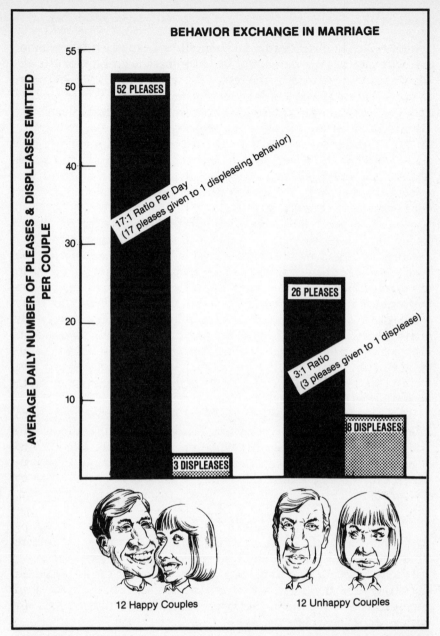

BEHAVIOR EXCHANGE IN MARRIAGE

AVERAGE DAILY NUMBER OF PLEASES & DISPLEASES EMITTED PER COUPLE

52 PLEASES

17:1 Ratio Per Day
(17 pleases given to 1 displeasing behavior)

26 PLEASES

3:1 Ratio
(3 pleases given to 1 displease)

3 DISPLEASES

8 DISPLEASES

12 Happy Couples   12 Unhappy Couples

Figure 4. Over a five-day period, 24 couples (12 happy and 12 unhappy couples) counted the number of pleasing and displeasing behaviors received from their mates. Compared to the unhappy couples, the happy group gave more positives and fewer negatives. Exchange of positive behaviors is the key determiner of marital happiness. Adapted from G. R. Birchler, R. L. Weiss, and J. P. Vincent, "A Multimethod Analysis of Social Reinforcement Exchange Between Maritally Distressed and Nondistressed Spouse and Stranger Dyads," *Journal of Personality and Social Psychology* 31 (1975): 349–360.

And research shows this to be generally true: When we compare behavior exchange in good and bad marriages, we find that couples who report their marriage to be happy also report they enjoy more P's and fewer D's than unhappily married partners. There's a definite link between a couple's happiness and their behavior exchange pattern."

"Another thing that shocks me," added Jean, "is that the pleasing-to-displeasing ratio is so lopsided between the two groups. In the case of the happy couples, for each annoying behavior, they offset it with seventeen good behaviors. But the unhappy ones exchanged only three nice behaviors to one irritation."

"Yes. The good-to-bad ratio was six times higher for the happy group. And that's the point I want us to remember most: Distress in marriage is caused by the imbalance in exchanges; there are just too many D's and not enough P's. You see, that's the crucial trait difference in couples: Happy couples show high rates of pleasing behavior and low rates of displeasing behavior. We call that a high P:D ratio. But if you were to watch distressed couples interact, you would likely find they reverse this ratio by delivering fewer positives and more negatives. That's called a low P:D ratio. The P and D trait clearly distinguishes good from bad marriages."

"Dr. Martin, if I hear you right, the biggest reason for our unhappiness was the P's caved in."

"Exactly, Tom. Many years ago, your happiness was due to your daily frequency of positive behaviors. But gradually, and unknowingly, the positive output got smaller while the negatives got larger. So to restore that happiness, we must change your interaction so you are giving many more P's than D's."

Partner-Pleasing Skills: The BEST

"I don't need any more research facts, Dr. Martin—I'm already convinced we need to put the P's back into our marriage. Where do we go from here?" Tom leaned forward as he waited for the response.

"Okay, let's spend the rest of our session learning how to please each other. The most effective way to do this is to use the Behavior Exchange Skills Technique."

"What in the world is a Behavior Exchange Skills Technique? It sounds pretty scary to me," said Tom as he raised his eyebrows.

"Let's take the scare out of it and just call it the BEST for short. BEST is a list of 304 events and behaviors that can occur in marriage subdivided into three categories—Positive, Negative, and Wanted. It includes behaviors you might do together or behaviors one of you might initiate, and it spans those conflict areas I gave you in the first session." Dr. Martin stepped to the flip chart and wrote out the thirteen areas.

"The purpose of the BEST is to help you re-experience the high care levels that were present when you first got married. These kinds of checklists are now being used with couples in counseling, and they have proven to be a great tool for helping couples recapture the positives and eliminate the negatives. Here's what the BEST looks like." Dr. Martin then handed Tom and Jean the first page of the BEST. This page shows two of the thirteen areas. (For a sample of the entire BEST, see pp. 178–210 (Appendix B) of this book or pp. 14–46 in *Traits of a Happy Couple Study Guide*.

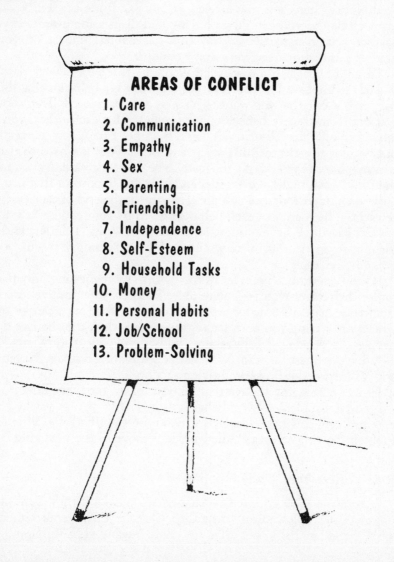

AREAS OF CONFLICT
1. Care
2. Communication
3. Empathy
4. Sex
5. Parenting
6. Friendship
7. Independence
8. Self-Esteem
9. Household Tasks
10. Money
11. Personal Habits
12. Job/School
13. Problem-Solving

RULES FOR THE BEST

Rule 1: Count Behaviors

Tom and Jean scanned the list as Dr. Martin gave some instructions. "There are six rules for filling out this checklist. First, each night for the next fourteen nights, read through the entire list—with the exception of the Problem-Solving section—and record the number of positive and negative behaviors you received from your partner during the past twenty-four hours. That is, did a behavior occur? how often did it occur? and did your partner's behavior please or displease you? Notice there is a row labeled Positive and one labeled Negative for each day so you can tally pleasing and displeasing events. If your partner acts in a particular way that has neutral impact on you—neither positive or negative—don't count it.

"You'll notice, also, a row called Wanted—that's for behaviors you'd like to see improved in your partner. A *Want* is a behavior that didn't happen but one that you want to happen or be increased. Even though you both want many behavior improvements for each other, you are limited to only *five* Wants each day. That's not five Wants per section, but five for the entire BEST each day. Sometimes it's hard to decide which behaviors you want your mate to begin or increase. As you mark the BEST each night, work independently. It's important that you observe each other fourteen straight days, and at the end of each day, you record the frequency of each behavior given by your spouse."

"Dr. Martin, I have a question about the Wants. I understand it's for things we wish our mate would do but isn't doing, but why do we get only five each day?"

"Good question, Tom. Here's the reason: By requesting only five—rather than many Wants—you're more likely to get a positive response from your mate. Too many behavior requests all at once can be overwhelming, leaving you both feeling frustrated when the changes don't happen. So decide carefully where you'll spend your daily Wants."

"I have a question, too. Why don't we mark Positives, Negatives, and Wants for the Problem-Solving section?"

"Jean, we're going to save that section for a later time. That is, you will count problem-solving behaviors only after you've learned specific problem-solving skills. So for now, use the BEST for all but the Problem-Solving category. All right, let's move to the next rule."

Rule 2: Rate Your Daily Happiness

"After you have counted behaviors and judged if they were pleasing or displeasing, indicate on a 0 to 10 scale your overall happiness with the relationship for that day. Zero means very unhappy, 5 is

BEST CHECKLIST
Daily Behavior Exchange Record---Week 1

CARE

		S	M	T	W	T	F	S
1. We exchanged back-scratching.	Positive							
	Negative							
	Wanted							
2. Partner gave me a hug.	Positive							
	Negative							
	Wanted							
3. Partner greeted me with hug and/or kiss when I came home.	Positive							
	Negative							
	Wanted							
4. Partner gave me a kiss.	Positive							
	Negative							
	Wanted							
5. Partner put his/her arm around me in public or at home.	Positive							
	Negative							
	Wanted							
6. Partner massaged my head, neck, feet, etc.	Positive							
	Negative							
	Wanted							
7. Partner reached out to hold my hand.	Positive							
	Negative							
	Wanted							
8. Partner gave me an "I love you" touch(non-sexual).	Positive							
	Negative							
	Wanted							
9. Partner rubbed my back until I fell asleep.	Positive							
	Negative							
	Wanted							
10. Partner...	Positive							
	Negative							
	Wanted							
11. Partner...	Positive							
	Negative							
	Wanted							

		S	M	T	W	T	F	S
12. Partner...	Positive							
	Negative							
	Wanted							

Care Totals:

	S	M	T	W	T	F	S
Positives							
Negatives							

COMMUNICATION

		S	M	T	W	T	F	S
1. We talked about an event we shared (movie, church, etc.).	Positive							
	Negative							
	Wanted							
2. We reminisced about a happy time in our relationship.	Positive							
	Negative							
	Wanted							
3. We laughed about something.	Positive							
	Negative							
	Wanted							
4. We talked about events that happened in our day.	Positive							
	Negative							
	Wanted							
5. We talked about a special topic (education, politics, religion, etc.).	Positive							
	Negative							
	Wanted							
6. We solved a problem.	Positive							
	Negative							
	Wanted							
7. Partner told me what was bothering him/her so I wouldn't worry.	Positive							
	Negative							
	Wanted							
8. Partner agreed with me on something.	Positive							
	Negative							
	Wanted							

neither happy nor unhappy, and 10 is very happy." Dr. Martin then handed Tom and Jean a special page and said, "You can put your happiness rating here on the BEST Weekly Summary record. Also, summarize your Positives (P's) and Negatives (N's) for the twelve areas on this same page. P's and N's are just another way of talking about pleases and displeases."

Rule 3: Compute P:N Ratios

"Figuring out your mate's P-to-N ratio is next. It sounds complicated, but it's just a matter of dividing the total number of Negatives into the total number of Positives. For example, Jean, let's say you have counted Tom's behavior on a given day, and he has pleased you 14 times but only displeased you 4 times. You then divide the 4 into the 14 to get an answer of 3.5. But to make it an easy-to-understand number, we round it off to 4. So Tom's P:N ratio on that day is 4 to 1. This means for each annoying behavior, he made you happy 4 times. Our aim, of course, is to achieve high P-to-N ratios for both of you each day. Remember that for happy couples, the average ratio was 17 to 1—that will give you something to shoot for."

"I'm almost afraid to find out about our ratios," confessed Tom.

"This isn't going to leave much doubt about where we are in our relationship right now, is it?" commented Jean.

"That's right. The P:N ratio is a benchmark or a road sign that reveals what's happening in the relationship and if it's getting better. At the beginning of our session, I said that the best test of a happy marriage is whether or not there is positive behavior exchange between partners. To find that out, we use the P-and-N ratio. It's a special number that tells an important story. It's an accurate measure of the good and bad things that take place between you every day. This number gives us some concrete information we can't get in any other way—namely, the patterns of interaction that go on at home. This number is vital—it reports your progress as a couple and reveals whether or not your marriage is moving forward.

"But there's a larger perspective you need to have about this critical number. P's and N's reflect your level of care for one another. P and N data not only help us measure objectively how close you resemble a happy couple, it represents how many loving events are being exchanged. You see, a high P:N ratio says, 'I care a lot about you.' Okay, let's go to the next rule."

Rule 4: Exchange BEST Checklists

"The fourth rule is to exchange your checklists. Each evening, I want you to set aside a short period of time to review and discuss each

BEHAVIOR EXCHANGE SKILLS TECHNIQUE SUMMARY---WEEK 1

RATING SCALE →

Marital Happiness Rating

0 1 2 3 4 5 6 7 8 9 10

Very Unhappy | Neither Happy nor Unhappy | Very Happy

S	M	T	W	T	F	S

Observation made by
Husband ☐ Wife ☐

POSITIVES DIVIDED BY NEGATIVES →

P:N Ratio (Categories A-L)
P:N Ratio (Problem-Solving)

S	M	T	W	T	F	S

		Positives/Negatives	S	M	T	W	T	F	S
A.	CARE	Positives							
		Negatives							
B.	COMMUNICATION	Positives							
		Negatives							
C.	EMPATHY	Positives							
		Negatives							
D.	SEX	Positives							
		Negatives							
E.	PARENTING	Positives							
		Negatives							
F.	FRIENDSHIP	Positives							
		Negatives							
G.	INDEPENDENCE	Positives							
		Negatives							
H.	SELF-ESTEEM	Positives							
		Negatives							
I.	HOUSEHOLD TASKS	Positives							
		Negatives							
J.	MONEY	Positives							
		Negatives							
K.	PERSONAL HABITS	Positives							
		Negatives							
L.	JOB/SCHOOL	Positives							
		Negatives							
CATEGORY A-L DAILY TOTALS →		Positives							
		Negatives							
PROBLEM-SOLVING TOTALS →		Positives							
		Negatives							

other's data. This step of partner-sharing gives you explicit feedback information about each other. For example, you can discover how well you succeeded in pleasing your spouse, and if not, to discuss the reasons why. Sharing BESTs helps you know precisely what behaviors pleased or displeased your mate; it takes the guesswork out of wondering what makes your partner happy or unhappy. The Wants will even provide you clues to what your mate would like you to do. From your past experience, you know how easy it is to misread or misunderstand your spouse's needs or wants."

Rule 5: Praise

"Each night when you exchange BESTs, also exchange appreciation. This means that you choose some behaviors from the list that pleased you and then tell your mate how much you liked that behavior. This is called positive reinforcement or positive feedback. When you first start giving positive feedback, you may feel uncomfortable. That's because you haven't been expressing praise for pleasing behaviors during your marriage. But even though you're out of practice with praising, it's vital that you both acknowledge each other's pleasing actions."*

Rule 6: Guard against Selective Tracking

"Finally, I want to caution you about a possible glitch that can occur in this process—it's called *selective tracking*. Selective tracking simply means you'll tend to see only the negatives in your mate. Because your history has been to exchange more negatives than positives, you're both susceptible to spotting only the bad and ignoring the good. You've had a lot of practice pointing out your mate's faults, so you'll have to retrain yourself to see the good things that are going on.

"In our second session together I told you that unhappy couples miss 50 percent of the nice things their mates do. They are less aware of the positive behaviors of their spouse. Well, that's what we're talking about here. My guess is that you have also screened out certain pleasurable behaviors and exaggerated the negatives. The checklist is designed to compete with your tendency to ignore the positive and focus on negative behaviors, but be on guard.

"Okay, those are the six rules for using the BEST. What other questions do you have?"

"Dr. Martin, I can see the value of counting P's and N's, but why do we have to rate our happiness each day?" asked Tom.

"Because I want you to see that behavior and happiness are linked.

---

* In the next session, Dr. Martin teaches Tom and Jean three praising skills. You might want to peek ahead to those now.

Keep in mind the lesson we learned from the graph—the strong connection between high P:N ratios and happiness. Tom, it may not mean much to you to calculate how happy you were for the day, but it's important for Jean to see that her actions directly affect your happiness—and vice versa. You will both come to realize that positive behaviors raise your mate's satisfaction and negative ones decrease satisfaction."

"My question has to do with the time involved in all this. It's going to take forever to go through all 304 items every night for fourteen days—and then do the summaries on top of it. I don't see how we're going to find time for all of it," sighed Jean.

"There's no doubt that recording your observations and sharing your positive, negative, and wanted data will be time-consuming. And I must warn you that at times it'll be dull and boring. I wish there were an easier way—but change is hard work, and it takes time. The thing to remember, Jean, is this: You are doing all this work to put your relationship back like it was during courtship and early marriage."

COMMITMENT TO CHANGE

"That does bring us to a crucial point, though. It's necessary for you to grasp that reviving a marriage—whether it involves this checklist or anything else I assign—is going to be one of the hardest things you'll ever have to do. It's taken you eighteen years to come to this point of disaster in your marriage, and you can't fix it overnight. It'll be the most emotionally exhausting work you'll ever be involved in. For that reason, it will take a strong, firm commitment from each of you. I realize that your willingness to return for counseling each week has indicated a commitment on your part, and I did ask you to commit to the thinking changes in the first session. But now you're beginning to see that revitalizing a marriage will require some behavior changes, too. You need to decide again if you're willing to put in all the time and effort this process will demand from you. Rebuilding a relationship is a priority and no effort should be spared. Think about it for a moment. Are you really dedicated to renewing your marriage no matter what it takes?" Dr. Martin folded his arms, locked his eyes on the couple, and waited for a response.

Tom broke the silence. "When we came in here three weeks ago, I had no idea what we were getting into. To be honest, I thought you'd slap on a few Band-Aids and send us back to the fight. I never really believed you could help us find happiness again. But that's changed for me. From what I've heard in the last four sessions, I'm beginning to believe there is hope for us. I'm willing to do whatever it takes to find that happiness. I know my life wouldn't be worth much without Jean and the boys." Tom reached over and squeezed Jean's hand. It was an emotional moment.

Jean wasn't able to speak right away and was silent as she regained her composure. "Thanks, Tom, you don't know how important it is for me to hear you say that. I've felt the same way, Dr. Martin. I expected you to give Tom some lectures on how to make me happy and we'd go on our way. But I'm finally beginning to recognize that I have contributed as much to our unhappiness as Tom has. I can identify with what you said about this being emotionally exhausting. I've never cried as much in my life as I have in the last few weeks. It's not easy to admit you've been wrong, and it's even harder to commit myself to some changes. In spite of all our problems, I love Tom. I want us to be happy the way we were during that first part of our marriage, and I'm ready to do the work to get there." Jean held tightly to Tom's hand.

"I want to thank you both for sharing your feelings about all this. It's important that I know where you are in your commitment, but it's even more important that each of you know where the other is. You've both done an eloquent job of doing that. I hope you'll remember your words and that they'll be an encouragement as you follow through on your assignments in the weeks ahead."

DR. MARTIN'S SUMMARY

"Okay, our time is up, but just before you go, let's do a very quick summary of our session. Today, we talked about the most important trait that characterizes happy couples—that's the trait of exchanging many positives and few negatives. Now that you understand that trait, how will you apply it in your marriage?"

"It seems clear to me that we need to please each other more," said Tom, "because that's what our relationship was like at its happiest time."

"But it's more than just increasing pleases," added Jean. "We also have to decrease the negatives—we have to stop annoying one another."

"You're both correct. To boost happiness, you've got to increase the number of positive interactions and decrease the ones that cause marital tension. The BEST will help you do both.

"Now, here are your BEST packets for the next fourteen days. When you come back for our next session, please bring your data so we can see if your P-and-N ratios are changing. This information is vital, so complete your behavior counting assignment every day. When you get tired of the record-keeping, remember the purpose of the BEST: It's to train you to behave like you did when you first met. What brought you together in the first place was the act of partner-pleasing. That created a bond, and now we're going to renew that bond in the same way—by learning to please each other. The boredom of this assignment will soon be forgotten as you see the happiness return to your relationship. Many couples find the BEST so helpful, they continue to use it beyond the fourteen days.

"Now, do you have any more questions about the assignment?"

"Sounds easy to me," said Tom. "Every night we count our partner's behaviors, rate them as positive or negative, check a few wants, show each other our scorecards, and discuss the results."

"But when we discuss the results, I'm guessing that you want us to spend most of our time talking about the positives, not the negatives."

"I'm glad you mentioned that, Jean. By all means, make an agreement with each other to focus your discussion on the pleases being exchanged rather than the displeases—the P's need to get most of the time. But it's also important to look at the N's your mate has checked. Really get acquainted with what annoys your partner, and then, of course, begin to make the efforts to reduce them. Research tells us that even a small reduction in the rate of negative interactions can lead to big increases in marriage happiness.

"Well, I'll be looking forward to hearing about your experiences with the BEST. But before you go, take another look at the BEST rules." Dr. Martin walked to the flip chart and began to write. After reviewing the BEST rules, Dr. Martin walked Tom and Jean to the door. "See you next session."

BEST RULES

1. Count behaviors.
2. Rate happiness.
3. Compute P:N ratios.
4. Exchange lists.
5. Praise.
6. No negative tracking.

ENRICHMENT ACTIVITIES FOR READERS

In this session, you have read about the importance of partner-pleasing as a means to renew marital happiness. To develop your skills in partner-pleasing, begin to use the BEST Checklist. (See pp. 178–210 in Appendix B of this book, or pp. 14–46 in *Traits of a Happy Couple Study Guide*.) Here are some special reminders about this assignment:

1. Use the BEST for *fourteen straight days*. (You and your spouse are encouraged to make photocopies for your personal use of the checklist in Appendix B or the one in the separate study guide.)

2. Follow the six BEST rules.

3. Deciding when to begin the twenty-four-hour behavior counting period is important. A good beginning and ending period is dinner time of each day.

4. Remember you are limited to five Wants each day.

5. Keep in mind why you are counting behaviors: You are focusing on positive exchanges simply because it was the positives that brought you together in the first place. Furthermore, the most important single factor in marital happiness is whether or not positive behaviors are being exchanged.

6. Do not count PROBLEM-SOLVING behaviors yet. Count the Positives and Negatives only in the first twelve categories.

SESSION FIVE

The Power
of Praise

"Well, folks, it looks like you survived your first seven days on the checklist," said Dr. Martin as he greeted the Andersons at the door to his office.

"Not without incident," responded Tom.

"That's why you're here. If something isn't going well with your homework assignment, let's talk about it. Let me see your BEST forms, and then you can tell me about what happened."

Jean responded first. "As you can see on our summary sheet, things went great on Monday, Tuesday, and Wednesday—we gave each other more positives than usual, and our happiness ratings were pretty high. But on Thursday, everything went to pieces. When we exchanged checklists that night, we got into a big argument because Tom didn't give me a point for something I'd done.

"After we left here last week, I kept thinking about the story of the P's and D's and the importance of doing nice things for each other. So I tried to think of behaviors that would please Tom. He did respond to the obvious things, but when I did a special behavior that he'd said was important to him, he didn't even notice it. In fact, I did it twice, and he overlooked it both times. I was so hurt and angry that I wanted to give up. I couldn't see any point in working so hard to please him if he didn't care enough to notice." Jean's anger was still obvious.

"You're right, Jean. It's hard to give pleasing behaviors if your mate is unmindful of what you've done. But I'm curious, what did he miss?"

"Well, you know how Tom is always complaining about my critical tongue. He's always harping that he wants me to be gentle instead of raising my voice—especially when we're trying to discuss a problem. I guess I've developed a bad habit in that area over the years, but it seems like that's the only way I can get Tom's attention.

"Anyway, as we were driving home last week from counseling, I decided I'd work on keeping my cool and not raise my voice to Tom. Thursday, I got my chance to try it out. That was the worst day I've ever been through. I had a flat tire on my way to work; Germs, our cat, threw up on the carpet; Billy came home needing his ball uniform washed for Friday's game; and our old washing machine stopped dead in the middle of a cycle. Tom said he'd fixed it a month ago, but no such luck. So I called Tom at work to tell him it had broken down again. I explained the problem calmly—without raising my voice or losing my temper—and he promised to look at it as soon as he got home. Instead, he walked into the house and went right to the TV set. First, I was hurt and disappointed—and then really mad!"

"I bet you were tempted to give him the old fangs-and-claws response."

"Was I ever!" Jean's eyes flashed. "But I just bit my tongue and stayed calm. Instead of coming unglued like Tom says I always do, I quietly walked over to him and in my sweetest voice, I gently reminded him about the washer. For the second time in the same day, I consciously tried to please Tom with gentle behavior. I looked forward to his reaction on the checklist that night, but he didn't even catch it. I acted gently—just like he wants—and he missed it both times! After that, I didn't feel like trying to please Tom with that behavior again. I'd lost my motivation."

"I understand, Jean. It's easy to get disappointed when you realize that certain efforts to be pleasing go unnoticed or unappreciated. I'm glad to hear you tried a new behavior—like having a gentle spirit and remaining calm during your conversations with Tom. We know happy couples are more likely to problem-solve in neutral, gentle, nondemanding voices than are unhappy couples. So it's important that you learn to confront Tom without anger. I applaud your efforts. But it's much better that Tom cheer you than me.

"Tom, you must feel like you're on the hot seat right now. Why don't you tell us your side of the story?"

"I really have egg on my face," admitted Tom with embarrassment. "No doubt, I goofed it. I just didn't pick up on the change. I don't know how I could have missed it—especially twice in one day. I guess I still see Jean as a feisty, Italian tornado with a sharp tongue. I just expect her to lose her cool all the time. It's hard to see her as a gentle person after all these years of being harsh with me. As I think back on it, it's true she didn't lose her temper, but somehow it seemed fake—

like she was gritting her teeth. I keep wondering why she never did it before. Why has she waited all these years to show me that behavior?"

"That's not fair, Tom! I did what you wanted me to. It's bad enough you were blind to my behavior, but now you're even criticizing me for it. That really discourages me from trying it again."

LEARNING FROM CONFLICT

Lession 1: How Mental Factors Cause Marital Stress

"All right, I know this conflict has disturbed you both, but instead of letting it block your relationship growth, we can use this conflict as a learning experience. There are three lessons we can learn.

"First, let's learn some more about the mental factors in marriage. They can play a key role in increasing or even causing marital conflict. Remember in our first session? I warned you that blaming attitudes and distorted thinking could easily disrupt our efforts to rebuild your marriage. Well, in this conflict, we're dealing with another negative mental factor—past perceptions. This factor can also get in the way of enriching your relationship."

"Past perceptions? You mean like the way I've always seen Jean as hot-tempered?"

"Yes, Tom. You're absolutely right. How you see Jean in your mind's eye—that is, your perceptions and expectations of her—can block out the actual behavior she's trying to show you.

"In your mind, you constantly play a video tape that pictures Jean as a person with a bad personality trait—an aggressive spitfire who is more inclined to criticize than congratulate you. This tape clouds your perception. You then miss those positive behaviors that run opposite to the image on your tape. If you expect to see harshness, you'll probably see harshness even when it's not there. I realize that Jean has acted aggressively in the past, but you can't let those past perceptions distort the positives she is giving you now.

"Tom, I'm not picking on you. Jean is just as susceptible to this kind of distortion; you'll both have to be on guard against the negative mental pictures you have developed of each other. The human mind has the mysterious ability to build up strong images about each other's faults. And the worst part about these images is that they keep the real world out—they block events that you need to let penetrate your mind. If you allow these images to continue, your partner will soon tire of trying to please you and give up—just like Jean did this past week. In short, past perceptions can tempt you to see the bad and miss the good."

"I can see now how I overlooked Jean's behavior, but the question is, How do I break the habit of seeing her from this negative viewpoint?"

"It's not easy, but it can be done if you do two things. First, be aware of the tricks your mind is playing on you. Become alert to the fact that negative perceptions about your mate can harm your relationship. Second, carefully follow all the BEST rules, especially the rule about not tracking negatives. I suspect after your experience with Jean this past week, you'll not be as likely to miss her positive changes in the future. Your nightly sharing time will give you each the opportunity to remind your mate of any good behaviors that might have been missed. Don't let this time generate into a fight—use it to erase those old tapes. As you continue to use the checklist, you'll be building a history of positive experiences that'll help you start seeing your mate in a new way."

Lesson 2: How to Use Reinforcement, Feedback, and Praise

"I think I understand now what happened with Tom last week. Next time, I'll try to be more patient when he misses something, but I have to confess that I need Tom to pay attention to what I do and respond to me in some way. It's not easy to change, and I'm learning something about myself—I get discouraged easily and start to give up if I don't think he's noticing."

"What you're saying, Jean, points out a second lesson we can learn from your conflict—*it takes two people to change one's behavior;* it takes reinforcement, feedback, and praise from your mate. We tend to look at change as an individual matter, but behavior change is really a joint task. Whether you want your spouse to start a new behavior like being gentle or stop an old habit like faultfinding requires that both of you act together as a team, initiating and responding. It takes both of you to change one of you.

"Let me illustrate the team approach to behavior change. Tom, you want Jean to change her harsh behavior to gentle behavior. But it isn't enough for you to tell Jean to change and then sit back, do nothing, and wait for it to happen. Behavior change is a mutual responsibility that requires two actions. Jean, you must initiate a positive behavior like gentleness; and, Tom, you must respond with a positive behavior. What I mean is, you need to see it, approve it, and verbally appreciate it. There has to be some positive reinforcement or positive feedback from you.

"Positive reinforcement is an extremely powerful method for improving or changing people's performance. In fact, long-lasting behavior change is impossible without some kind of reinforcement or feedback. In positive reinforcement, we *add* something to a situation. The 'something' that is added is called a *positive reinforcer*. A rat pressing a lever for food pellets, a worker doing a job for money, a student studying to get good grades, or a child being good to earn parental approval are examples of the effects of positive reinforcement. The positive reinforcers in these examples are food pellets, money, good grades, and parental approval. When these somethings follow a response, they strengthen that response and make it more likely to be repeated. But if something doesn't follow a response, that response is not likely to be repeated.

"Here's how it worked in your case last week. Jean, you acted in a gentle way. Tom, that was an ideal opportunity to strengthen Jean's new behavior with a well-deserved reinforcement—a warm word, a smile, or a hug. Instead, because of your past negative perceptions and being unskilled at delivering positives, her behavior went unnoticed. With no positive feedback, it destroyed Jean's motivation to keep up that behavior.

"It's a well-established law of human behavior that if a behavior isn't rewarded, recognized, or reinforced in some positive way, we eventually stop doing it.

"It's like telling a joke to your friends. If they laugh, you'll repeat it to another group. But if it's a bomb, you'll never tell it again. We stop doing things that have no payoff for us. We think, *This action isn't doing me any good, so why do it?*

"Now that I've explained the crucial law of reinforcement, I want to stress the responsibilities you each have. Jean, I know it's hard to keep on being gentle when Tom ignores you. When you don't get anything for your hard work, you're tempted to quit. But you can't! Your responsibility is to continue to start new behaviors. Tom's ability to notice will improve. I know he'll get better at both identifying and responding to your new actions.

"And, Tom, here's your responsibility. You need to put on a new pair of glasses—glasses that are not fogged up by past perceptions—so you can catch Jean doing good. And then, reinforce her—thank her, acknowledge her efforts, or say something to her so she knows that you know she's tried to please you. This kind of positive feedback helps Jean keep her activity level up. On the other hand, if you criticize or fail to respond positively to her changed behavior, you snuff out the very behaviors you want and need—so you lose. Each of you must realize that criticism and the inability to give credit, appreciation, and praise will kill motivation. The point is that the role of the receiver is just as important as the giver. That is, you both have to learn to be effective givers and effective receivers of pleasing behaviors.

"Tom, something else happens when you fail to acknowledge Jean's progress: Her new behavior will taper off, and she is likely to relapse into her old, harsh patterns. This sets in motion one of those negative cycles that has entrapped you in the past. Jean criticizes you for something, you escape to the TV or golf, she interprets this as indifference, and eventually a raging conflict results. Over time, these cycles increase bad feelings about each other and the relationship. Both of you contribute to those cycles, and both of you have to cooperate to end them by exchanging a high number of pleasing behaviors followed by a high number of positive reinforcers."

Lesson 3: Learning Positive Feedback Skills

"There's another lesson that can come from your conflict, and that has to do with learning how to give positive feedback. Since most couples have never been taught how to use reinforcement principles in their daily interaction, let's spend the rest of our session practicing the skill of giving positive feedback to each other. There are three ways to acknowledge, reinforce, or praise your mate's efforts.

"The first one is simply called *Reading Positives*. Here's how it's done: Pick a day and a category from the BEST where you checked a number of positives or pleases received from your mate." Dr. Martin gave them a few moments then said, "Jean, what day and category did you choose?"

"I'm looking at the 'Self-Esteem' area for Sunday."

"Okay, now I want you to turn to Tom and share with him how he pleased you in that category. Just read the positive behaviors you checked."

"Well, Tom, you said I was attractive, and you especially pointed out that you still liked my freckles and brown eyes. You said I was a good cook, and you praised me for making a wise decision on the new dress I bought. You also noticed that I had cleaned out the junk drawer in the kitchen. Those five things really pleased me."

"That's good, Jean. Now, Tom, it's your turn. Tell Jean what category you picked and what she did that day to please you."

"In the category of 'Household Tasks,' it pleased me when you made that good meal on Monday—you know how much I love your lasagna with spinach filling. And I was pleased that you cleaned the bathroom. You know how I hate to johnny-mop the toilets. I was also pleased when you straightened up the house and did the laundry."

"Okay, you're off to a good start," encouraged Dr. Martin. Now let's practice the second feedback skill. It's called finding the *Best Positive of the Day*. Look over your checklist again, and in a different category for any day find the thing your partner did that pleased you most. Then I want you to share it enthusiastically with your mate. Jean, you go first. What category and day did you choose?"

"I'm looking at 'Parenting' on Tuesday. Tom did several things I liked in that area on that day, but the Best Positive was 'Partner disciplined child firmly but without harshness.' On that day, Tom had to discipline Chris because he hadn't cleaned his room like he'd been told. Usually, Tom loses his temper and scolds him so fiercely I have to come to the rescue, and then, of course, we get into a fight about my interference. But this time Tom handled it firmly, without yelling or losing his temper."

"Now, Jean, I want you to turn to Tom and tell him what you've been telling me. Share it as enthusiastically as you can."

"Well, Tom, you know how important it is to me that you discipline the boys in a mild-mannered way. It's difficult for me to explain, but when you come on so strongly with them, it frightens me, and I feel like rushing in like a mother hen to protect my chicks. You had every right to be mad at Chris for his messy room, but you handled it really well—you were firm, you told him there would be no TV until his room was cleaned up, and you didn't lose control. That was the best thing of the day and the Best Positive of the whole week."

As Jean finished she reached out and squeezed Tom's hand. Tom smiled a big grin as he received Jean's appreciation. As Dr. Martin watched Jean communicate the Best Positive with words and human touch, he knew that in the future Tom would be more apt to discipline the way Jean wanted.

"Jean, that was an excellent way of sharing your Best Positive with Tom. Feedback given with both warm words and physical touch has a great impact on us. Now, Tom, let's have you share with Jean what she did on that same day that pleased you most."

"That's an easy choice for me. It's in the 'Communication' area. I checked 'We agreed on something.' Remember Jean, when I read that article on TV viewing that told how hard TV was on family life? We've always disagreed in the past about how much TV the boys should watch, but that day, when I suggested the boys watch less television so they could get their homework done, you agreed with me. I was so surprised when you said, 'That's a good idea; I'm all for it.' It really makes me happy when you agree instead of challenging or disagreeing with me. I need your support in some of those tough decisions that aren't popular with the boys. That was definitely the best thing you did for me on that day."

"You both did a good job expressing the Best Positive of the day to one another. Remember, you can pick a Best Positive for each day from any category. But there's a third way to strengthen your mate's behavior so that it will happen again. You can use *Appreciation Notes.*"

Dr. Martin then handed Tom and Jean a three-by-five-inch index card and instructed them to write these words on their card: "I appreciated it when you . . ." He then asked them to write an ending to this sentence about their partner's behavior for that day.

Dr. Martin gave them a minute to fill out their cards and then said, "Okay, now exchange your appreciation notes with each other."

Upon trading notes, they broke into wide grins as Tom remarked, "I didn't even know that you had noticed." Jean's appreciation note to Tom read, "I appreciated it when you cleaned the toilet this morning."

Jean's grin was from embarrassment as she said, "I could have guessed this one." Tom's Appreciation Note to her read, "I appreciated it when we had sex this morning."

"Sounds like you're getting into the swing of this," chuckled Dr. Martin. "Now I want you to keep it going by giving each other a note like this every day for the next week. It'll be part of your homework assignment as long as you're using the checklist, but it might be something you'll want to continue indefinitely."

"I have a question," said Jean. "Are we to use all three of the positive feedback skills every evening?"

"Yes. You need to do all three every day, but you can write the note at any time during the day and leave it where your mate will find it. Make that part of it fun.

"Well, you've both done well in our practice activities today. The three feedback skills are not complicated, but couples sometimes feel uncomfortable giving feedback because it hasn't been a natural part of their daily interaction."

"It was a little awkward last week trying to follow the Praise rule, but I'm certainly feeling better about it now. It really helps to have some specific things to do to help us get started. I especially like the Appreciation Notes—it's a fun way to say 'thanks.' I know we don't do that enough."

"Right, Jean. There are so many wonderful things we never tell each other. The praise rule and the feedback skills give you chances to say things which often go unsaid. I hope you can see how vital this rule is to your marriage. Silent gratitude doesn't help anyone."

"After the problem we got into this week, that's one rule we're not likely to forget," laughed Tom.

DR. MARTIN'S SUMMARY

"Well, I'd planned to spend this session looking over your checklists from last week, but I think it's been more valuable to deal with this problem area instead. As you can see, conflict is not always bad—sometimes we can learn from it.

"I hope you'll remember the three lessons. The first is to be aware of some thinking factors—like negative past perceptions—which can lurk in your mind and cause you to overlook your mate's positive behavior.

"The second lesson had to do with understanding how positive reinforcement works in marriage. Reinforcement, feedback, and praise are such powerful events in rebuilding a marriage. I can't emphasize enough how vital it is that you acknowledge each other's pleasing behaviors; Keep this in mind: If a partner ignores his mate's new efforts or, worse yet, finds fault with them, they will dwindle. But if you acknowledge the good things your mate does, you'll motivate him or her to keep at it. Always try to praise a pleasing action.

"And the third lesson was learning three specific ways to feedback positive information to your mate about his or her good behavior. Reading Positives, choosing the Best Positive of the day, and giving Appreciation Notes are reinforcers which motivate your mate to repeat pleasing actions. Each of you needs to hear how you pleased your spouse.

"Our time is up, but if you'll leave me last week's summary sheets I'll look over them before we meet next week. We'll spend more time talking about your checklists next time, as well as giving you some more strategies to help you increase the number of positive, pleasing behaviors. Now, go home and have some fun catching each other doing good. I'll see you next session."

Tom helped Jean on with her coat and opened the office door for her. As Dr. Martin watched them walk toward the exit, Jean slipped her arm into Tom's. By learning the power of praise, they had taken another step toward becoming a happy couple.

ENRICHMENT ACTIVITIES FOR READERS

1. Continue to use the BEST for a second week. It should be used for *fourteen* straight days.

2. Try to increase your P:N ratios each day. The higher they get, the happier you'll be.

3. Expand your range of P's. Use the long list of BEST events to find new ways of pleasing your mate. Raising the number of pleasing events and adding novelty and variation are both important.

4. Apply the three feedback skills daily.

SESSION SIX

Care Days and Cookie Jars

Dr. Martin welcomed Tom and Jean to their sixth counseling session. "There are two things we need to do in this session. First, I want us to focus on the benefits of counting behavior, and second, I'll show you some other ways to increase your positive behavior exchanges. But to begin with, did the BEST work any better this week? How do you feel about all this hard data collecting?"

"It sure went smoother this week," responded Jean cheerfully. "I'm beginning to see why you kept prodding us to add positives to our marriage. Counting nice things on our checklist has really helped."

"Jean's right," confirmed Tom. "It's been a great week."

"I'm glad to hear things have improved. Now, let's look at your Weekly Summary pages to see what's been happening."

Tom and Jean handed Dr. Martin their summaries. He laid them on the table so they could study them together.

VALUES OF EXCHANGING POSITIVE BEHAVIOR

Value 1: Finding Balance in Positives

Dr. Martin studied the pages briefly and said, "It's easy to see why you're happier this week. I notice several good things about your data. For one thing, your P's went up and your N's went down throughout the week. That's a big reason why you're feeling good—remember, the number of P's and N's is linked to daily happiness. No doubt about it, you're starting to put positives back into your marriage. And you're

BEHAVIOR EXCHANGE SKILLS TECHNIQUE SUMMARY---WEEK 2

RATING SCALE

Marital Happiness Rating

0 1 2 3 4 5 6 7 8 9 10

Very Unhappy — Neither Happy nor Unhappy — Very Happy

	S	M	T	W	T	F	S
	3	4	6	7	8	9	9

Observation made by: Husband ☐ Wife ☒

POSITIVES DIVIDED BY NEGATIVES

	S	M	T	W	T	F	S
P:N Ratio (Categories A-L)	1:1	3:1	5:1	7:1	14:1	14:1	15:1
P:N Ratio (Problem-Solving)							

		S	M	T	W	T	F	S
A. CARE	Positives	1	2	1	2	2	3	3
	Negatives	0	0	0	0	0	0	0
B. COMMUNICATION	Positives	2	2	2	3	3	3	2
	Negatives	1	2	1	1	0	0	0
C. EMPATHY	Positives	3	3	4	4	4	4	5
	Negatives	1	1	0	0	0	1	0
D. SEX	Positives	1	1	2	0	3	3	3
	Negatives	1	1	0	0	0	0	0
E. PARENTING	Positives	1	2	2	2	2	3	2
	Negatives	1	1	0	0	0	1	0
F. FRIENDSHIP	Positives	1	2	2	2	3	3	2
	Negatives	1	1	0	0	1	0	0
G. INDEPENDENCE	Positives	1	1	1	1	1	1	1
	Negatives	0	0	0	0	0	0	0
H. SELF-ESTEEM	Positives	1	2	3	3	3	3	4
	Negatives	1	0	1	0	0	0	0
I. HOUSEHOLD TASKS	Positives	2	2	2	2	3	2	3
	Negatives	1	0	0	1	1	0	1
J. MONEY	Positives	0	0	3	0	1	0	1
	Negatives	1	0	0	0	0	0	0
K. PERSONAL HABITS	Positives	1	1	1	1	1	2	2
	Negatives	2	1	2	1	0	0	1
L. JOB/SCHOOL	Positives	0	1	0	1	1	1	1
	Negatives	0	0	1	0	0	0	0
CATEGORY A-L DAILY TOTALS	Positives	14	19	23	21	27	28	29
	Negatives	10	7	5	3	2	2	2
PROBLEM-SOLVING TOTALS	Positives							
	Negatives							

BEHAVIOR EXCHANGE SKILLS TECHNIQUE SUMMARY---WEEK 2

RATING SCALE → Marital Happiness Rating

0 1 2 3 4 5 6 7 8 9 10

Very Unhappy   Neither Happy nor Unhappy   Very Happy

	S	M	T	W	T	F	S
	4	5	7	8	8	9	10

Observation made by Husband ☒ Wife ☐

POSITIVES DIVIDED BY NEGATIVES →

	S	M	T	W	T	F	S
P:N Ratio (Categories A-L)	3:1	5:1	4:1	7:1	7:1	15:1	15:1
P:N Ratio (Problem-Solving)							

Category			S	M	T	W	T	F	S
A. CARE	Positives		1	2	1	3	2	3	3
	Negatives		0	0	0	0	0	0	0
B. COMMUNICATION	Positives		2	2	2	2	2	2	2
	Negatives		1	1	1	0	1	0	0
C. EMPATHY	Positives		4	4	4	4	5	5	6
	Negatives		1	0	1	1	0	0	1
D. SEX	Positives		2	2	3	0	3	3	3
	Negatives		0	0	1	0	0	0	0
E. PARENTING	Positives		2	3	2	2	3	3	2
	Negatives		0	1	0	0	0	1	0
F. FRIENDSHIP	Positives		1	2	2	2	3	3	2
	Negatives		1	1	0	0	1	0	0
G. INDEPENDENCE	Positives		0	0	1	1	1	1	1
	Negatives		0	0	0	0	0	1	0
H. SELF-ESTEEM	Positives		1	2	2	2	3	3	3
	Negatives		1	1	1	0	0	0	0
I. HOUSEHOLD TASKS	Positives		3	4	3	4	3	4	5
	Negatives		1	0	1	1	1	0	1
J. MONEY	Positives		0	0	1	0	1	0	1
	Negatives		0	0	0	1	0	0	0
K. PERSONAL HABITS	Positives		1	1	2	1	1	2	1
	Negatives		1	1	0	0	0	0	0
L. JOB/SCHOOL	Positives		0	1	0	1	1	1	1
	Negatives		0	0	1	0	1	0	0
CATEGORY A-L DAILY TOTALS →	Positives		17	23	23	22	28	30	30
	Negatives		6	5	6	3	4	2	2
PROBLEM-SOLVING TOTALS →	Positives								
	Negatives								

cutting down on the displeases—getting rid of even a few negatives can make a big difference in how happy you are.

"But there's another good sign. When you compare each other's P:N ratios, what do you find?"

"Well, except for the first two days, they look about the same," answered Jean. "That surprises me. In the past I always thought I was giving more than Tom, but the chart shows we're pretty even."

"You're right. The record shows that one person isn't doing all the giving while the other person is doing all the taking. In the lives of unhappy couples, we often see a huge inequity—one spouse gives a high number of P's while the other gives only a few; inequities in P's are a major reason why they are unhappy. But your give-and-get is equal. Checking for balance is one of the real values of the BEST. Have you noticed other ways it's been helpful this week?"

Value 2: Preventing Conflict

"I think it's saved us some fights," answered Tom. "Like Jean has just said, she often believed she was doing most of the giving, and I was doing all the taking. Her I'm-better-than-you-are attitude would lead to a fight—I'd get defensive and try to count up all my good behaviors to prove she was wrong. But with the checklist, a simple counting of P's shows what really goes on between us. We don't have to rely on memories—it's there in black and white."

"That's an excellent point," said Dr. Martin. "The checklist keeps the record straight about who's doing what. It gives you a precise history of P's and shows what the true interaction pattern looks like. It helps to head off a spouse's protest of 'Why should I work to put out more pleases? I'm already doing more than my share.'

"Besides preventing conflict, counting behaviors can also help you battle some of those negative mind games we've discussed. As I've mentioned, unhappy couples are not accurate observers of the behaviors being exchanged—they see the bad and miss the good. But daily records of P and N behaviors can clear up distortions, shift thinking, change attitudes, and build positive images about your mate."

Value 3: Understanding the Happiness-Behavior Link

"Now, let's look at your summary charts again. Do you see a connection between your P:N ratios and your happiness ratings?"

"It's pretty clear that when the ratio is low our happiness is low, but when it gets higher, our happiness goes up, too," answered Tom.

"That really shouldn't be a surprise," added Jean. "You've been telling us all along that would happen. Our happiness really is tied to how well we treat each other. I can see why you spent so much time urging us to add more P's and subtract N's."

"I'm glad you've spotted the connection between happiness and behavior. When couples recognize how their behavior affects their mate's happiness, they usually become more committed to increasing pleasing behaviors and decreasing displeasing behaviors. And once a couple consciously changes their exchange pattern, their marital happiness changes, too—and that, of course, is where we're headed. Boosting positives and reducing negatives is a proven way to get a marriage back on track. Okay, what other values do you see in behavior exchanging?"

Value 4: Learning More about Your Partner

"One of the things I like about the BEST is that I don't have to be a mind reader anymore. In the past, I got mad at Jean because she expected me to know intuitively how to please her. Now, by reading Jean's checklist, I don't have to guess how to make her happy—with the Positives, I know what behaviors she likes; with the Wants, I know what changes she desires; and with the Negatives, I know what behaviors get her goat. For instance, I'm getting much smarter about how I displease Jean in the 'Money' area—she gets real insecure when I don't keep the checkbook up-to-date or when I spend beyond the budget. Knowing these things about her gives me confidence and makes it less likely for me to fail as a partner. In fact, it's been a relief learning what it takes to please Jean. From the feedback I get on the checklist, I know how my efforts are best spent and what behaviors to work on."

"I feel like I'm getting to know Tom better, too. When we talk over the results on our checklist every night, I find out just what's important to him. Even after all these years of marriage, I'm learning new things about him. I've always known how important sex was to Tom, but I didn't realize that certain kinds of caring, attention, and touch were so important. For example, he likes it when I initiate a hug, put my arm around his waist, or give him a little pinch. Now I know that when I increase my behaviors in the areas of both sex and caring, it sparks his happiness.

"Another thing I've noticed," continued Jean, "is that the BEST has alerted me to our differences. I always thought Tom liked what I liked, but the BEST has helped me find out that what makes me happy may not be what makes him happy. For example, I always like to have the grass cut and the house straightened up before company comes, but I've discovered that Tom couldn't care less. I guess that's my need, not his."

"It sounds like the BEST is helping you learn some important lessons about one another. For one thing, you are recognizing the impact you have on each other—both positive and negative. You're starting to see the effect your behavior has on the receiver, and you're paying attention to those actions that have a major influence on your mate's happiness. Isn't it strange that you can live together all these years without knowing your partner's 'hot buttons'? I hope you are also coming to see that you do have control over your relationship—you can change it with your P and N behaviors.

"Another lesson is that you're learning about one another's preferences. Jean, as you have discovered, there are key differences between you. Often, we act on the belief that our sources of happiness are the same. That kind of thinking can get us into trouble because it leads to significant omissions. That is, we miss some good opportunities to please our mate. But with the BEST, you can avoid making assumptions that your partner's preferences are similar to your own. This is one of the values of the checklist—it helps you pinpoint what really makes each other happy."

"But just discovering these things isn't enough. Don't we have to act on our new learning?"

"Yes, Jean. Real love in a marriage means that each spouse is responsible for learning about and responding to his or her mate's needs. Tom, with your new insight about Jean's security needs, it's vital that you give new behaviors in the 'Money' area. And, Jean, now that you've learned that your caring behaviors are so important to Tom, it requires you to give more in that area. Understanding your mate's needs and then acting to meet those needs are two key partner-pleasing skills. So by all means, support your new knowledge with new behaviors—increase the positives and cut down on the negatives.

"Now, what other advantages do you see in the behavior exchange assignment?"

Value 5: Improving Care Levels

"I'd have to say the increase in caring. For the first time in months, I feel like Tom really cares about me. I've loved all his attention this past week—I just hope it lasts."

"I've noticed that, too," agreed Tom. "Jean's been showing that she does care for me. I think this has been the happiest week in our marriage for a long time. How can the BEST help us to turn things around so quickly?"

"That's a good question, Tom. Here's my answer. When you came into counseling, you were both extremely stressed-out. For months, you'd been hammering on each other trying to get change but going about it all wrong. All your energies went into making conflict instead of caring for one another. So you began to feel deprived of

love, affection, and gratification. You felt unappreciated for the efforts you had made. As a result, you were hurt, angry, frustrated, and
dissatisfied with each other. Quite simply, your basic need to be
cared for was unmet, and your reservoirs of relationship energy were
depleted."

"That describes us perfectly," said Tom. "We were out of gas emotionally, and were we hostile! Anger was stacked up all over the house."

"When I see unhappy couples like you who are exhausted and angry, the best thing I can do is first, help you overcome blame and distortion; second, help you see the good in each other; and third, put
you on a program to increase positive exchanges. Remember, it was
positives that bonded you together in the beginning, so we had to get
you back into the habit of exchanging P's.

"Exchanging P's gave you a quick 'shot in the arm' of marital pleasures which helped revitalize your empty stores of relationship energy.
Exchanging P's helped you re-experience some positive aspects of the
relationship that had disappeared over time. Exchanging P's helped you
behave the way you did when you first met. So if there's any magic in
BEST, it's because it put you on the receiving end of some benefits
you've been missing. According to last week's record, you both did a
good job of trading positives and applying the skills of partner-pleasing.
You both got lots of P's—which are acts of care, love, and concern.
That's why you're feeling up. That's my analysis, Tom, of what's been
happening."

"That helps. I can see that we were in pretty bad shape. We were
both hungry for care and support."

"Hungry?—I'd say we were starving," said Jean.

"Each of us is dying for care and love," said Dr. Martin, "and we
don't know how to go about getting it. Almost everything we do is
affected by these longings. Both of you want to be loved, liked, and
cared for—but you went about it in the wrong way. Because these
human needs are so strong, we had to arrange your home setting so
that you would again start pleasing and caring for each other. And
that, in fact, happened. As your P's went up and N's went down, you
sent a powerful message to one another saying, 'I care for you.' The
BEST has created a caring, supportive environment where your needs
are now being met.

"Okay, what other good experiences have you had with the BEST?"

Value 6: Increasing Motivation

"It's a funny thing, Dr. Martin, but when I sensed that Jean was
starting to care for me this past week, I got motivated to care back. My
feeling was, 'I'll try to please you since you are trying to please me.'"

"You mean, Tom, you felt like reciprocating?" paraphrased Dr. Martin.

"Right. That's sure a turn-around. We've been at each other's throats for so long trading negatives, and all at once, we start to care for each other. Like last Sunday, I was washing the car, and suddenly, there was Jean with a sponge and pail cleaning that muddy car right alongside me. When we finished, I dug up the flower bed she's been wanting for so long. I actually volunteered to do it—she hadn't even mentioned it. It was fun working on that together. Is it normal that two people can affect each other like that?"

"Yes, Tom. I think we've forgotten one of the most basic laws of human behavior: Love breeds love and establishes a positive cycle. You may remember that in our third session, I explained it this way: *Positive actions cause positive reactions, first in the attitude of your partner and then in his or her behavior.* What simply happened, Tom, was that when Jean acted in a caring way, she affected your attitude. And when you felt cared for and appreciated instead of criticized, it motivated you to reciprocate—to give back in like manner."

"That law sure worked on me," said Jean. "When I noticed Tom was changing his P's and N's, it really did influence me. It made me want to please him back. But there was something else. A big part of my motivation came because we started using the praising ideas you taught us last session. Reading our Positives, sharing the Best Positive, and exchanging Appreciation Notes really stirred me to show care for Tom. When he thanks me for something, I want to please him even more."

"That was true for me, too," agreed Tom. "On Wednesday, Jean put an Appreciation Note in my lunchbox thanking me for balancing the checkbook. I thought about her all afternoon wondering what I could do to make her happy. I ended up buying her some roses on the way home."

"He hasn't done that for years, Dr. Martin. That was really special. But the big surprise bonus came when he said he was glad he was coming to counseling with me instead of going golfing on Saturdays. That made my day."

Dr. Martin smiled as he listened to Tom and Jean talk about their new-found motivation to please each other. It was clear that the BEST experience was having a good effect on them. It had prompted reciprocity attitudes—they were motivated to care and give back. The BEST was also giving the couple opportunities to acknowledge one another's efforts, and by giving positive feedback and recognition, their resolve to reciprocate was strengthened. And as Tom and Jean started to act more positive toward each other, they seemed willing to invest more energy into the hard job of rebuilding their

marriage. But Dr. Martin was equally happy to see that the couple
had been able to push blame to the background and bring about
relationship changes with a cooperative effort. They were working as
a team to increase P's.

"Now, just before we move to the next part of our session, let's summarize briefly our discussion on the values of the BEST. Whatever we
choose to call it—reciprocity training, partner-pleasing, or behavior exchange—the BEST is a necessary tool for renewing a marriage. I'll list
the six advantages here on the flip chart.

"*First*, the BEST helps to identify if partner-pleasing is balanced. If
it's unequal, then that spouse can be encouraged to raise his or her rate
of P's. *Second*, behavior counting gives us an accurate picture of what
the behavior exchange pattern really is, not what we feel it is; and this
objectivity in a relationship can help prevent conflict and distortion.
Third, the BEST helps you learn which behaviors please or displease
your partner. Therefore, you come to understand how to influence
your mate's happiness. *Fourth*, it helps you learn about the unique
needs of each other. *Fifth*, the BEST boosts care levels and charges your
relationship batteries. And *sixth*, it motivates you to give love—thus
recreating a relationship that resembles the marriage you once had."

MERITS OF THE BEST

1. Shows if partner-pleasing is balanced.

2. Prevents conflict and distortion.

3. Raises understanding of the happiness-behavior link.

4. Gives insight to your partner.

5. Improves care levels.

6. Boosts motivation.

OTHER METHODS TO INCREASE POSITIVES

Care Days

"You've had success with the BEST. Now we're ready to learn some other ways to increase your positive behaviors. The first one is called *Care Days*.

"The Care Day is a special day for caring exchanges. On that day, it's your job to increase the number of positive things you do for your mate. These are not just small increases in P's but rather large spurts of pleasures—the giver of a Care Day is to double his/her output of pleasing behaviors."

"You mean you want us to increase our positive behaviors 100 percent?"

"Yes, that's right."

"Well, how do we decide when to give a Care Day?" asked Tom.

"You each decide what day of the week you want to be the giver. It's like a secret decision, but the receiver should be able to tell at the end of the day if he or she has received a Care Day."

"I get it. If you are on the receiving end of a Care Day, there will be more marks on your BEST, and there should be a big jump in your happiness rating."

"Exactly, Tom. If you're the person giving a Care Day, you'll know if you've succeeded because your mate's daily happiness rating will have peaked."

"It sounds like fun, but isn't it going to be hard to double the number of positives in one day?" asked Jean.

"Don't forget, the checklist provides a large menu of pleasing events to use on a Care Day. This'll give you the chance to try some you haven't gotten around to yet. But if you feel overwhelmed by giving a total Care Day, try a smaller amount of time, like a Care Hour or a Care Evening. Whichever one you do, the goal is always the same— make the time exceptionally pleasing for your mate."

Cookie Jars *

"Another method to help you increase positive exchanges is the *Cookie Jar*. With this method, each of you will develop a pool of desired events that you would like to receive from your partner. These events could include such items as receiving a box of candy, having your spouse clean the garage, or getting a back rub. You simply

---

* Dr. Robert Weiss at the University of Oregon Marital Studies Program developed the "cookie jar" method of increasing positive exchanges.

write your items on color-coded slips of paper (for example, yellow for one spouse and green for the other) and store them in a cookie jar or any container with a lid. Whenever you want to do something nice for your spouse, you just draw the appropriately colored slip from the jar and follow the instruction written on the slip.

"This is a good way to keep positives in your marriage, but you'll need to follow some guidelines to make it work. First, the desired events should not include requests for sweeping personality changes like 'Be an extrovert.' Second, the requests should ask for an increase in a behavior, not a decrease. Events like 'Stop smoking' or 'Don't yell at the kids' won't work.

"Third, you need to put the Cookie Jar in an easy-to-see place so it'll be a constant reminder to use it. The idea is that anytime you want to do something nice for your spouse, you pull out one of his/her slips from the jar and do what it says. Do you have any questions about this activity?"

"The Cookie Jar sounds like the same thing as the Want column on our checklist," said Jean.

"They are similar—both focus on behaviors you want to receive. But there's a difference. When you respond to a Want from the checklist, you're doing something that's expected of you. But when you use the Cookie Jar, it's spontaneous—you do it because you really want to. That'll mean even more to your mate."

DR. MARTIN'S SUMMARY

"We have about five minutes left, so I want to help you get going on the Cookie Jar by starting a list of wants." Dr. Martin gave Jean a sheet of yellow paper and Tom a sheet of green paper on which to write their lists.

When Tom and Jean had completed their lists, Dr. Martin announced, "Our counseling time is up for today, but before you go, I want to summarize where we are in our relationship-building. In the last three sessions, our goal has been to help you develop a marriage where there are more positives than negatives. As I've said, happy couples reciprocate positive behaviors more frequently than unhappy couples. That is, in a good marriage, the partners trade many P's. Because of this fact, I've tried to help you structure your daily lives to include a lot of positive exchanges.

"To accomplish this, we've learned three ways to generate more P's—the BEST, Care Days, and Cookie Jars. You've now had fourteen days of using the BEST, so this week try the Care Days and Cookie Jar. With another successful week of exchanging positive behaviors, you'll be ready to learn another trait commonly found in the lives of happy couples—the trait of using positive behavior change skills. Have a good week."

ENRICHMENT ACTIVITIES FOR READERS

1. If you've followed Tom and Jean's counseling schedule, you should have completed fourteen days of using the BEST. If your P:N ratios are high and you are feeling happy about your relationship, stop counting behaviors. Instead, keep the positives going by trying *Care Days* and *Cookie Jars*.

2. If you feel your P:N ratios are not high enough yet, continue the BEST for another seven days.

3. Invent your own pool of *Cookie Jar* behaviors. Here are a few to help you get started:

Brag on me to the kids.
Give me a scalp massage.
Say something that would make me feel proud or happy.
Shampoo my hair.
Read a book with me.
Take me to a romantic movie.
Let's go to a coffee shop and try new coffees.
Help me buy some new home decoration (picture, painting, etc.).
Take me to an antique shop.
Make my favorite dessert.
Tell me you love me.
Compliment me with an honest praise.
Put some money in our vacation piggy bank.
Help me do a hard chore.
Help me work on my favorite hobby or craft.
Let's go browsing in a book store.
Help me plan a party or dinner for friends.
Let's take some donuts and visit friends.
Do one of my chores for me.
Exchange back scratches.
Help me wash the car.
Tell me some news you know I would enjoy hearing.
Make me a homemade pizza with lots of stuff on it.
Go window shopping with me.
Help me plan or work on a home improvement project.
Help me do the bills.
Make love to me.

SESSION SEVEN

Changing Your Mate

"Come on in, folks. Today, we're going to spend time talking about a second trait that distinguishes happy from unhappy couples: Happily married partners use positive methods to change their mate's behavior, but unhappy couples go about it in a more negative way. I'll write this key trait difference here on the flip chart to help us remember."

"Dr. Martin, when you talk about happy couples using positives and unhappy ones using negatives to change each other, what exactly do you mean?"

"Tom, I briefly mentioned these methods in session three, but this is a good time to review them. When family scholars made studies of how happy couples control each other, they found that happy partners use positive reinforcement—things like praise, approval, affection, sex, or a favorite dessert. In contrast, studies of unhappy couples showed that these couples seldom use these positive control techniques. Instead, troubled couples rely on negative pressure tactics or coercion like threats, intimidation, criticism, yelling, silence, and withdrawal. Being constantly hit with these negatives plays a big part in the breakdown of a marriage."

"I have a question about this behavior change you're talking about," said Jean. "I've always heard you shouldn't try to change your mate. You married him for 'better or worse,' so it's a mistake to try to change him."

"I know there are people who believe that, but I think they're missing the real essence of marriage. Marriage is a place to exchange benefits—to give and take positive behaviors. It's a place to meet each other's physical and emotional needs. So when one person feels he/

96

she is not receiving benefits, then the relationship must be changed or adjusted in some way. The point is this: It's normal in marriage that situations occur when you will be disappointed by your mate, and so you will want him/her to behave differently.

"Just look at your own case, for example. Jean, you've wanted Tom to change by spending more time with you, and Tom has wanted you to change from a critical person to a gentle, affirming wife. These are legitimate changes to desire from each other—neither of you should apologize for wanting them. Just think how happy you'd be if your mate were to change and become the person you wanted!"

"I see what you mean. I guess that's why we came to you in the first place—we wanted change from each other, but we couldn't get it."

"Right, Jean, and the biggest reason why you couldn't get change is because you went about it in the wrong way. You began coercing instead of reinforcing each other. Jean, you'd nag and criticize; and Tom, you would use silence or withdraw from the conflict. Unfortunately, neither of you knew there were more constructive ways to get change. So you kept relying on these old, useless tactics, and they brought a lot of unhappiness into your marriage. You see, that's part of the education you've missed. You've never learned the positive skills to control your mate. Today, I'm going to teach you these skills. When you learn these positive methods for behavior change, it will move you closer to becoming a happy couple."

METHODS FOR CHANGING BEHAVIOR

"For the rest of our time today, we'll be working on these methods. Did you notice that I said 'methods' with an *s?* That's right, there is more than one. Some couples believe it's impossible to change their mate, but usually that's because they have tried only one way—which is the only one they know—and it didn't work. Naturally, they get frustrated with their mate and feel powerless to control the relationship when this happens. Restricting yourself to only one change tactic is risky; you need a wide variety of methods to choose from. The more you have, the better your chances to find one that will work with your spouse. It's like having more than one arrow in your quiver—if the first shot doesn't score, you still have others to use. So let's look at six different ways you can bring about change."

Change Method 1: Using the Checklist

"By using the BEST *checklist,* you've learned that it's a way to give and get pleasing behavior. But it's more than just a tool to help you express care for each other—it will also help you change one another's behavior. Can you think of any ways the checklist has already worked to change anything about your partner?"

"I can think of one," responded Jean. "One night, I checked a Negative in the 'Money' section because Tom didn't have the checkbook up-to-date—that same old problem again. He still didn't understand how frustrated I get when he doesn't pay bills and I have to deal with angry creditors on the phone. For one of my Wants that day, I checked where it referred to bills being paid on time, because I really wanted Tom to do that. It's one thing if we don't have the money, but usually the money is right there in the bank, and he just hasn't gotten around to writing the checks. Anyway, marking those two things on the list must have had an influence, because the next night he sat down, paid all the bills, and balanced the checkbook."

"When I saw it on the list, it was easy to do," explained Tom. "In the past, Jean's tried to talk me into doing it, but when she comes across cranky, I get stubborn, and we end up in a fight. But this time, there wasn't a big fuss. I didn't feel defensive; I just changed and did what she wanted. Besides, there was a payoff—she gave me points in the

Positives row and left an Appreciation Note on the bathroom mirror."

"That's an excellent example of how you can use the BEST check-list to get change from each other," affirmed Dr. Martin.

Change Method 2: Positive Reinforcement

"I'm glad you mentioned the Appreciation Note because that leads us into the next method for behavior change—*positive reinforcement*. We've already covered this in detail, so I just want you to see how it fits in with the other methods of change.

"The situation with the checkbook is a perfect example of how part-ners cooperate to get change, but it also demonstrates how to use posi-tive reinforcement. Jean, you used the checklist to show Tom where you wanted him to change. He responded without resistance, and then you reinforced his change in two positive ways—you checked the Posi-tives and gave him a note to tell him how much you liked his efforts.

"Tom, it sounds like Jean's recognition and approval of your good deeds had an impact on you."

"You're right about that. It's great when Jean sees good things in me. When I get her praise and thanks, I feel like redoubling my efforts to please her. But criticism just won't work on me. Even though I know I should change, I just get stubborn. It brings out all my defenses, and I fight back."

"I understand. Most of us respond the same way. Criticism only inflames the conflict and fails to bring about long-lasting change, and that's true of all the coercion tactics—frowns, angry words, accusa-tions, blame, humiliating comments, demands, depriviations, harsh penalties, and threats. But positive reinforcement is more likely to motivate people to change. You'll almost always succeed in changing people by recognizing their positive efforts, good behaviors, and con-tributions."

"I see how Jean used approval instead of criticism to get me to change, but I'm not sure how I can do the same thing with her. I wish I could get her to stop putting me down in front of the boys when I'm disciplining them. I want her to support me and not interfere or challenge me. But how do I get her to do that with this positive reinforcement?"

"First, Tom, start paying attention to those times she does support you—it may not happen often—but I'm sure it does occur. Then, when she supports you, reinforce her immediately. Remember the law of reinforcement we talked about? You have to *add* something to that situation—a smile, congratulations, affectionate touch, enthusiastic praise—that tells her how good it makes you feel. That way, there'll be a payoff for her in doing what you want. And when you give her any of these positive consequences, it causes her to support you again in the future.

"Let me explain positive reinforcement in a different way. Tom, I'm sure there have been days when you've played some really terrible golf—days when nothing went right. You hit balls into trees, water, sand traps, or out-of-bounds. If you managed to make it through the course, you swore you'd never play again. Then, almost miraculously, you hit a great drive off the tee. It's a magnificent shot that just missed a hole-in-one. Suddenly, you're inspired, and the game is wonderful. That one shot revitalized your love for the game. You start thinking great thoughts about yourself—*you're a pretty good golfer after all*. That one shot raises your self-confidence. You can't wait to try it again next week.

"The point is, Tom, that great golf shot is a positive reinforcement, and it motivates you to stay with the game and not give up. You see, when Jean does what you want and you give her a positive consequence like praise, it acts just like your golf shot—it raises her self-esteem and motivates her to increase a behavior. Even though the change may be hard for her, your praise and encouragement help her keep at it. In a nutshell, that's how positive reinforcement strategies change behavior."

"If I hear you right, you're saying that to change or improve each other, we just watch closely for the good behaviors and then reinforce them."

"Yes, Tom, it's that easy, and there are many reinforcers to use—Appreciation Notes, thank yous, hugs, back rubs, a foot massage, gifts, flowers, chocolates. Even sex can be used if you're both in the mood. Just be sure that the reinforcers you use are the ones your mate likes."

"But what if we're not sure?"

"If you don't know what Jean enjoys, ask her. And when you find out, use her favorite things often to reward her new behaviors. But if you're ever in doubt, the best reinforcers are in the area of appreciation. I say this because one of our deepest human needs is to be appreciated. We all need to be approved of and affirmed. Approval is always a good consequence to follow a good behavior. It'll motivate your mate to make the changes you want."

Change Method 3: Positive Specific Requests (PSR)*

"Let's move on to another way you can influence your partner's behavior by learning to make requests in a positive way. I sometimes call this the *Positive Specific Request Rule* or the *PSR*.

* The "Positive Specific Rule was developed by J. O'Farrell and Henry S.G. Cutter. See "Behavioral Marital Therapy for Male Alcoholics: Clinical Procedures from a Treatment Outcome Study in Progress," *The American Journal of Family Therapy* 12 (1984): 33–46.

"We tend to think behavior change rests only on the willingness of one partner to change. But it's equally important that the other partner have the ability to ask for change in a manner that makes it easy for the spouse to respond. When you seek change, you have three key responsibilities. First, *be positive*—state what you want, not what you don't want. Second, *be specific* and clear so there's no confusion about what you want. *Specific* means what, where, and when. Third, *make requests*, not demands, threats, or statements that try to coerce your partner to change. This means to say it in a friendly, noncritical tone that shows the possibility for negotiation and compromise. The point is, some problems don't get solved simply because the asking spouse doesn't have the social skills to make a PSR. Instead, he/she asks in a negative, vague, or abrasive manner that creates resistance in the mate.

"To help you understand the PSR Rule, here are nine guidelines." Dr. Martin then handed a page of guidelines to Tom and Jean. He explained each one and then said, "The best way to learn to make a PSR is to practice making one. So let's take a few minutes and use some of these guidelines on a real problem. What kind of behavior changes would you like from each other? Jean, what about you?"

"One of the changes I'd like Tom to make is in personal habits. After he takes a shower, he leaves his clothes in a pile on the bathroom floor and expects me to take care of them."

"Okay. Now, request that change from Tom."

"Tom, I'd like you to hang up your clothes or put them in the hamper after your shower," asked Jean calmly.

"Tom, what's your response?"

"No problem. I'll be more careful from now on to keep my clothes picked up."

"Now, that behavior change wasn't too hard to achieve, was it? And the reason, Jean, is that you did a good job of stating your request. It was positive, you pinpointed the behavior specifically, and it wasn't a demand."

"Most important to me was that Jean didn't get mad or raise her voice," commented Tom. "I'm a real pushover when she puts sweetness in her voice."

"Okay, Tom, it's your turn to make a request."

"Well, I'd still like Jean to stop interfering when I'm disciplining the kids. We get into lots of fights because she keeps rescuing them when they need to be punished."

"Tom, that request doesn't fit guideline 5," said Jean. "I mean, we've had some real knock-down-drag-outs about that discipline thing."

"Jean's right. That's a problem, not a request. You'll have to save that for a later problem-solving session. Besides, you've asked her to stop a behavior instead of starting or increasing one. Try another request."

GUIDELINES FOR MAKING POSITIVE SPECIFIC REQUESTS

1. Begin your request in a nonthreatening, nondemanding way. To increase the chances of getting a cooperative response, communicate the request effectively by using any of these three openings:

> "I would appreciate it if you . . ."
> "I would like you to . . . "
> "Would you please . . . "

2. State your request in a neutral, noncritical way. To prevent hooking into your mate's defensiveness, keep your tone of voice calm, gentle, and without emotions.

3. State your request in specific terms. Don't force your mate to be a mind reader or play a guessing game because of a vague, ambiguous request. For example, instead of saying, "I want you to take more responsibility for raising our son," state the request in precise terms that pinpoint the behavior and the frequency: "I would like you to spend from noon until three on Saturday taking care of the children."

4. Use the BEST. A simple way of learning to make requests is to refer to the BEST. It is usually easy to select a behavior that is clearly identified on the list as something you would very much like to receive. After you have chosen a behavior, restate it as a request.

5. Confine your requests to behaviors that have no negative emotional history. It is important to differentiate between requests and problem-solving issues. Any behavior that has been the subject of repeated discussions or has been the source for intense conflict should not be requested. Those behaviors are to be earmarked as issues to be saved for later problem-solving discussions.

6. Request behaviors that can be performed by your spouse at minimal cost. Help your mate succeed at what you are asking him/her to do.

7. Requests should focus on behaviors which, if carried out, would increase your pleasure rather than just remove irritations. Instead of saying, "I would like you to stop yelling at the kids," try "I'd really like it if you would keep your voice calm when disciplining the children." Ask for increases, not decreases in behavior. It is easier to reinforce increases.

8. The behavior chosen must be one that can be completed within the upcoming week.

9. Avoid negotiations. Stay away from requests that involve counter-proposals and compromises. The request should be uncomplicated so that the person of whom the request is made can simply agree to what she/he is willing to do.

"Okay, I've got one: Jean, I'd like you to start greeting me at the door with a kiss and hug when I get home from work each night."

"That request really surprises me," said Jean. "I never realized they were that important to you. I stopped years ago because I thought it was just a habit without meaning. But I'd love it. I've missed that, too."

"That was a good choice, Tom. You included the three key parts of the PSR Rule. That'll help Jean do just what you want. And, Jean, that was a good response. You agreed immediately without getting into negotiations. We can tell you were successful with your change requests because you both agreed to do what your partner asked. By the way, keep in mind that the more agreements you can make, the happier your marriage will be."

"Dr. Martin, I have a question. What if I follow all the guidelines and Tom still says no?"

"That could happen, Jean, but it's rare. If you're gentle, specific, avoid conflict topics, and keep all the guidelines, Tom will say yes nine out of ten times. If he says no, maybe your timing is not right. Try the same request again, at a different time—I predict he'll comply."

Change Method 4: Touch and Tell

"Now, let me explain a fourth change method. This one is called *Touch and Tell*. Jean, when you want something from Tom, go up to him, look directly into his eyes, give him a big hug, and then make a PSR. The part I want to emphasize is the hugging—positive physical touch is a great resource. When you combine warm words and affectionate touch, it's hard to say no to a request."

Change Method 5: Written Contracts

"Just one more question. Tom has agreed to start picking up his clothes, but what if he doesn't? What do we do then?"

"Good question. I have two answers. First, reinforce any change immediately. When he hangs up even one thing, be quick to notice it and express your pleasure. Remember, failure to acknowledge progress will cause a new behavior to wither and die.

"Second, put your agreement into a simple written contract that can include rewards and penalties. Let's take some time to learn how to write behavior change contracts." Dr. Martin then gave the couple a page of Guidelines for Contracting (see p. 104). Then after discussing the guidelines, he helped them put their new agreements into writing. (See Figure 7.)

After the verbal agreement was placed into written form, Dr. Martin said, "Written agreements have five advantages. Here they are briefly:

GUIDELINES FOR CONTRACTING

1. Written contracts have three parts: Behavior to be changed, rewards to be earned when behavior is completed, and penalties to be applied if behavior is not completed. Rewards and penalties, however, are *optional*.

2. The behavior which is the target for change should be one that can be increased, not decreased.

3. Rewards are divided into two groups: Partner rewards or environmental rewards. *Partner rewards* come from your mate and could include gifts or services (e.g., five-minute backscratch). Before deciding on using a particular partner-given reward, be sure your partner agrees to give it so there is no problem when it is actually earned as part of completing a contract. *Environmental rewards* do not involve your mate. They could include buying a record, going to a movie, etc. In either case, the spouse receiving the reward decides what the rewards will be.

4. Penalties come from two categories: Giving up positive things and doing disagreeable tasks. *Giving up positive things* could include a favorite TV show or dessert. *Disagreeable tasks* include fixing a leaky faucet, cleaning the basement, or giving the dog a bath. In either case, your partner is not linked to the penalties.

5. Use a wide variety of rewards: Joint activities, money, gifts, services, recreation, physical pleasures, etc.

6. Do not use sex as a reward unless you are both in the mood.

7. Rewards must be affordable, practical, and available.

8. Penalties must not be extreme or drastic.

9. Partner rewards should be reasonable—the items should have a low response cost for the partner giving the reward.

10. Partner rewards should not include behaviors that the partner regularly does.

11. Contracts are usually saved to cover more difficult behavior change areas.

12. Post your written agreement so it is easy to see.

BEHAVIOR CHANGE CONTRACT

WIFE	HUSBAND
BEHAVIOR TO INCREASE:	**BEHAVIOR TO INCREASE:**
Jean will give Tom a kiss and hug each night when he gets home from work.	Tom agrees to keep his clothes picked up off the bathroom floor each time he takes a shower.
REWARD:	**REWARD:**
Tom takes Jean out for a special dessert if she does it everyday for a week.	Jean gives a 2-minute backscratch or deposits 25 cents in Tom's golf ball piggy bank each time.
PENALTY:	**PENALTY:**
Jean will vacuum whole house next day.	Tom will mop and clean the bathroom floor and johnny mop the toilet.

Signed:

_Jean_____ (Wife)

_Tom_____ (Husband)

Date: __1/11/88_____

Figure 7. This is an example of how to make a contract with your mate to change a specific behavior. Written contracts should be used only for those behaviors that are hard to change.

First, since they are usually more precise in language than are verbal agreements, the potential for confusion and conflict is decreased. Second, with contracts, you don't have to rely on memory. Third, by posting the written agreement on the refrigerator door or bathroom mirror, it can be a visual cue reminding you to change. Four, a written contract is tangible evidence that you're committed to improving your marriage and making each other happy. Finally, written contracts are another way to add positives to a marriage. That is, they are really behavior exchange agreements where each mate agrees to please each other more."

Change Method 6: Positive Problem-Solving Skills

"The last way to get your partner to make changes is by using positive problem-solving skills. This method you'll save for the really tough problems, and we'll get into that next session. I just wanted to mention it now so you can see how it fits in with the other change methods.

DR. MARTIN'S SUMMARY

"Well, our time is almost gone, so let's summarize what we have talked about. Our purpose today was to learn six positive procedures for bringing about change in your mate. Do you have any comments or questions?"

"This has been a good session for me," said Jean. "When I think back on it, I can see that my frustration and anger stemmed not only from Tom's annoying behaviors, but it also came because I didn't know how to change him. I have to admit, I was not a good sender of my problem, and so Tom couldn't be a good responder. But the most helpful part of today's session was when you said that marriage is a place to trade good behaviors, and when those things stop, it's okay to ask your partner to start them again. Sometimes in the past, I've felt guilty for wanting Tom to be different. But now, you've given me permission to seek change and methods to go along with it."

"Yes, Jean, marriages thrive on exchanged benefits. In good marriages, the partners reciprocate—they swap or return favors. So when the favors decline and the give-and-get becomes lopsided, you have a perfect right to realign the relationship by using one of the behavior change methods we've discussed today.

"Maybe it'll help to remember that change is the third partner in your marriage—the lifeline of your marriage. Being able to adapt and change is a requirement for a happy relationship. But also, you need to be skilled at helping your mate change. Unfortunately, most couples don't have positive skills, and so they rely on negatives to control their mate. They use negative pressure tactics like criticism, demands, guilt, complaining, tears, the silent treatment, threats of leaving, nagging, and whining. But when they try to force change on their mate, it only causes unhappiness. Coercing your spouse only makes you a source of pain instead of pleasure. How you go about getting change affects marital happiness.

"Tom, what about you? How are you feeling about this session?"

"I've got to confess that I've used some of those negative tactics on Jean—like running off to play golf was a way to punish her for being critical. I can see that withdrawing and giving her the silent treatment was wrong, but I didn't know what else to do. I had no idea there were half-a-dozen ways to get Jean to change. Now I'm excited to get home and try out these new ideas; they'll sure beat the fights and put-downs we've used in the past. I just wish we'd known a better way of being negative."

"Right, Tom. In fact, you don't have to be negative with each other. Now, when your mate annoys you or differences in needs arise, instead of reacting with critical feedback, you can use six positive options. They're too important to miss, so I'll put them on the flip chart.

HOW TO CHANGE YOUR MATE

1. Use the BEST.
2. Praise changes with positive reinforcement.
3. Use the PSR Rule.
4. Touch and Tell.
5. Write contracts.
6. Use positive problem-solving skills.

"*First,* use the checklist to identify the changes you want. *Second,* reinforce small changes with praise and appreciation. *Third,* learn to make Positive Specific Requests (PSR's) which motivate your mate to comply, not resist. *Fourth,* you can use warm words and positive touch. *Fifth,* you can contract with each other for specific changes. And *sixth,* you can become effective problem-solvers; that's our agenda for next session. Getting the most from each other is easier than you think if you can remember to apply these strategies for change.

"Just a final thing before you go. Today, we've talked about another trait that separates happy from unhappy couples—the trait of using positive behavior change methods. Happy mates rely on positives and rarely use coercion. But unhappy couples control each other by using many negative tactics and few positive ones. Okay, see you next session, and don't forget to follow through on your behavior change contract."

ENRICHMENT ACTIVITIES FOR READERS

During the next few days, practice behavior change skills.

1. You have already been using the *"Wanted"* part of the BEST to identify behaviors you want started or increased. But you might want to go back and mark other wants.

2. Practice making positive specific requests. Be sure to use the nine guidelines as you make simple verbal agreements.

3. If you feel you have had success getting behavior changes with the BEST Wanteds and with PSR verbal agreements, move to more difficult changes by using written contracts. (Use the contract in Figure 7 as your guide.) Rewards and penalties may be included—they are optional. But if you choose to include rewards, be sure you give them to your mate as they are earned. The biggest reason written contracts fail is because rewards earned are not delivered. Examples of rewards and penalties are given on page 109. Keep in mind that contracting for change is a complex skill and should be saved for the hardest-to-change behaviors. Make contracts only for issues that have a long and difficult history.

4. Whether you achieve behavior change through the BEST, by making PSR's, touch and tell, or through written contracts, remember to *reinforce* all changes with praise, approval, appreciation, or tangible rewards.

EXAMPLES OF REWARDS AND PENALTIES
FOR WRITTEN CONTRACTS

REWARDS

One hour free time while
mate babysits

Breakfast in bed

Mate cooks breakfast or dinner

Shower/bath together

Body massage

Backscratch

Gift under three dollars

Home-baked bread or dessert

Fresh flowers

New dress/shirt

Ten dollars toward new clothing

Free evening out

Buy book or tape

Buy hobby supplies

Money toward jogging shoes

Bag of favorite cookies/candies

Dinner at a restaurant

Attend movie, play, concert

Undisturbed bubblebath

Ice cream, sundae, or banana split

PENALTIES

Clean oven

Clean garage

Wash/clean car

Mop/wax one floor

Wash dishes

Polish silver

Paint fence

Clean garbage can

Give dog bath

Clean basement

No dessert

Do yard work which
is being put off

Weed flower bed

Miss golf date/
bowling night

Fix leaky faucet

Shampoo rug

Wash windows

SESSION EIGHT

Solving a Parenting Problem

"Good morning, folks. I'm glad you're a little early today. We have a lot of ground to cover in this session. Grab a cup of coffee if you like, and we'll get started.

"First, tell me about your week. Did the contract work?"

"We did great on the two requests we put in the contract. We had all rewards and no penalties," reported Jean. "I thought I was going to catch Tom one day, but he ran back a minute later and got his clothes before I had a chance to say anything."

"I couldn't believe what a hard habit that was to break. The threat of those penalties was what kept me going the first few days," said Tom. "But the rewards made it all worthwhile. Those good times with Jean were really special."

"I almost felt guilty for taking a reward for something as enjoyable as kissing Tom. Anyway, our success with those two changes encouraged us to try some others. Tom's remembering to take out the garbage before leaving for work, and I'm putting the newspaper back together for him if he hasn't read it. So far, so good."

"I'm glad to hear that. It sounds like you needed the contract to keep you going, Tom, while Jean could have made her change without it. You're obviously having fun with this—keep at it."

GETTING READY TO SOLVE PROBLEMS

"Okay, let's move on. Today we're finally going to get into problem-solving. Your relationship has improved steadily, and I think you're

110

now ready to tackle some of the major problems that still need to be settled. Jean, as I recall, when you first came into counseling, the conflicts over money, children, and sex were the main reasons you came for help. I know you were frustrated that we didn't deal with those issues immediately."

"You're right about that. I was pretty annoyed when you put us off. In our third session, you told us that good communication and happiness go together. So if that's true, why wait till now to learn how to talk to each other? Why didn't we begin with problem-solving?"

"Jean, there were three goals that had to be met before we could start solving problems. *The first goal was to deal with those blame attitudes.* As I've said, blaming your partner for a bad marriage is the most destructive force in rebuilding a relationship. But it's clear that you've made a mental shift away from blame and toward cooperation. For example, you worked together successfully in the partner-pleasing assignments, and now you've learned how to team up to get behavior changes. I think you're realizing that healing a marriage is a mutual responsibility. Some couples never arrive at this perspective."

"I have to admit it wasn't easy changing my mind about our unhappiness. But now I can see that Tom and I both caused our sick marriage— so it'll take both of us to make it healthy again."

"*The second goal we had to meet before starting our problem-solving training was to learn to put positives back into your marriage.* And you've done a good job there, too. You were able to get some good P and N numbers. Those high Positives and low Negatives were optimistic landmarks on your road to recovery. They meant you were taking on the qualities found in happy couples and that your relationship was beginning to resemble your courtship and early marriage. Most importantly, a high-pleasing-to-displeasing ratio was a sign you were showing more care, and caring has to come before you can learn effective communication skills."

"That part I don't understand, Dr. Martin. Why does caring come before problem-solving?"

"It's like this, Jean. Problem-solving is a special kind of communication that helps a couple solve specific relationship problems. It is the highest form of human cooperation, coordination, and teamwork. It requires the ability to compromise and make concessions. But if care is missing in a relationship, it's hard to concede a point to your spouse or change your behavior. You see, the essence of problem-solving is making behavior changes, and if you don't feel cared for, you resist change. However, when you feel cared for, it's much easier to see your partner's side of the problem and cooperate with him. As your basic emotional needs for care are met, you gain new energy to work patiently through hard problems. Does that help, Jean?"

"I see where you're coming from. When we came for help, I was so mad at Tom and blaming him for everything that I probably wouldn't have listened to a word he said. But now that he's shown he does care for me, I think I'll be in a better frame of mind to work things out with him."

"*The third goal we had to work on was to get some changes started.* So far, you've succeeded in getting behavior changes by using the BEST and written contracts. That's an excellent beginning. Behavior changes reduce tension, build trust in one another, and help you gain confidence in your ability to control your relationship. In summary, learning new conflict resolution skills is a difficult task, but it's made easier in an environment where there's no blame, lots of care, and successful changes."

POSITIVE PROBLEM-SOLVING:
A TRAIT OF HAPPY COUPLES

"Now, just before we get into our problem-solving training, I want to summarize one very important fact about communication in marriage. Working from videotapes, family scholars have been able to watch both happy and unhappy couples interact when solving conflicts and dis-agreements. These tapes clearly show that they resolve problems differ-ently. Happy couples use many positive problem-solving behaviors and few negative ones; this style helps them reach a speedy agreement. In contrast, troubled couples are high on negative problem-solving behav-ior and low on the positive ones; this pattern not only keeps them from solving disputes, but it also breeds new ones. In short, positive conflict resolution is a key trait that distinguishes these couples."

"Dr. Martin, I hear you saying that positive communication and good marriages go together."

"Right, Jean. And the flip side is just as true—negative communi-cation and bad marriages go together. If a couple doesn't have positive skills to solve problems, resolve fights, and negotiate conflicts, prob-lems stockpile and unhappiness sets in. The research with the two groups of couples clearly shows that communication skill deficits are a major cause of marital stress."

"I've got a question. When you say that happy and unhappy couples differ in how they solve disagreements, are you saying that the happy ones never fight?" asked Tom.

"Oh, they fight all right. Happy couples have problems just like other couples; it's just that they don't destroy each other in the proc-ess. They handle their fights differently. What makes them good problem-solvers is that they rely on more positive and fewer negative communication behaviors than do unhappy couples. That way, they don't upset their mate."

"I have a hard time believing Jean and I could ever have a difference of opinion without a big fight."

"I understand how you feel, Tom, and I agree that right now you couldn't because you don't have the necessary skills. But the good news is that you can learn to do just that. I can teach you how to solve problems the way happy couples do.

"By studying the videotaped interaction, we've been able to identify a set of twenty-five communication behaviors that help couples reach agreement. I like to call them *Helpers* because they help make problem-solving easy. Happy couples tend to use these at a high rate, and that's why they have fewer problems. The opposite behaviors I call *Killers* because they kill or make problem-solving difficult. They bring the process of communication to a dead halt. Unhappy couples tend to use more Killers than Helpers, and that's why their problems pile up.

"Here's a list of the twenty-five Helpers and the twenty-five Killers. It should give you a better understanding of what I'm talking about." Dr. Martin handed them each a copy of the communication behaviors, and they spent the next few minutes discussing each one (See p. 114. Also a complete definition of each behavior is found in the Appendix. Familiarize yourself with that information before reading on).

THE PROBLEM-SOLVING DIALOGUE:
TOM AND JEAN PRACTICE

After they had discussed the page of problem-solving skills, Tom said, "That's quite a big list, but I have to admit that you've really lost me when it comes to knowing how to use them in a fight. I wouldn't know where to begin."

"That's why we're going to practice, Tom. I want you both to try applying these skills to a real problem. Pick a problem you are dealing with right now in your marriage and then try to work through it here while I watch you. Work as hard as you can to reach a solution that you both can live with. As you work on the problem, I'll tape record your interaction. There will be times when I'll stop your problem-solving so we can discuss what's happening."

As Dr. Martin prepared the tape recorder, Tom and Jean decided to work on a parenting problem. "Parenting sounds like a good choice. Tom, why don't you begin?"

"Jean, I think the reason we have so many problems dealing with the boys is that you never support me when I discipline them. It's important to me that you stand behind me when I tell them something. Like

COMMUNICATION BEHAVIORS AND PROBLEM-SOLVING SKILLS

HELPERS Behaviors That Facilitate Couples' Communication (common to happy couples)	KILLERS Behaviors That Block Couples' Communication (common to unhappy couples)
1. Positive Problem Description	1. Negative Problem Description
2. Validation	2. Cross-Complaining
3. Active Listening; Summarizing*	3. Interrupting
4. Accepting Responsibility	4. Denying Responsibility; Excuses
5. Compliance	5. Noncompliance
6. Approval*	6. Criticism
7. Agreement*	7. Disagreement
8. High Agreement-to- Disagreement Ratio	8. High Disagreement-to- Agreement Ratio
9. Composed	9. Complaining
10. Seeking Information	10. Making Assumptions
11. Accurateness	11. Exaggeration
12. Positive Mind-Reading	12. Negative Mind-Reading
13. Taking Turns	13. Overtalk
14. Cooperation; Collaboration	14. Blaming
15. Negotiations; Contracting	15. Excessive Counterproposals
16. Compromise	16. Polarized
17. Brainstorming	17. Limiting Options
18. Proposing Solutions*	18. Problem-Oriented
19. Paying Attention*	19. Divided Attention
20. Tracking	20. Sidetracking
21. Positive Specific Requests	21. Negative Vague Demands
22. Social Support*	22. Put-Downs; Rejection
23. Positive Physical Touch	23. Aloofness
24. Positive Nonverbal Communication* (smile, gentle voice, etc.)	24. Negative Nonverbal Communication (angry voice, angry face, etc.)
25. Positive Reciprocity	25. Negative Reciprocity

Happy couples out perform unhappy couples especially in these categories.

yesterday when I had to scold Chris for his lousy report card, and you just sat there like a bump on a log. You could have said something to back me up, but you didn't. You just dumped the whole responsibility in my lap. Sometimes I feel so alone, like I'm out on a limb by myself trying to teach them values."

As Tom continued, his voice became emotionally charged. "But what really gets my goat is when you interfere and contradict me right in front of the kids. That means I not only have a problem with the boys, but now I have a new problem with you because you interfered. You've got to stop . . ."

Before Tom could finish his sentence, Jean interrupted with loudness in her voice. "No, Tom, you've got to stop! You know I can't stand it when you yell and scream at the boys. I can't support you as long as you do that. You're always out of control when you discipline them." Jean shook her finger at Tom and continued, "Besides, you never consult me before you punish them. Then when you do punish, it's always overkill. Like last week when Chris left his bike in the driveway—'grounding' his bicycle for a whole month was more punishment than he deserved. That's why I can't support you. You're too extreme in how you handle the boys. You just never . . ."

"Well, I wouldn't have to come down on them so hard if you didn't let them get away with murder," interrupted Tom, raising his voice even louder. "I have to overdiscipline because you're so permissive and lax—so I come out looking like the bad guy. And you're wrong when you say I *always* holler at them. Just a few weeks ago, here in our counseling session, you said you were pleased with the way I disciplined Chris. It makes me so mad when you make these sweeping generalities. You're doing just what Dr. Martin warned us not to—you see my negatives and not my positives. You just don't give me a fair evaluation. According to you, I never do anything right—I'm a rotten parent, a rotten lover, and I can't even manage the money right. Isn't there anything good . . . ?"

Once again, Jean jumped in before Tom could finish. "Now that you mention it, yes, you could be a better sex partner. You think only of your sexual needs and never consider me with your 'wham-bam-thank-you-ma'am' approach to sex. You're so selfish!"

It was obvious to Dr. Martin that Tom and Jean would never reach an agreement. They were using Killer messages and none of the Helpers. The parenting problem which they were supposed to solve was only escalating into a destructive war of words. He called a halt.

"Okay, stop action! Let's take some time now to look closely at your problem-solving behaviors. I'll rewind the tape, and then I want each of you to listen to what you said and how you said it. Then we'll evaluate. As we listen, see if you can spot what Helpers or Killers you used."

COMMUNICATION BEHAVIORS

Interrupting

Dr. Martin played the tape, allowing Tom and Jean to listen to their short and unsuccessful attempt at problem-solving. "Now that you've listened to yourselves, what communication behaviors happened during your talk time?"

"The first thing I noticed was that Jean interrupted me before I finished explaining my side of the problem. That really ticks me off! When she butts in like that, I get so mad I almost forget what we're fighting about. I start thinking about the new problem of being interrupted."

"But, Tom, you interrupted me, too!" protested Jean.

"I'm afraid the tape shows you are both guilty of interrupting. That behavior is a big communication killer. There are three reasons why it damages your problem-solving efforts. First, interrupting is a selfish behavior. It usually means that you've been too busy mentally rehearsing your own problem to listen to your mate's problem. It says, 'I don't have time to listen to your needs.' The end result of selfish behavior is that partners fail to recognize or meet each other's needs.

"There's a second reason why interrupting spoils communication.

It will diminish your mate's self-esteem. When someone fails to listen and steps on your sentence, it is as if the interrupter were saying, 'I don't respect your opinion,' 'I don't value your thinking,' or 'Your ideas are not worthwhile.' These messages bruise egos and trigger defensiveness, resistance, resentment, and counterattack.

"And you're right, Tom. Being interrupted can cause you to focus on new problems. That's a third way that interruptions block communication. They drag you away from your original problem and force you to pursue a self-esteem problem. Now, instead of having only one problem to resolve, you have created another problem—the problem of hurt and angry feelings. Both of you have a strong desire to be understood; that's a basic human need. But you can't be understood if you're not listened to. So for all these reasons, listen."

The Psychology of Problem-Solving. "Dr. Martin, it sounds like you're saying that anytime we problem-solve, we have to be aware of both the problem and our emotions."

"You've hit it right on the head, Jean. Problem-solving is not just an intellectual task but a deep psychological event as well. I'll picture it here on the flip chart. Problem-solving is like a two-sided coin. On one side, we have the issue—like sex, money, companionship, or parenting. Dealing with these topics takes our best brain power, mental energy, and creativity. But on the other side of the coin are the basic, human emotional needs—being respected, accepted, valued, approved of, supported, and understood. This emotional side of the problem-solving coin requires that we be very sensitive to the psychology of our mate. That means that we must consciously avoid using the twenty-five Killers because they trigger negative emotional responses in our spouse—rejection, hurt, anger, and inferiority. When that happens, conflict will quickly escalate, resolution will elude you, and your problems will double. You'll end up fighting over matters that are beside the point. But if you practice the twenty-five Helpers, you protect your mate's positive emotions."

"As I look at the list of Killers," said Tom, "it seems like many of them could grab our negative emotions. Interrupting isn't the only Killer we have to worry about."

"Good point, Tom. Killer messages—like criticism, blaming, and negative mind reading—will either bring problem-solving to an abrupt halt, inflame tempers, open doors for new conflicts, or leave you looking at a mountain of unresolved issues. The worst part is that chronic failure to solve problems puts great stress on your relationship; it wears you down. The pileup of problems is a subtle reminder that you're failing as a couple. These unsuccessful problem-solving events make you doubt each other and tempt you to see your mate as a bad person. Unsolved issues can cause permanent damage to a marriage."

"That sure sounds like us. If we could just learn to fight successfully so we could get rid of the backlog of problems. It's like a minefield at home where we keep stepping on unsettled disagreements."

"I understand, Tom. Each unsolved problem is like an inflamed nerve which, when touched, gives rise to hurt, rage, and resentment."

"I feel the same way about our conflicts," said Jean. "I'd give anything if we could learn how to talk through a problem without fighting. But our discussions suddenly erupt, even over little things. They become irrational wars where we start being mean to each other. It leaves me feeling exhausted—like a failure. Can we learn to do it better, Dr. Martin?"

"Yes, you can, Jean. That's one of the most heartening findings in marriage research—unhappy couples can learn to be good problem-solvers. Right now, the main reason why you're being defeated in communications is because of your skill deficits, not because of any personality disorder in your mate. It's a simple case of using too many negative communication behaviors and not enough positive ones. As you start practicing the Helpers and stop using the Killer messages, your problem-solving will be a successful experience, not a failure event. If you can just remember that problem-solving is not a battlefield where you are trying to hurt each other. Instead, it's a place to solve an issue, and at the same time, defend your mate's fragile psyche."

Active Listening and Summarizing

"I can see how these Killers have caused us to fail at problem-solving. But you're asking us to change a habit we've had for eighteen years. Can we break it right away?" asked Jean.

"One of the best ways to break old habits is to learn new alternatives. That's why I gave you the list of Helper and Killer skills. Every time you identify a communication Killer, just look on the skill sheet for its opposite behavior and practice it. Now you have choices you didn't have before. For example, what is the opposite of interrupting?"

"Listening."

"Right, Jean. But it's not referring to a passive, relaxing event like listening to the radio. This kind of listening is active. You summarize or paraphrase what your partner has said. Let's practice this skill. Jean, summarize or restate in your own words what Tom said earlier about the discipline problem."

"Well, I guess Tom is saying that he wants me to back him up and be more supportive when he disciplines the boys. But I can't do that when he comes on so strong with them. It scares me."

"Tom, is that an accurate summary?"

"Kind of. I just need her to say something in front of the boys that will show them that she agrees with me. Discipline's no good unless they feel we're both behind it 100 percent. But also, I don't want her to interfere."

"Now, Tom, summarize what you heard Jean say about the parenting problem."

"Jean said that she can't support my discipline because it's too harsh."

"Is that right, Jean?"

"Yes, that's it. But I also want to have some say in the kind of punishment he gives them."

"Okay. You both did a good job of summarizing. During our problem-solving training, there may be times when I'll have you stop and summarize what you heard your spouse say, so be an active listener."

Accuracy versus Exaggeration

"Now, look at the skills page and see if you recognize any other communication behaviors you used in your discussion."

"Well, I have to admit that I did use the words *always* and *never* quite a few times when I was talking about Tom's behavior. That's probably number 11—exaggeration."

"Yes, Jean. Those two words are common exaggerations that can easily disrupt problem-solving. It was obvious they made you mad, Tom."

"You bet they did! I just see red when Jean says I 'always do this' or 'never do that.' It makes me look like a total failure. I feel like I have to defend myself, and then we get off the real problem."

"Exactly. It's natural to become defensive when someone makes exaggerated statements about us. And when we put all our efforts into defending our self-esteem from unfair attacks, we just don't have time for problem-solving. That's why we have to make accurate statements."

Validation versus Cross-Complaining

"Now I'm going to replay the tape again because I want you to hear some other communication problems." After the tape played, Dr. Martin asked, "Tom, when you explained your problem about lack of support, what did Jean do?"

"Well, she came back with a problem of her own, and it made me feel like she really didn't want to do anything about my problem."

"That's right. You raised a problem, and then Jean raised another one—that's called *cross-complaining*. I know you both want to get your point across, but back-to-back problems will only destroy your efforts. Good problem-solving means working on one problem at a time. When you both start unloading your complaints, problem-solving stops and fights start.

"Jean, while Tom was explaining his problem, the best behavior on your part would have been to actively listen to what he said, and then show Tom you understood him and wanted to help him solve the problem. Tom's need at that point was to know that you were sincerely interested in his problem, cared about his feelings, and would be responsive to the problem. Instead, your first action was to cross-complain with a problem of your own. You came back with five sentences, none of which validated Tom's feelings. Nothing you said told Tom you had any interest in helping him solve his problem."

"But when do I get to explain my problem to Tom?"

"The appropriate time is after you have validated Tom. I don't want either of you to cross-complain because you talk right past each other. Hear and respond to complaints. Don't counter with one of your own."

"Okay, but I'm not sure I understand what you mean by *'validating'* Tom. How do I do that?"

"That's a good question. There are five validation skills. First, you can just *listen* and then *summarize* what your mate has said. Second, *accept responsibility* for your behavior that might be causing the problem. Third, *comply* with his request that you do something. Four, *approve* of something Tom did or said. And five, tell him you *agree* with what he has said. Agreement sentences are extremely important in problem-solving. In fact, happy couples use many more agreement than disagreement statements when solving conflicts. Any of these five responses will send a forceful message to Tom that says, 'I value you.' How you respond to your mate's problem can determine whether or not you will be able to proceed through the conflict."

Sequencing: The Order of Events. "So far, I've encouraged you to make frequent use of Helpers and drop the Killers. Besides the frequency with which you use Helpers, sequence is also important. *Sequencing* is the order of communication events that happen between you. For example, your interaction pattern was a sequence of conflict— interrupting and cross-complaining—not a sequence of support— 'How can I help you?'

"The best chain of events would have been a *problem-validation-solution sequence.* Tom, you would state a problem. Then Jean would listen and validate. Finally, you would both move toward proposing a solution. But instead, your communication pattern was a *problem-problem sequence* that went like this: Tom, you raised a problem. Jean, you interrupted and cross-complained. Then Tom, you followed by raising another problem. Suddenly, you are both overwhelmed with problems. In fact, you had seven problems to deal with—support, yelling, overpunishment, interference, sex, money, and fair evaluation. This is one of the biggest pitfalls for couples when they start to solve an issue. They get themselves entangled with too many problems at the start. You can only deal effectively with one problem at a time."

Tom and Jean looked at each other and nodded their heads in silent agreement as Tom said, "No wonder we never can work through a problem—we've been trying to deal with a whole kitchen sink full of problems. That's been one of our worst communication errors, but I couldn't put my finger on it. There were times I'd get so frustrated that I'd just give up and walk away from our talk."

"And when you walked away, to me that meant you didn't care about me or our marriage. That's why I always ended up so hurt and angry at you. I had to get angry because I was afraid I'd be ignored."

"But it's important, Jean, that you reinterpret Tom's behavior. He does care. And Tom must learn to state the problem without blaming. It's just that when you both use these ineffective problem-solving styles, it brings out the worst in you. You both come across to each other in unloving, uncaring ways."

Nonverbal Communication

"All right, let's turn our attention to another area. When couples communicate, they communicate on two levels—the verbal and the nonverbal. Up to now, we've talked only about verbal communication behaviors such as interrupting, exaggeration, and cross-complaining. But words are not the only communicators. Words are accompanied by a group of nonverbal behaviors, some of which can interfere with good problem-solving. If we had a videotape of your interaction today, you would immediately recognize some of them."

"I know what you're talking about, Dr. Martin. Tom sure used some. He started out sounding so critical—like I was to blame for the whole problem. And then he started to raise his voice at me. And one more thing, when I tried to explain my problem, Tom physically turned his back on me, as if he didn't want to hear what I was saying."

"Uh, huh, I understand. It sounds like when Tom tells you something in a harsh, loud voice, it's easy to interpret his remark as a criticism. Jean, how did those nonverbals make you feel?"

"I was mad! I just wanted to get back at him."

"Now, Tom, what about you? Do you recall any of Jean's nonverbal behaviors that affected you?"

"Yes, she did her usual thing: She got that dirty look on her face and wagged her finger at me like I was a naughty little kid. When I see her angry face and pointing finger, I don't even hear her words. I just can't pay attention to what she's saying because of those other things."

"You've both given good examples of nonverbal behavior, especially the negative ones. By talking about them, I hope you're becoming more aware of this significant part of human communication. Research in marital communication tells us that couples don't fully appreciate the power of their nonverbal messages. This is especially true of unhappy couples—they use a high number of negative nonverbals while happy couples use a low rate. The troubled couples just don't understand the fact that the nonverbal Killers seriously disrupt communication."

"I have a question," said Tom. "Is this nonverbal stuff the same as body language?"

"To a large part, yes. We communicate our attitudes by how we use our bodies. For example, Tom, when you turned away from Jean and your shoulder became a barrier, you told Jean you were angry and didn't want to listen to her. You may also have been telling her that her ideas were dumb and stupid. And, Jean, when you sent a message accompanied by a hostile gesture of finger pointing, it came across as a put-down. I don't think you realize the potent impact that behavior has on Tom. Posture, gestures, spacing, amount of eye contact, facial expressions, and amount of touching are all examples of body language. But we also communicate our attitudes nonverbally by the tone of voice and by its loudness or softness. All of these make up the important area of nonverbal communication."

"Dr. Martin, it seems that *how* we say what we say is just as important as *what* we say."

"Actually, Jean, we have to be more careful about *how* we say it. Up to 75 percent of the information we receive comes from nonverbal signals. That means that words are less important than how the words are used. We may not be conscious of it, but as a listener we pay more attention to the way the message is delivered than to the message content itself. And if we perceive hostility, a fight is on. Just like in your interaction today, you sent messages with loud voices, hostile gestures, and sarcastic, belittling tones. And it had a negative impact—a fight broke out and problem-solving got scuttled. It's almost impossible not to be affected by your mate's nonverbal behavior; nonverbal behavior can have a great effect on how the words are interpreted and the response which will follow them. How you nonverbally send your verbal message is vital to your success in problem-solving. So when you discuss issues in your marriage, avoid the negative nonverbals like annoyed sighs, yelling, and angry looks. Instead, use the positive nonverbal behaviors like a gentle voice, positive touching, and smiling."

Positive and Negative Reciprocity

"Okay, let's talk about another communication behavior that happened in your problem-solving—negative reciprocity. In an earlier session, we talked about the word *reciprocity*, which means to exchange or trade behavior for behavior. If you remember, I explained that in a happy marriage, couples exchange positives on a reciprocal basis; that is, if one mate sends a nice behavior, the other mate returns a nice behavior. But now, we are dealing with the reciprocity of negative exchanges.

"Simply put, negative reciprocity is the tendency to give back the same kind of negative communication behavior that you've just received. Here's how it happened in your dialogue: Jean, when you interrupted Tom, he responded in the same manner by interrupting you. And, Tom, when your voice became loud, Jean got loud, too."

"It sounds like you're saying that if you get zapped, you're likely to zap right back," concluded Tom. "It's an eye for an eye."

"Right. If you're gruff, you'll probably get gruffness in return. If your voice quality is blaming, it'll cause your mate to bristle, and he/she will tend to give back in like manner. If you punish your spouse with a criticism, interruption, or rejection—look out, because those behaviors are coming right back."

"I think it's awfully hard not to get hooked by your mate's negative talk behavior."

"It is hard, Jean. It takes a real sensitivity to *how* you're talking to each other. You have to pay close attention to your process of communication and become aware that the negative reciprocity is happening. But it also takes a special kind of personal strength not to return a punishment when you've just been punished."

"Well, so far in learning these communication skills, we're batting zero," said Tom. "We didn't start out very well, did we?"

"No doubt, the Killers dominated your problem-solving, but remember you carried some liabilities into your relationship; you had some premarital skill deficits that resulted in later stress. You started marriage without knowing how to settle conflicts, and over the years, you've developed some ineffective habits for dealing with disagreements—you've had years of bad practice. This is the first time you've had supervised training, and as I've said, you can't expect to change wrong communication habits and become skillful problem-solvers in just one session. Mastering all twenty-five skills for positive conflict resolution will take some time."

STEPS IN SOLVING PROBLEMS

"Are you ready to try another round of problem-solving on the parenting issue?"

"Let's go for it!" responded Tom enthusiastically. "I think you've taught us a lot about how to communicate better. Anyway, we can't do any worse than the first time around."

"Up to now, we've talked about what communication behaviors will help you in problem-solving and which ones get you into more trouble. But we also need to look at a step-by-step approach for solving conflicts." Dr. Martin handed them a page to look at.

Here's a flow chart that shows eight steps that should be followed when you're solving a problem. It's an orderly, common-sense method that begins with defining the relationship problem and moves to the final step of taking and evaluating actions. It may look a little complicated at first, but with practice, it can become second nature to you. When you follow these steps and use the Helpers rather than the Killers, you can be a success at solving any problem. Let's give it a try on this next round."

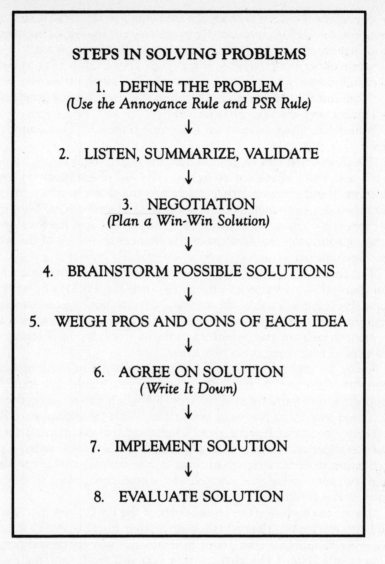

STEPS IN SOLVING PROBLEMS

1. **DEFINE THE PROBLEM**
(Use the Annoyance Rule and PSR Rule)
↓

2. **LISTEN, SUMMARIZE, VALIDATE**
↓

3. **NEGOTIATION**
(Plan a Win-Win Solution)
↓

4. **BRAINSTORM POSSIBLE SOLUTIONS**
↓

5. **WEIGH PROS AND CONS OF EACH IDEA**
↓

6. **AGREE ON SOLUTION**
(Write It Down)
↓

7. **IMPLEMENT SOLUTION**
↓

8. **EVALUATE SOLUTION**

Step 1: Define the Problem

"This time, I want you to be especially careful about how you start. The most critical time in problem-solving is at the beginning when you define the problem—that's when communication frequently breaks down. How you describe the problem to your mate at the outset can determine whether or not the problem erupts into a fight or gets solved peacefully.

"A good method for describing a problem is to use what is called the *Annoyance Rule.** It includes three parts—the X-Y-Z. This method says, 'I feel X when you do Y in Z situation.' I'll show you what I mean. Jean, remember the conflict you had with Tom a few weeks ago when he didn't notice your pleasing behavior? To describe that, you would say, 'Tom, I feel hurt and angry (X) when you don't see my good behavior (Y) in a very stressful situation (Z).'"

"You mean all we have to do is say one sentence? That sounds too easy."

"It's almost that simple, Jean. There's no need to go to great lengths to tell your mate what's annoying you. The X-Y-Z is a short expression of feeling about a behavior that upsets you and that you'd like changed. But this is the step where couples make their biggest errors. They dwell too long on defining the problem. And, if you are long-winded in defining your problem, it increases the chances that some of the Killers will creep in.

"But there's something else. After you've used the Annoyance Rule, you then ask for a behavior change by using the Positive Specific Request (PSR) Rule. That is, the annoyed person requests positive action from his/her mate that would eliminate the source of annoyance. Let's apply both rules to the parenting problem. Tom, try to describe your problem to Jean using these two rules."

"Okay, I'll give it a go. Jean, I feel angry when you're silent while I discipline the boys. What I want is that you would say something supportive that shows you agree with me when I'm scolding them."

"Good job, Tom. You used both rules. With the Annoyance Rule, you described your feelings, Jean's behavior that caused that feeling, and the situation. Then you added the PSR Rule—you stated a positive action desired rather than what is not desired; it was specific in that you stated what you wanted and when; and finally, it was a request, not a command.

"I want to emphasize the request part of the PSR. Keep in mind that problem-solving is a time to ask your partner for changes, so *how* you ask is very important. Tom, your tone of voice was gentle and friendly. This greatly lessens the chances that you will hurt your mate's self-esteem and cause a fight. If you'd been critical, Jean would feel attacked and be less responsive to the request. It's so easy to create undue antagonism by the manner in which we express a problem. Remember, your goal is to solve problems, not offend your mate."

* The "Annoyance Procedure" was developed by N.H. Azrin, V.A. Besalel, R. Bechtel, A. Michalicek, M. Mancera, D. Carroll, D. Shuford, and J. Cox. See "Comparison of Reciprocity and Discussion-Type Counseling for Marital Problems," *The American Journal of Family Therapy* 8 (1980): 21–28.

Step 2: Listen, Summarize, Validate

"Now that you've heard Tom describe his problem, Jean, what should you do?"

"Well, I'd still be tempted to rush in and air my problem, but since I can't cross-complain, I should validate him. I need to *listen* and be able to *summarize* what he's said. I could *accept responsibility* for not backing him up on discipline. I could *comply* with something he might want from me. I could *approve* of something he did or said, or I could *agree* with how he sees the problem."

"Perfect, Jean. Any of those behaviors would have shown Tom that you cared about him, and that you were willing to work on the problem that was annoying him. Just knowing you are trying to understand will defuse some of his resentment. After you validate, you are then free to raise your problem. Now after validation, what's the next step?"

Step 3: Negotiate a Win-Win Solution

"According to the chart, we need to start looking for a solution," answered Jean.

"Right. Now you both focus your energies on proposing solutions to the problem. That's where the real behavior change happens. Too often, couples keep describing problems and never get to solutions."

"I'm surprised to see the word *negotiations* on the flow chart. It's hard to see how that word relates to marriage. At work, I'm involved in labor relations and sit on the union side. In my experience, negotiations can be a nasty time of arguing over money and trying to out-fox the other side. How do negotiations fit into marriage?"

"Tom, I'm not advocating that kind of adversary climate. Negotiating in marriage simply means that whatever solution you agree on must meet the needs of both parties—a good solution satisfies everybody. If the solution meets only your needs, Tom, and not Jean's, she'll not be committed to carry it out. The same is true if only Jean is satisfied—you'll probably drag your feet. The point I'm making is this: To negotiate in marital problem-solving means that you work together to find a win-win solution—one that's good for both of you. It's a certain kind of attitude. When there is a win-win outcome, instead of a husband-wins-while-wife-loses, the relationship improves."

Step 4: Brainstorm to Find Solutions

"Now we're going to look for that win-win solution to your parenting problem. The best way is to come up with as many different possible solutions as you can. The more you think of, the more likely you will be to stumble on one that satisfies both of you.

"The method you'll use to generate those solutions is 'brainstorming.' Let's practice. Your goal will be to list five to ten possible answers for the parenting problem. Be as creative as you can, and don't stop to evaluate or criticize the ideas until you've completed the list. I'll give you about five minutes to come up with as many alternatives for the problem as you can while I write them down. Go!"

"How about if Jean handles all the discipline for Chris, while I take care of any problems with Billy?" suggested Tom.

"What? You've got to be kidding! That's a really stupid idea. You know Chris is a lot harder to handle than Billy. How could you even . . ."

"Whoa!" interrupted Dr. Martin. "You've forgotten the key rule to brainstorming—don't criticize a solution until you have finished your list. Jean, if you jump on Tom's idea, he'll get protective, defensive, and reluctant to suggest other solutions. And, Tom's ideas won't be at a high quality level. Scientists who have studied the brain tell us that criticism 'freezes' brain cells. If you send a critical, harsh sentence to Tom, his thinker goes out-of-order; it shuts down his thinking factory and paralyzes creativity. So hold your criticism until all possible ideas have been developed. Now, let's try brainstorming again."

Following Dr. Martin's admonishment, Tom and Jean then cooperated to generate a list of possible solutions to their parenting problem. (See flip chart p. 129.)

Step 5: Weigh Pros and Cons

"That was a great job of brainstorming solutions. Your joint effort resulted in eleven ideas in five minutes. Now we're ready to take the next step, which is to decide the merits of each solution. This process of elimination should give you the best possible answer to your problem.

"In choosing the best solution, your first task is to eliminate the worst solutions. After that, compare each solution against several criteria: (1) Is the solution practical—can it be carried out easily? (2) Does it meet Jean's needs? (3) Does it meet Tom's needs? (4) Does it agree with your values? (5) Does it require equal responsibilities for change—will both of you have to make behavior changes? If a solution requires a maximum amount of effort from one of you and only a minimum amount from the other, it's not a good solution. You can choose all kinds of criteria depending on the problem, but these will do for now.

"So let's take your eleven solutions and rate them against the five criteria. An easy way to achieve this step is to use what we call a *Decision Chart*." Dr. Martin handed them a blank chart and helped them complete it. (See p. 130.)

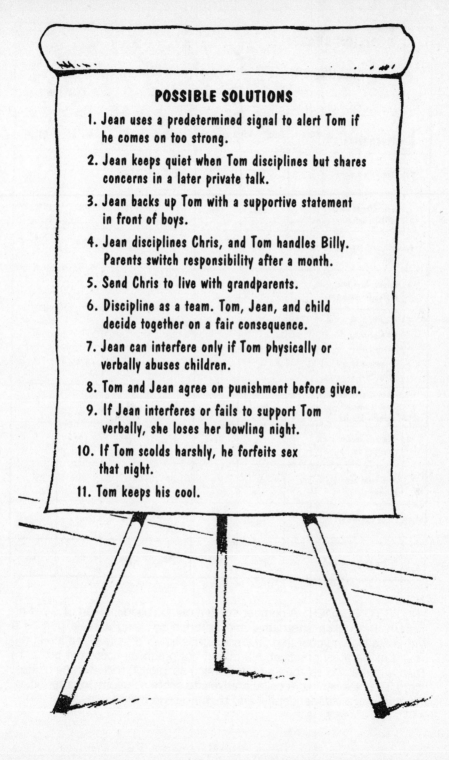

POSSIBLE SOLUTIONS

1. Jean uses a predetermined signal to alert Tom if he comes on too strong.

2. Jean keeps quiet when Tom disciplines but shares concerns in a later private talk.

3. Jean backs up Tom with a supportive statement in front of boys.

4. Jean disciplines Chris, and Tom handles Billy. Parents switch responsibility after a month.

5. Send Chris to live with grandparents.

6. Discipline as a team. Tom, Jean, and child decide together on a fair consequence.

7. Jean can interfere only if Tom physically or verbally abuses children.

8. Tom and Jean agree on punishment before given.

9. If Jean interferes or fails to support Tom verbally, she loses her bowling night.

10. If Tom scolds harshly, he forfeits sex that night.

11. Tom keeps his cool.

DECISION CHART*

Selection Criteria → ↓ Alternative	Practical/Easy to Carry Out	Agrees with Couple's Values	Meets Jean's Needs	Meets Tom's Needs	Equal Responsibility for Change	SUM
1. Jean uses a signal.	yes	yes	yes	yes	no	4
2. Jean remains quiet but talks later.	yes	yes	yes	yes	yes	5
3. Jean says something positive.	yes	yes	no	yes	no	3
4. Parents have total charge for each boy.	Inadequate					
5. Send Chris to grandparents.	Inadequate					
6. Discipline as a committee.	no	yes	yes	no	yes	3
7. Jean intervenes if Tom is physically or verbally abusive.	yes	no	yes	yes	no	3
8. Tom and Jean consult and then punish.	yes	yes	yes	yes	yes	5
9. Jean loses her bowling night.	no	no	no	Does Not Apply	no	0
10. Tom forfeits sex.	no	no	Does Not Apply	no	no	0
11. Tom keeps his cool.	yes	yes	yes	yes	no	4

* NOTE TO READER: A number system can be used instead of a yes-no system. Rate each alternative and criterion by using a scale of 1 to 5 with a 5 a high number (e.g.; if a solution is highly practical, put a 5 in the box. If moderately practical, a 3, and if not practical, score the box a 1.) Then add the scores across to see which solution(s) receives the highest score. Couples can work collaboratively to score solutions to criterion, or they can work independently, and then average their scores.

Step 6: Agree on Solution (Write It Down)

As Tom and Jean looked over the list of possible solutions, they quickly eliminated two of the solutions because they were inadequate. As they discussed the remaining options, the Decision Chart helped them see that two solutions met all the criteria and two others were close to perfect. As a result, they agreed to combine these four alternatives into one solution.

"You've done an excellent job of discussing your alternatives, and I believe you've reached a win-win solution. You have both made a commitment to change. Now it's important that you record the agreement made in this problem-solving session. If you try to rely on your memories, you could end up in another conflict trying to remember who was to do what. Write your solution on this three-by-five-inch index card. In the future, you may wish to keep all such solutions in a small notebook, but for now we'll use the card. We only need four main pieces of information: Date, problem discussed, outcomes achieved, and your signatures." (See Figure 8.)

Step 7 and 8: Implement and Evaluate Solution

After Dr. Martin helped Tom and Jean record their solution, he explained the last two steps in problem-solving, namely, to carry out the solution and then evaluate it. Here are the guidelines he gave for evaluating solutions:

1. The couple should arrange to talk about the solution within one week of implementing it.
2. During this talk, review progress, and if necessary, make changes in the agreement. Decide to continue the solution, modify it in some way, or switch to another solution from the Decision Chart.
3. When you have this evaluation discussion, start with what has worked, and then discuss what has not worked.

DR. MARTIN'S SUMMARY

After Dr. Martin shared the above guidelines, he said, "Well, this has been a long session today. We've covered much material, and you've had your first practice session in learning new problem-solving skills. We all realize that there is still much room for improvement, but I feel you have made a good start in learning how to handle disagreements constructively.

PROBLEM DISCUSSED

Tom upset with Jean for not supporting him when disciplining. Jean also interferes and rescues the boys. Jean upset with Tom because he's too harsh and doesn't consult her.

OUTCOME/ SOLUTION

Jean agrees to use a "peace" sign to signal Tom if he scolds too harshly. She promises not to interfere. Together, they will agree on punishment before it's given. Tom commits to a calmer approach.

Signed: *Jean*
(Wife)

Tom
(Husband)

Date: 1/17/88

Figure 8. Agreements made during a problem-solving session should be placed in writing and kept permanently. Such records prevent conflicts, and they are good reminders to the couple that they have succeeded in solving problems.

"During this next week, here are your homework assignments: First, of course, I want you to implement your solution to the parenting problem. Second, I want you to go home and spend fifteen minutes each day practicing these communication skills on some real problems. Just be sure the problems are easy ones so you can achieve success. Avoid major conflicts like your sex problem; we'll work on that one together next session. Be sure to write down your agreements in a notebook or on three-by-five-inch cards.

"The most important part of your daily practice is to use the BEST. That is, use only the Problem-Solving section. You don't need to keep recording the other BEST sections at this time. However, follow most of the usual rules. Look for both positive and negative problem-solving behaviors used by your mate, record these behaviors, and compute P:N ratios. Each time you problem-solve, try to improve your Positives and Negatives.

"Finally, as you practice this week, keep in mind that the work of a marriage is to solve problems, and the best way to do that is to apply the Helpers and eliminate the Killers.

"Also, remember that couples who report much happiness are likely to use many positive problem-solving behaviors and few negative ones. But it's just the opposite for disturbed couples. They use too few positives and too many negatives; that's a big reason why they're unhappy. Negatives don't work. Positives do. Okay, I'll see you next session."

ENRICHMENT ACTIVITIES FOR READERS

During this week, choose three to four nights to do problem-solving with your mate. Follow these procedures:

1. Limit your practice sessions to fifteen minutes only.
2. Work on small, minor issues. Don't tackle any big "monsters" yet until your problem-solving skills are better developed and you've read the next session.
3. Use the "Problem-Solving" section of the BEST to count your P's and N's (don't count behaviors in any other section).
4. As you finish each practice time, follow most of the BEST steps—record problem-solving behaviors used by your mate, figure P:N ratios, exchange lists, discuss, and praise. If there are problem-solving behaviors wanted, you are limited to two at each discussion.
5. Your goal in each problem-solving time is to solve a problem and raise your P:N ratios. If your numbers are changing in the positive direction, that's good news! You're becoming better problem-solvers.
6. Keep a problem-solving notebook. Each problem solved is a tangible sign or reminder that your relationship is improving. Each solution you record will give you confidence and strengthen your belief that you can make it.

SESSION NINE

Solving a Sex Problem

TOM AND JEAN SOLVE SOME MINOR PROBLEMS

"Well, I've been thinking about you this week," began Dr. Martin as Tom and Jean settled into their chairs. "I was especially curious to find out how you were doing as you practiced some of the new communication skills."

"You told us to stick to solving little problems and not take on any biggies so that's what we did," responded Tom. "On Monday, we talked about the problem of Jean forgetting to put gas in the car after she uses it for shopping or errands. There have been many mornings when I leave for work with the gas gauge on empty, wondering if I'll run out of gas on the way to the plant. I'm a nervous wreck by the time I get to work."

"How'd you solve that, Tom?"

"Well, I just made a simple request—a PSR—asking Jean to put gas in the car any time the gauge reads less than half empty, and she said okay; it was that easy. And on Tuesday, we discussed a problem that Jean's had with me about my habit of leaving chores incomplete. I agreed to a solution of not starting a new chore until I've finished the one I've been working on."

"That habit has been a real pain to me," said Jean. "At any one time, Tom can have a half dozen unfinished jobs in the air. Part of the landscape is in grass and the other part is still in clods waiting to be seeded; he'll clean up half of the basement and leave the other half messy. Things like that really annoyed me. I'll be so happy if Tom keeps this new agreement!"

"On Thursday, we solved one of our money problems. Jean has complained about my not paying the bills on time. But we came up with a solution that requires that we both change our behavior. Jean agreed to help me on bill-paying night. After I write out the checks, she's going to stuff them into the envelopes, lick the stamps, and seal them up. Then, we balance the checkbook together. That may not sound like a big deal, but with that kind of moral support, I'm almost looking forward to paying the bills next time."

"Dr. Martin, I bet you'll be pleased to know that our P-and-N problem-solving numbers went up each day, and our happiness ratings went up, too," reported Jean. "We're feeling quite proud about that. I'm especially feeling good because some nagging little problems are finally getting solved."

"Well, it sounds like you've had a good week with your homework assignment. And thanks, Jean, for sharing that news. You know how important numbers are to me. I always get excited when the Positives rise and Negatives drop. A change in numbers is the best way to measure progress in your marriage skills. When I hear your problem-solving ratios are improving, it can mean only one thing—you're learning how to handle conflict in your marriage."

TOM AND JEAN TACKLE A SEX PROBLEM

"Okay, let's continue skill-building in communication. During this session, I want you to resolve another real issue. My guess is you'd like to try solving that sex problem you've mentioned before."

"That's right, Dr. Martin. I've been looking forward to having you help us deal with this one, but I think it's going to be much harder than the parenting problem we solved last session."

"Well, let's get started then. We'll use the same method as we did for the parenting problem—I'll let you try out your new skills while I observe and tape record the session. Every now and then, I'll break in to give some instructions or feedback. Now, remember, your goal is to find a solution that meets the needs of both of you. A good solution is one that satisfies everybody—you both win. Are you ready?"

"Well, Jean, where do you want to begin?" asked Tom.

"There are several problems I have with our sex life, Tom. To say it in X-Y-Z, I feel hurt and angry when you pressure me into sex when I'm tired. And I'm also upset when you get in such a hurry to meet your own needs that I don't get satisfied—you just turn over and go to sleep, leaving me frustrated. I want to be fulfilled sexually, too."

"It sounds like you have two problems with me," summarized Tom.

"I don't take your tiredness into consideration when I want sex, and I don't allow you time to reach an orgasm."

"That's it exactly. I don't feel you really understand how tired I am at the end of the day. I work part-time at my secretarial job, and then I come home to do the cooking, cleaning, and laundry for the whole family while you just sit and watch TV. And then you expect me to jump into bed and be a responsive sexual partner. Then, to make matters worse, you forget about my sexual needs. I wish you'd satisfy me, also."

"You're probably right, Jean. I guess you can't enjoy sex when you're too tired and too mad. You've been doing more than your share—working at your job and at home. On the fatigue problem, I admit I don't really understand why sex and tiredness don't mix. From my viewpoint, I'm always ready for it.

"But I also have my side of the sex problem," continued Tom. "I want to have more sex, and I want some variety. We should try different sex techniques, not just the same old way each time."

"All right, let me step in for a few minutes to say a couple of things," said Dr. Martin. "First of all, I want to say that you're doing a great job of dealing with a very volatile conflict like sex. Jean, you applied the Annoyance Rule—you described the problem briefly and precisely pinpointed the behavior that was annoying. And you used the PSR Rule—you told Tom what behavior you wanted more of. Also, you confronted him without setting off sparks. You didn't show any negative nonverbal behaviors—you didn't raise your voice, show disgust on your face, or shake a finger disapprovingly at Tom."

"Yeah," affirmed Tom. "You said it gently—not turned up two octaves. It was easy to listen. I don't feel attacked when you're calm and your voice is friendly. That makes a good problem-solving mood for me."

"But you also helped the problem-solving process, Tom. You were an excellent listener. You could have reacted immediately by bringing up your own problem of wanting more and different sex, but you didn't. Instead, you validated Jean."

"You mean I didn't cross-complain?"

"That's right, Tom. After Jean stated her problem, you validated her in two ways. You gave her a summary sentence showing that you understood her problem, and then you gave her an agreement sentence about her fatigue problem. That was a good sequence. Jean surfaced a problem and you then validated her. Only then did you bring up your problem.

"Now you're ready for the fun part, which is to search for solutions that you can both live with. Okay, let's have you continue your discussion."

Tom resumed, "Well, it sounds like we have four problems to settle—your tiredness and feeling sexually unsatisfied and my wanting more and different sex."

"I hadn't thought of it like that, Tom, but I agree—we do have four problems."

"I guess we should look for solutions next," suggested Tom. Let's brainstorm and see if we can come up with some win-win solutions that would make us both happy."

"I agree," said Jean enthusiastically.

In the next five minutes, Tom and Jean contributed possible solutions to their sex problems. During this time, they shared equally in creating the list. Dr. Martin facilitated their brainstorming activity by writing all of their solutions on the flip chart. Here are their potential solutions.

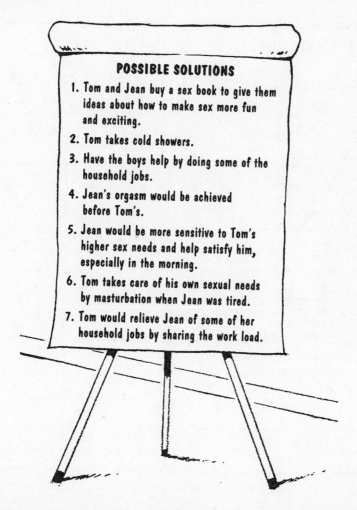

POSSIBLE SOLUTIONS

1. Tom and Jean buy a sex book to give them ideas about how to make sex more fun and exciting.

2. Tom takes cold showers.

3. Have the boys help by doing some of the household jobs.

4. Jean's orgasm would be achieved before Tom's.

5. Jean would be more sensitive to Tom's higher sex needs and help satisfy him, especially in the morning.

6. Tom takes care of his own sexual needs by masturbation when Jean was tired.

7. Tom would relieve Jean of some of her household jobs by sharing the work load.

After the brainstorming activity, the solutions were placed on the Decision Chart. Instead of using a "yes-no" method for evaluating the merits of each alternative as they had done in the parenting problem, Tom and Jean used a number system. They rated each alternative against a criterion by using a scale of 1 to 5. In this method, a 5 means that any given alternative-criterion is highly likely to solve the problem; a 3 means that the alternative-criterion is moderately likely; and a 1 means that it is not likely to solve the problem.

Tom and Jean worked as a team to rate each alternative. When they added up the numbers for each alternative, they found that five of the seven received the highest scores. As a result, they agreed to combine these five into a single solution. The solution was then recorded in their problem-solving notebook as shown in Figure 9.1.

DECISION CHART

SELECTION CRITERIA →

ALTERNATIVES	Practical/Easy to Carry Out	Requires Change from Both Mates	Meets Jean's Needs	Meets Tom's Needs	SUM
1. Buy a sex book.	5	5	3	5	(18)
2. Tom takes cold showers.	3	1	Does Not Apply	3	7
3. Boys help do household jobs.	4	5	5	5	(19)
4. Jean's sexual satisfaction is achieved before Tom's.	3	4	5	4	(16)
5. Jean meets Tom's sex needs in the morning.	3	3	3	5	(14)
6. Tom masturbates.	4	1	Does Not Apply	3	8
7. Tom shares household jobs.	4	2	5	3	(14)

PROBLEM DISCUSSED	OUTCOME/ SOLUTION
Jean upset with Tom because he wants sex when she is tired and because he doesn't satisfy her sexual needs. Tom upset with Jean because he wants more sex and creative sex.	Tom and Jean will involve the boys more in doing household chores. Tom commits to satisfying Jean sexually. Jean agrees to meet Tom's sex need in the morning. Tom will help do laundry 2 times each week. Together, they will shop for a new sex book and try new sex techniques that are mutually satisfying.

Signed: _Jean_   _Tom_
         (Wife)   (Husband)

Date: 1/24/88

Figure 9.1. This is another example of how to record agreements. As agreements mount, they become positive feedback to the couple that their skills in problem-solving are improving.

TOM AND JEAN SUCCEED AT PROBLEM-SOLVING

After Tom and Jean had completed their problem-solving, Dr. Martin said, "Well, you've just solved a very difficult problem, and you did it without my help. To move from a sex conflict to resolution takes some real skills. You're both to be congratulated!"

"Dr. Martin, I'm simply amazed at what we just did," said Jean. "We've been plagued by this for months, and it's caused so much tension between us. It's hard to believe that we were able to get a solution and do it in such a short time. If we can just carry out these solutions, it will be one of the best things that's happened since we started coming to counseling."

"I feel the same way. To think that we could solve a big issue like sex without ripping each other or getting into a fight is really great. We couldn't have done that a few weeks ago, and it seemed so easy. What's made the difference?"

"Tom, you're asking an excellent question. There were several reasons why you were successful. Let's take a little time to look at these. The first reason has to do with the fact that you used positive rather than Killer messages. In particular, you used what I call the *positive trilogy*—listening, approval, and agreement. These are the building blocks of effective problem-solving. Tom, you were willing to hear Jean's complaints—you listened to her needs and showed a genuine interest in meeting them. And then you showed approval of her as a working mother. And, Jean, I counted four times that you agreed with Tom. Those three communication behaviors created a good atmosphere for solving issues."

"Now that you've brought that to my attention, I do remember Jean agreeing more than disagreeing. That did have a good effect on me."

"Yes, Tom, that's the communication skill called *high agreement-to-disagreement ratio*. And Jean's ratio was excellent—four agreement sentences to zero disagreements. Using more agreement than disagreement sentences will almost always influence your mate in a positive way. But if the talk time is heavily sprinkled with more disagreement sentences, problem-solving can erupt into a big fight.

"The second reason for your success in problem-solving was that you avoided the *negative trilogy*—interruptions, criticism, and disagreements. As I explained last session, the three most frequently used verbal messages used by troubled partners are interrupting, criticizing, and disagreeing; and that's a big reason why these partners have difficulty solving their differences. But instead of using this trilogy, you concentrated on their positive counterparts—listening, approving, and agreeing.

"The third reason for your success was that you used positive non-verbal communication. We've talked about this before, but it's so vital that I want to review it again. While we communicate with words, wordless parts of communication are also important. In fact, some communication experts say that nonwords are more powerful than the actual words. Up to 75 percent of your communication effectiveness is due to your nonverbal skills. This is because we listen with our 'third ear.' That is, we hear the words of a message, but we also hear and see the wordless parts—and these nonverbals can determine how we will respond to the message. For example, if we hear a hostile, loud voice or see an angry, scowling face from our mate, we will usually respond negatively to his or her message.

"Happy partners are much more likely to communicate nonverbal messages of 'I care,' 'I'm interested in your ideas,' 'You're so smart,' or 'I'm glad I married you.' In contrast, unhappy mates tend to communicate wordless messages of 'I don't care,' 'Your ideas are stupid,' or 'Why did I marry you?' When couples perceive these Killer nonverbals with their third ear, they can feel their self-esteem attacked. As a result, they counterattack, and the problem mushrooms into a major conflict.

"Unfortunately, most couples aren't mindful of the tremendous power of their nonverbal behavior and how it influences the solution-making climate. This is especially true of unhappy couples. They simply fail to see that their negative, nonverbal actions can dominate and become the overwhelming message that's received by their mate, totally canceling out their words."

"Run that by me again, Dr. Martin; I'm not sure I understood that last part."

"What I'm trying to say is that you can become overpowered by how something is said and not hear the words. You can be distracted from the words by *how* a person talks to you."

"Okay, I see what you mean now. That's sure been true for me. In the past, I've tried to listen to what Jean said, not how she talked to me, but it was impossible, especially when I got an angry voice, dirty looks, and an accusing finger pointed at me. Those nonverbals would affect me so much that I'd either want to run away from the discussion or fight back."

"That's often the case, Tom. When you're on the receiving end of a loud voice, angry face, or hostile gestures, it can prompt you into one of two responses—escape from the anger or fight.

"But the point I want to make is that your nonverbal behavior was positive today. Jean, you're improving the ways in which you send messages. I know you've been pretty uptight about the unsolved sex problem, but you didn't let it show in a negative nonverbal way; you did a splendid job of handling it. I wish I had a videotape replay to show you how well you did in that area. It was really a contrast to last week's session. Your facial expression, which is the most powerful aspect of human nonverbal behavior, was friendly. And I didn't detect anger in your voice or see a wagging finger; you didn't fall back into those old coercive habits. That helped Tom. Jean, you may not have realized before how dominant your nonverbal behavior was or what it did to Tom. But now, you're learning the skills to convey your message appropriately."

"I know in the past there have been times that I did come across too strongly when I explained a problem, and I guess that did repel Tom. But today, I made a special effort not to do that. Even though the sex thing has been festering for a long time, I haven't been so uptight about it lately. I think that has to do with Tom's new attitude toward me. I've been feeling much better about our relationship, and when there's less tension between us, problems don't seem quite so bad. I guess it's like you said in the last session, I'm a better problem-solver when I feel cared for."

"That's right, Jean, and it points out the fourth reason why you succeeded in your problem-solving. When care levels are up and your needs are being met, there's less anger and frustration and more good will. That helps you relax and pay attention to your mate. You focus less on your own pain and start to listen more carefully. When the environment at home is one of love, support, and care, problems don't seem so overwhelming. In fact, sometimes a conflict evaporates as care goes up. What's happening is simply this: You're both delivering more P's and fewer N's, and that helps create a positive climate for solving problems. Caring puts you in a frame of mind to make concessions, compromises, act cooperatively, and be friendly. Feeling cared for is an antecedent for effective problem-solving. That's the reason why I had you learn partner-pleasing skills before you learned problem-solving skills.

"There's one more explanation to why your problem-solving went well, and that's because you spent more time on solutions and less time talking about problems. One of the big communication differences between happy and unhappy couples is that distressed couples keep on describing problems. They seldom move toward solutions. Let me show you a real example of what I mean."

Dr. Martin then gave Tom and Jean a copy of a computer print-out (see Figure 9.2) showing the results of another couple's problem-solving interaction. Dr. Martin explained that couples can now be videotaped or audiotaped for ten minutes while they solve real relationship problems. The interaction is then scored by trained observers to see how many of the twenty-five verbal and nonverbal

HUSBAND

	IRRELEVANT	DESCRIBING	BLAME	PROPOSING CHANGE	VALIDATING	INVALIDATING	FACILITATING
7.		D					
6.		DDD					F F F F
5.		DDDDDDDD					F F F F
4.		DDDDDDDD					F F F F
3.	X	DDDDDDDD	B B B	C C C	V V V		
2.		DDDDDD		C C	V V		
1.	X X X						
CATEGORY	IRRELEVANT	DESCRIBING	BLAME	PROPOSING CHANGE	VALIDATING	INVALIDATING	FACILITATING
Category Totals:	4	46	3	5	5	3	10
Rate per Minute:	.40	4.60	.30	.50	.50	.30	1.00
Percentage:	5	61	4	7	7	4	13

WIFE

	IRRELEVANT	DESCRIBING	BLAME	PROPOSING CHANGE	VALIDATING	INVALIDATING	FACILITATING
7.		DDD					F F F F
6.		DDDDDDDD					F F F F
5.		DDDDDDDD					F F F F
4.		DDDDDD					F F F F
3.	X		B B B B	C C C		- - -	F F F F
2.	X				V	- - -	
1.							
CATEGORY	IRRELEVANT	DESCRIBING	BLAME	PROPOSING CHANGE	VALIDATING	INVALIDATING	FACILITATING
Category Totals:	2	36	4	5	1	8	19
Rate per Minute:	.20	3.60	.40	.50	.10	.80	1.90
Percentage:	3	48	5	7	1	11	25

Figure 9.2. This graph shows communication behaviors of a husband and wife during a ten-minute problem-solving session. The category frequencies show the strengths and weaknesses of a couple's interaction. This graph is part of the Marital Interaction Coding System (MICS) developed by Dr. Robert Weiss at the University of Oregon Marital Studies Program.

behaviors happened during the ten-minute period. The communication behaviors are counted in terms of rate per minute and percentages and then placed into seven categories. The final result of this analysis is this computer print-out. It shows both the kind and frequency of communication behaviors used by a husband and wife.

Dr. Martin took special time to point out that this couple had spent too much time in the problem description stage and not enough time in finding solutions and proposing changes, thus leaving them with an unsolved problem. He explained to Tom and Jean that this problem-solving pattern is typical of many unhappy couples who get into a problem-orientation habit rather than being solution-minded.*

DR. MARTIN'S SUMMARY

Following the discussion of the computer print-out page, Dr. Martin said, "Well, our time is up for this session. You worked together as a team in solving a pretty hard problem, and I want to compliment both of you. As we've discussed, your success in solving the sex problem can be attributed to five reasons: First, you used some positive communication behaviors like listening, approving, and agreeing. Second, you avoided Killer messages such as interruptions, criticism, and disagreement. Third, your verbal messages were accompanied by positive nonverbal behaviors. Fourth, you're feeling cared for; that defuses hurt and anger and motivates you to become a cooperative problem-solver. And fifth, you concentrated on solutions, not problems. Together, this communication style will help you succeed at problem-solving.

"I wish I could tell you that you'll never have problems again, but of course, I can't say that. Some conflict, unhappiness, frustration, and anger is inescapable in every marriage relationship simply because they are in the fabric of all human relationships. But what I can say is this: If you'll keep these five things in mind, you will have some powerful tools that will help you work successfully through any problem. With these new skills and insights, you will be able to interrupt fights sooner so they don't become physically or emotionally destructive.

"Finally, here's your homework assignment. Continue to do your fifteen-minute problem-solving activities. Since your skills are getting better, solve some issues that are moderately hard, but don't take on any major problems for now. Before too long, however, your skills will

---

* For information about how you can take advantage of this new communication measurement technique by having a problem-solving session scored, see p. 211.

have improved to the point where you can tackle any issue, easy or hard. Remember to compute your P:N ratio in the Problem-Solving category. Keep up the good work at home, and I'll see you next time when we discuss the topic of self-esteem and how it affects marital happiness."

ENRICHMENT ACTIVITIES FOR READERS

1. During this next week, complete at least three fifteen-minute problem-solving sessions with your mate. Work on small-to-medium-hard conflicts. Try not to take on any big "monster" problems yet while you continue to develop your conflict resolution skills.

2. Continue to use the BEST, but only the "Problem-Solving" section. Compute your P:N ratios, exchange lists, and discuss. As a goal, try to raise your P:N ratios each time. As these numbers change in the positive direction, you know you're becoming skilled at solving problems.

3. Keep your Problem-Solving notebook up-to-date. Each solution you record is evidence of your ability to cooperate and work as a team.

Building Self-Esteem in Marriage

Dr. Martin began the counseling session. "In several sessions, I've explained how thoughts and beliefs play a big role in the success of a marriage. For example, we've looked at how blame, distortions, and focusing on your mate's negative behaviors can interfere with marital happiness. Conversely, we've discussed how cooperation, realistic perspectives, and focusing on your spouse-positive behaviors can revitalize a marriage. Today, I want us to look at another mental factor that affects marriage—self-esteem.

"A good way to start is by having you recall some of the major successes you had when you were growing up. Here's a paper for each of you. At the top, write the words *My Early Successes*. In the next few minutes, list at least five achievements that you had early in life. These are accomplishments that may have happened when you were a child or a teenager, and they can be successes that you experienced either at home or school."

Tom and Jean began the assignment eagerly, but after a few minutes, Dr. Martin noticed that their enthusiasm for the task had quickly faded. Tom looked out the window and chewed on his pencil. Jean stared at her paper with a pained look on her face. Dr. Martin could tell that not much was being written on their lists.

After a short time, he announced, "Okay, let's see what each of you has put on your 'Success List.' Tom, what about you? What early successes do you recall? I'll write them here on the flip chart."

"Well, I only have one on my list. I earned a junior varsity letter in baseball, but I wasn't good enough for the varsity."

"One is better than none, Tom," encouraged Dr. Martin.

"What I remembered most were my school failures. They seemed to stand out in my mind. Like I was horrible in arithmetic. My fifth grade teacher, Mrs. Kennedy, used to get so exasperated because I couldn't learn division problems. She tried everything—special workbooks and chalkboard drill—but it wouldn't sink in. One day she tried to motivate me by saying, 'Tom, if your brain was in a bird, it would fly sideways instead of straight ahead.' All the kids laughed, and I felt pretty stupid.

"And to make matters worse, my dad tried to help me learn numbers at home. To teach me fractions, he'd use my mom's measuring cups, but that didn't work either. He'd just get mad and say, 'How many times do I have to tell you?' I'd end up feeling like a real dumb bunny.

"In high school, it was more of the same. I just couldn't make friends with math. To this day, numbers cause me lots of headaches. At the plant, I always worry about understanding the computer spoilage report. I wonder if my early problems with numbers is why I hate to work on keeping the checkbook balanced?"

"That could be, Tom. Failure experiences of the past can affect your current motivation and performance on certain tasks. What else do you remember about school?"

TOM'S EARLY SUCCESSES

1. Earned a JV baseball letter.
2. ?
3. ?
4. ?

"Well, besides math, I wasn't too good with books. I was a fast reader but a slow understander. I was so bad that I was put into a remedial class with other kids who couldn't read. What a wasted class that was; when teacher's back was turned, we sailed paper airplanes, matched pennies, and shot spitballs at each other. I even had problems in music class. Once, my report card said, 'Tom helps our group singing by being a good listener.' When it came to grade school, the only thing I was good at was cafeteria and school bus."

"Thanks, Tom, for sharing that. It takes some real courage to talk about your failures. How about you, Jean? What outstanding personal achievements can you think of?"

"My sense of accomplishment comes from two things—in the eighth grade, I won the Spelling Bee, and in high school, I played the piano in the orchestra. But I have the same problem as Tom. The pains of my childhood are easier to remember than my successes.

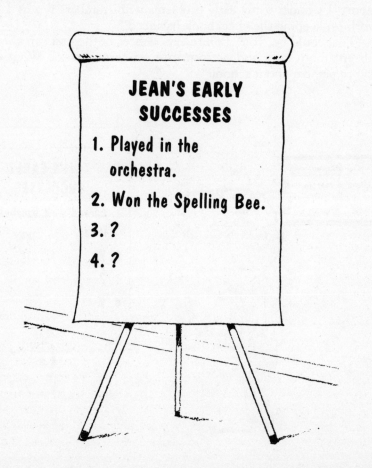

"My dad was an alcoholic, and many nights he'd come home from work drunk and start hitting me or yelling at me with that angry look on his face. I especially remember one night, he beat me because I spilled milk all over the table. I can still hear him screaming at me. I was so scared that my body shook and my heart nearly thumped out of my chest.

"Living with my mom wasn't much better. She'd always compare me to my oldest brother, who was a real brain, and call me stupid. Even when I was good in spelling, she'd never notice it. She would constantly complain and say I wasn't good enough. That's what I remember most about growing up."

WHAT WE KNOW ABOUT SELF-ESTEEM

"I want to thank both of you for sharing these very personal things with me; I know it's not enjoyable to think about failures and painful events. Before we look at how these negative experiences may have influenced your marriage, I want to briefly explain five things we know about self-esteem. Then, we'll discuss how some of these relate to your marriage."

1: What Is Self-Esteem?

"First, let's begin by defining self-esteem. There are several terms that mean the same as self-esteem: *self-image, self-confidence, self-concept,* and *self-evaluation.* Whatever name you choose, it describes satisfaction or respect for oneself. It is mentally how we see ourselves. This estimate of ourselves may be the most important value judgment we ever make because it affects our psychological development, our motivation, and our ability to relate successfully to others. Self-esteem could be the most valuable psychological resource human beings possess."

2: Self-Esteem Is Learned

"Second, we are not born with self-esteem. It is learned. Our self-evaluations are developed mainly from the evaluations others give us, especially parents. For example, if we have received acceptance, respect, concerned treatment, and success reports from parents, we will probably have a positive self-esteem. But if there's been an accumulation of rejections and a reflection of failures, we'll likely have a negative self-image. This is especially true if the negative events are interpreted to mean rejection by the significant adults in our lives at that time."

3: Self-Esteem Is Changeable

"Fortunately, since self-esteem is learned or acquired, it is also changeable. We can reverse the way we think about ourselves. This is done by focusing on certain kinds of information. There are two main sources of information that help us change self-evaluations from bad to good: Self-information that we have about our own successes and others' information—that is, positive feedback that comes to us from others. The point is, fears and self-doubts that are educated into us can be educated out. We'll spend more time talking about this later in our session."

4: Personality Characteristics of High and Low Self-Esteem People

"Another thing we know is that people with high self-esteem have different personality traits from those with low self-esteem. People with positive self-concepts are flexible, adaptable, and open to others' feedback. They trust others, accept responsibility, and can focus on the needs of others. People with a low self-esteem are just the opposite. They are rigid, resistant, and threatened by feedback. That is, they are not strong enough to receive negative feedback; they can't handle being wrong and tend to see a behavior request as a criticism. Other telltale signs include being suspicious, ego-centered, or selfish. They also tend to blame and distort reality."

5: Happy and Unhappy Couples Differ Psychologically

"The fifth point is that positive self-esteem precedes successful adjustment in a variety of social relationships—the greater our self-confidence, the better we relate to others. There's no better example of this than in marriage. In their research with good and bad marriages, family scholars have discovered that mental health and marriage happiness are inseparable. Couples who report happiness in their marriage also report strong self-esteem, but troubled couples are more likely to suffer low self-esteem. In short, we know that self-esteem is one of the key traits that set happy and unhappy couples apart. When you appreciate and like yourself, it's easier to be a better mate. I'll say more about this idea later."

TOM AND JEAN'S SELF-ESTEEM

"Dr. Martin, I have a question about number two. Since Tom and I were able to recall more rejections and failures, it must mean that we grew up with poor self-concepts."

"Yes, Jean, that's the sad conclusion we'd have to make—your self-esteem development got off to a shaky start. Home and school, the two most powerful sources for influencing how our self-esteem is shaped, have had a strong impact on each of you. Jean, from what you've told me, your parents did not provide you with a very safe environment for growing a healthy self-concept. You may have not thought of it like this, but you suffered a traumatic childhood of being physically and verbally abused. Those physical beatings and the fact that you were frequently yelled at and criticized have likely left some negative marks on your self-esteem; that kind of cruelty and rejection can convince you that you are no good.

"Tom, it wasn't much better for you. Your school experiences were not the kind that would have facilitated positive attitudes about yourself. Constant school failures can bruise a person's self-esteem and leave him with feelings of inferiority, inadequacy, and self-doubt.

"The point is, your self-esteem backgrounds were very similar. You both grew up with a lot of negative feedback with adults telling you that you were incompetent, worthless, and not good enough. All that negative information about yourself can crush self-esteem and cause you to doubt your abilities. What you needed instead was approval—school and home should have provided you with feelings of being competent, significant, and okay. But that didn't happen. When these vital emotional-psychological needs go unmet as a child or teenager, you can develop into an adult with a low self-esteem."

SELF-ESTEEM IN MARRIAGE

"Now that I've given you a quick analysis of your self-esteem, I'll show you how low self-respect can threaten happiness in marriage. This happens in three ways."

Threat 1: Overlooking Self-Esteem Needs

"The first has to do with not recognizing the esteem factor in people. When you got married, neither of you fully understood your own basic human needs. That's true for most of us—we really have little insight to who we are and what we need. Sexual needs are an exception; those demands grab our attention. But beyond that physical craving, we are not aware of our own psychological needs to be accepted and approved of; it's not unusual for partners to go through an entire lifetime together insensitive to their needs for a positive self-esteem. Self-esteem needs, unlike sexual drives, are subtle and can easily be overlooked."

"It looks like we bagged some self-esteem problems into our marriage and didn't know it."

"It seems that way, Tom. Neither of you had totally healthy personalities at the start of your marriage; you both had self-esteem deficiencies. And because you were not conscious of your own esteem needs, you naturally didn't detect that need in your mate. It was much easier to pay attention to your other roles and responsibilities. For example, Jean, you saw your role as cook, mother, and sexual partner. And, Tom, you concentrated on your role as breadwinner and father. But neither of you recognized this other major assignment—to express emotional support, to build each other up, to praise and celebrate your mate's efforts and achievements; neither of you perceived that one of your key duties was to help your spouse develop a positive self-esteem. Somewhere along the way, we neglected to tell you that esteem-building was an essential task for marriage partners. Furthermore, we forgot to tell you that marriage is a place to meet the psychological and emotional needs of your mate. So the bad result was that nurturing and protecting each other's psyches didn't become a part of your job description."

"Dr. Martin, I have to admit that I rarely gave thought to that area. You're right—no one ever told me that I'd have to learn how to deal with Tom's self-esteem needs. And I guess I thought that adults weren't supposed to have self-esteem problems—self-esteem is only for children."

"That goes for me, too. I never knew that I was to help Jean build her self-esteem. But what surprises me most is that she had an esteem problem all these years. Why this is the first time she's ever shared that horrible childhood with me. Not only was I oblivious to my own need for a good self-esteem, but I didn't notice that Jean had the same problem."

"But, Dr. Martin, even if I had been aware of my low esteem problem, I doubt if I would have ever shared that with Tom. I'd be afraid to share that kind of secret for fear that he wouldn't accept me."

"I understand, Jean. That fear is called *self-disclosure anxiety*, and it adds another problem to a marriage. You see, low self-esteem spouses are very reluctant to disclose deep hurts and psychological needs to each other. It's too threatening—you might get further rejected and put down. And to make matters worse, if there is negativity, distrust, and hostility in a relationship, partners are even more reluctant to be transparent with each other. So they clam up, carry their esteem burden alone, suffer in silence, and fail to get that much needed support from their mate.

"But the picture is just the opposite for high self-esteem people. They have a peculiar courage or ego strength that makes them less sensitive to subtle rejection cues that come from their mate. They open up, and by sharing their psychological problems, they have a better chance to get emotional help from their partner."

"I'm beginning to see how our low self-esteem caused so much trouble in our relationship. We came into marriage feeling worthless and insecure and not even realizing it. And because we weren't wide awake, we couldn't talk about it. To think that for eighteen years we've had these esteem problems and didn't see them. It's so easy to forget the self-esteem needs of our mate."

"Yes, Tom. Like so many couples, you moved right through marriage oblivious to the self-esteem factor. And here's the real tragedy: Because you didn't appreciate or understand the role of self-esteem in marriage, you failed to exchange important esteem-building behaviors in your daily interaction—supportive behaviors like praise and positive feedback. This is the reason why the BEST includes a 'Self-Esteem' section."

"Dr. Martin, with the kind of background Tom and I had of growing up without praise and acceptance, we probably needed more positives than most couples."

"I think you're right on that, Jean. All of us have self-esteem needs when we marry, but you and Tom had extraordinary needs because of your deprived backgrounds; you didn't have a big storehouse of positive memories to make you strong. You both needed mega doses of approval—cheers, affirmations, compliments, and pats on the back. You needed to hear your mate frequently say, 'I love you; you're a special person.' But that did not happen. So those self-esteem needs only festered over the years."

Threat 2: Self-Esteem Affects Behavior Change

"There's a second way that self-esteem affects marital happiness, and that has to do with the area of behavior change. In our session on behavior change methods, I explained that change is the salvation of a marriage—couples must be able to change and adapt. But we must be careful about the approaches we use to get change from our mate. One of the basic truths about human beings is that we are more likely to modify our thoughts and behaviors when we are surrounded by positives rather than being assaulted by negative change tactics. That is, it's easier to get people to change in an atmosphere rich in approval and acceptance. The reason for that is because honest praise and positive reinforcement uplift our self-esteem. When people make us feel competent, significant, and cared for, it strengthens our self-image. When we have those good feelings about ourselves, we are more likely to be receptive to change requests from our mate. The point is, appreciating and liking yourself makes you a better mate—one who is more sensitive and responsive to your mate's change requests.

"But negative change tactics have just the opposite impact on our self-esteem. For example, just consider what the tactic of criticism does to us. A critical sentence is like a knife that cuts into our self-esteem and produces an emotional hurt. That kind of pain 'bleeds' and must be healed immediately like any physical wound. What kind of healing treatment do human beings use on psychic injury? We quickly apply 'Band-Aids'—we make excuses, get angry, counterattack, or refuse to change. While it is normal for us to use these behaviors to protect our self-esteem, these Band-Aids only create impasse and status quo instead of healing. In the final analysis, criticism destroys motivation to change. And when change is restricted, a marriage is threatened."

Threat 3: Low Self-Esteem and Distortion

"As I mentioned before, low self-esteem people have a tendency to distort messages they receive. This personalitmcharacteristic can cause a stormy cycle of misunderstanding between a couple. I'll create an example to show you what I mean. Tom, let's say that you send a message to Jean asking her to lose some weight. Your message is simply this: 'Please change in one area.' Jean, because of your low self-esteem, you exaggerate the problem and distort Tom's message: 'He's trying to hurt me by saying that I'm a totally bad person.' Feeling hurt and rejected, you respond with a message based on your misperception: You counterattack with anger, accusation, and resistance. Tom is taken off-guard. He doesn't understand that he's pressed your low self-esteem button. From his perspective, all he wanted was a small behavior change; but instead of compliance, he gets blasted. Tom concludes that he's married to a hostile, resistant wife who does not want to please him. So now, you're both hurt and angry. As this cycle continues, behavior change is blocked, conflict heightens, and good feelings evaporate—all because of one person's low self-esteem."

"Dr. Martin, how does a couple stop this cycle?"

"Well, one of the partners—probably the one with the higher self-esteem—must take the initiative to interrupt this cycle by saying, 'What's going on here?' or by communicating empathy and care. But if that chain of distortions is left to run its natural course, it can cause great harm to the relationship."

"Dr. Martin, it seems to me that those distortions can be set off by both the words we say and the way we say the words. I mean, if Tom were to ask me to lose weight with a tone in his voice that said I was fat and ugly or showed an angry look of disrespect, I'm sure I'd really feel an attack on my self-esteem. I can see how self-esteem problems are tied to communication problems."

"Good point, Jean. When a couple says, 'We can't communicate,' it usually means they're sending a barrage of Killer messages that attack each other's self-esteem. That attack can occur in the words said or in the nonverbals that are delivered with the words. Both levels of communication can trigger the distortion cycle."

DEVELOPING SELF-ESTEEM

"Well, we've been looking at the negative side of self-esteem. Let's shift gears and take some time to consider how to overcome the problem of low self-concept. Remember the good news—self-esteem is changeable. There are two ways to change self-esteem. They are both based on key sources of information that you need to reflect on. The first one has to do with focusing on information from the past."

Self-Esteem Source 1: Information about Past Accomplishments

"We started out today's session by having you think about successes you had during your childhood or teen years. I have another activity that is similar, but this time, I want you to think about your triumphs that you've had as an adult; I sometimes call these your 'mastery experiences.' And, instead of having you work alone, I want you to work as a team. Tom, let's begin with your adulthood. What successes, outstanding personal achievements, or mastery experiences can you recall? Jean, if Tom gets stuck on this task, help him think about these kinds of events."

Tom was silent for a few moments and then said, "I understand what I'm supposed to do, but it's just not coming. I'm drawing a blank about my adult achievements."

"Dr. Martin, I've got one that fits what you're talking about. Several years ago, Tom was on the union bargaining team at the plant, and he helped head off a labor strike by talking the union members into accepting a new labor contract. There was lots of strife and the union was divided; Tom worked night and day to try to keep peace. If a strike had occurred, the men could have lost their jobs and many families would have suffered. But Tom helped keep the union together. He showed a good ability to communicate with the members and to motivate them to accept the contract. Several wives called me afterwards and said they were glad that Tom had helped to keep the men on the job. To me, that was a great accomplishment for him. If I were Tom, I'd count that as a tremendous feather in my cap."

"I agree, Jean. That sounds like a good example of a past achievement. Tom, how about that?"

"You know, I completely forgot about that event. Now that I think back to it, I do feel good about what I did then. That was a high pressure time—management had threatened to shut down the plant. It could have been a long strike, but I was able to coax our union to ratify the contract. I guess that was one of my personal achievements."

"And, Tom, there's another one that I bet you've forgotten—that's the time you passed the apprenticeship program at the plant. That was not long after you first went to work there. I remember how hard you studied for months, and when you passed all the tests, your department gave you a special award. Plus, your hourly wages went up. We really needed the money then because I was pregnant with Chris, and we knew there would be extra expenses with our expanding family."

"You're right again, Jean. I did work hard during that apprentice program. I learned to repair heavy equipment and operate both the metal lathe and the fork lift machine. Knowing these three jobs gave me more job security at the plant. How come I can't remember those things, Dr. Martin? Is it normal to forget our successes?"

"Yes, Tom. Consciously thinking about our past victories doesn't come naturally. We get so busy moving on to the next goals in life that we forget how good we've been. And, of course, our society doesn't let us dwell on success because it's considered to be boasting."

"When you tell us we must think of our past, it sounds like you're saying that we have a rear-view mirror that we can look into to find out what successes we've left behind us."

"That's a good way of saying it, Tom. We need to resurrect and re-experience successes that have been buried and forgotten. Paying attention to past performance achievements is an excellent way to build positive feelings about ourselves in the present tense. And when your self-esteem is at a high point—when you're feeling happy and satisfied about yourself and respect who you are—you become more receptive and responsive to your mate's needs. But when you are plagued by self-doubt and feelings of inferiority, you get stubborn and unresponsive.

"The fact is, dwelling on our past triumphs is absolutely necessary if we want a good marriage. One of the laws that affects all of us is this: Our current self-esteem is directly linked to our past accomplishments.

In other words, respecting, appreciating, and liking ourselves now is largely a result of what we've achieved in the past. To apply that law to marriage means that we must take stock of our performance histories and note what we've mastered. These past successes are building blocks for a positive self-esteem, and when we have a good self-image, we're less likely to focus on our own needs; instead, we are more open to meeting our mate's needs. Feeling good about ourselves allows us to make behavior changes that our mate wants.

"Okay, with Jean's help, we've been able to recall two of your successes, Tom. I'll put them here on the flip chart. Now, let's do the same for her. What kinds of adult successes can you remember, Jean?"

"It's still easier to think of myself as just plain old me, but I suppose one of my accomplishments was being the PTA president for two years in a row. I had been treasurer earlier, and while that job had taken a lot of time, being president was a real burden. What I feel

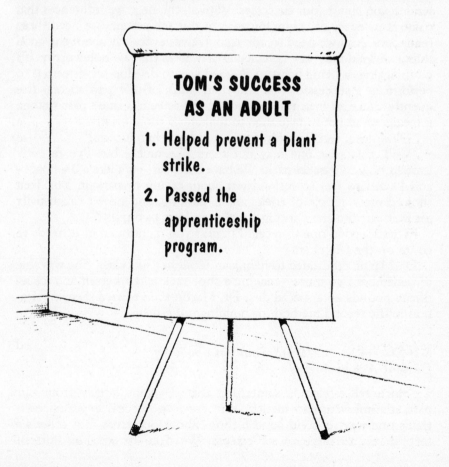

**TOM'S SUCCESS
AS AN ADULT**

1. Helped prevent a plant strike.

2. Passed the apprenticeship program.

most proud about was that our school carnival raised $10,000, and we used that money to buy new playground equipment."

"Jean, I think Dr. Martin should know that you did so well that the community parents gave you a 'Great Person Award' for being such a good leader during those two years."

"I'd nearly forgotten all about that award, but now that I think back to it, that award meant a great deal to me. I was so proud that I hung it on the kitchen wall, but I finally took it down because I thought guests might think I was bragging or just showing off. It's stuffed in an old cardboard box down in the basement."

"Jean, I encourage you to dig it out and put it back on the wall. And, Tom, if you can find your old junior varsity baseball letter and your special recognition award from the plant, put those on the wall, too. It is so vital that you both display visually the tangible awards that represent your past performance accomplishments. Awards—things like ribbons, trophies, and certificates—reflect real achievements that help to remind you about your successes. With all the negative influences that come at us every day chipping away at our self-esteem, we need these reminders. And we need to talk to ourselves every day about the good things we've done—the spectacular as well as the less noteworthy; it's not bragging or being boastful. A good way to develop self-esteem is to perform in a successful way and then think of that past success frequently. Since an important source of self-esteem is one's past victory, it means we've got to take time to remember those events.

"Okay, Jean, can you think back on any other success?"

"Well, this next one may not seem like much, but I've recently learned how to parallel park. We have a big car—it's like a big boat—and I used to feel so intimidated about trying to park it. But Tom showed me a couple of tricks about parking, and now I can usually get that car into the parking space in at least two tries."

"That's a good one to recall. I'm glad you mentioned it. It needs to go up on the flip chart."

Dr. Martin continued to help Jean recall her successes. She was able to remember two more—making a shoe rack all by herself and losing fifteen pounds on a special diet. Dr. Martin then turned the conversation to the second method for building self-esteem.

Self-Esteem Source 2: Information about Current Achievements

"Since self-esteem is something that develops largely from our past, it's important to identify our previous success experiences—that's one way to build good feelings about ourselves. But there's a second way to improve self-esteem: We need to consider current

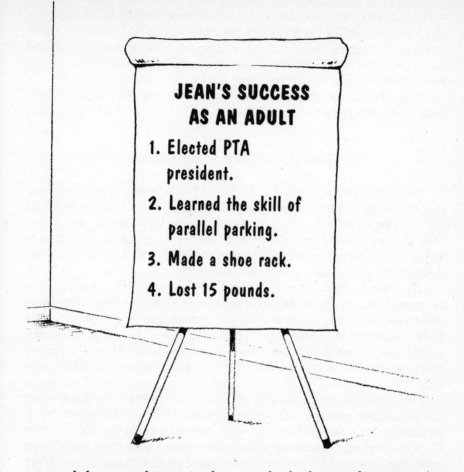

**JEAN'S SUCCESS
AS AN ADULT**

1. Elected PTA president.
2. Learned the skill of parallel parking.
3. Made a shoe rack.
4. Lost 15 pounds.

accomplishments; that is, we have to think about information that reflects daily successes. A good way to do this is by using the self-esteem section of the BEST. In that section, there are more than thirty different self-esteem events that focus on here-and-now achievements. You've already had a chance to use this category. How do you feel about that part of the BEST?"

"I think the self-esteem checklist has been one of the most helpful parts of the BEST," responded Tom. "It's helped me pay attention to behaviors on my part that boost Jean's happiness. For example, I'm much more alert to complimenting her on her appearance, telling her I love her, and not overlooking her special efforts to please me."

"Dr. Martin, I like that section also. It's opened up my thinking to the many ways I can bolster Tom's self-esteem. With that checklist, I've learned how important it is to laugh at Tom's jokes, ask his opinion, brag about him to the children, and point out his positives."

"Good. I'm glad to hear that the self-esteem checklist has been valuable. You're probably at the point now where you don't have to mark items on the list each day. Instead, you can make your daily interaction pattern one that includes the giving of positive feedback and approval messages to each other. So put away your pencils and the checklist and just start living out the esteem-building behaviors on a regular basis. Make it a normal part of your relationship."

DR. MARTIN'S SUMMARY

"Well, our time is nearly up. Let's take a few minutes to summarize our discussion. During this session, I wanted you to learn to appreciate the role of self-esteem in marriage. I especially wanted you to see that positive self-esteem is a crucial asset in marriage and to understand that low self-esteem can cause problems. What questions or comments do you have about our session?"

"Dr. Martin, I've got some mixed feelings about the session. The bad part is facing up to the fact that we came into marriage with poor self-concepts; I can see how that can almost doom a marriage right from the beginning. And, then, because Tom and I were blind to our esteem needs, we didn't build each other up when all the time, we desperately needed it. It's sad to think that for eighteen years of marriage we lived each day secretly hoping that our mate would affirm us and say something pleasant and praising; it bothers me to think of all the supportive messages we never said to each other. We had so many chances to help each other cope with low self-esteem but didn't do it. But the good part is hearing you say that there's a cure for self-esteem problems. It would be awfully discouraging to go through life with no hope of being able to change our self-concept."

"I appreciate what you're saying, Jean. You could easily get depressed if you focused on both your painful early years and the missed-opportunity years when you didn't exchange esteem-building messages; most couples are just like you—they pass up chances to enrich their spouse's self-esteem, thereby endangering their marriage. But I'm glad you've caught the idea that self-esteem can be improved, and we do that in two ways—by reflecting on past successes and by exchanging positive feedback in our daily interaction. The point to remember is that the past and the present are both important in changing a poor self-esteem."

"Dr. Martin, when you talk about the past and present, that means that Jean and I can't bring up each other's negative past histories, and we can't continue to use negative change tactics on each other. Past and present negatives will only stir up our feelings of inferiority and cause us to resist each other."

"Precisely, Tom. Those two behaviors only crush self-esteem: reminding your mate of his/her past failures and using communication behaviors that include criticism, harsh negatives, and Killer messages. But there are two opposite behaviors that will boost self-esteem: thinking about successful, mastery experiences and nurturing each other's self-image with warm words, honest praise, and enthusiastic hugs."

"Dr. Martin, as you've explained self-esteem building, it seems that you're saying that Tom and I can't improve our self-esteem alone—we need each other."

"That's right. It's hard to build self-esteem by ourselves; the people around us help to define us. That means, Jean, that your self-definition is influenced by Tom as he reflects your achievements back to you. And you help Tom define himself by telling him about his successes. You can't develop positive self-evaluation on some desert island by yourself. You need each other's positive feedback—recognition of your efforts and performances. Esteem-building is a process that happens as one person relates to another person."

"When you say it like that, we don't have any choice—Tom and I must be each other's biggest fans and cheerleaders."

"I like the way you've said that, Jean. Yes, it's vital that you make a commitment to each other's mental health and psychological wellness. Jean, you've got to focus on Tom: Help him be strong psychologically. Praise him. Agree with him more than you disagree with him. Look for ways to applaud him. Remind him daily of his successes. Remember, he wants to be appreciated, not criticized. Be his number-one support person. And, Tom, you perform the same function for Jean. Focus on her. Nurture her psychological health. Give her the kind of information feedback that helps her feel loved, valued, esteemed, and appreciated. As you both support each other and build self-esteem, your marriage will be happier.

"Here's something else to consider. Remember, you both have some negative experiences and ghosts of the past that can interfere with your current happiness. But you can't exorcise those demons of defeat, self-doubt, and inferiority alone. You need a supportive partner to overcome those harmful histories. And by support—I'm talking about communicating positive information—that kind of information acts as a countermeasure for those early negative years. Positives help heal the hurt of the past. However, all couples need esteem-building in their relationship; even healthy husbands and wives have doubts about themselves and need regular affirmation from each other. Can you think of anything else you'd like to bring up before we end our session?"

"Dr. Martin, I have a question about something you said earlier. Didn't you say that good marriages and bad marriages have different amounts of self-esteem?"

"Right, Tom. Happily married couples have better mental health. It's one of the key traits that distinguish them from disturbed couples. Scientists are just now showing us this crucial link between self-esteem and marital happiness."

"Well, if that is true, it means that if our self-respect improves, so will our marriage."

"Right again. Those two events happen together; there's no doubt, self-esteem is a big factor in marital adjustment. Happy marriages require individuals high in self-esteem. But I want to quickly point out that you can't put all your happiness eggs in the self-esteem basket. The best way to assure marital happiness is to improve the other four traits also: More P's and fewer N's, practicing positive change methods, using positive communication behaviors, and spending more time together. Improving the total cluster of traits will have an enormous impact on your happiness.

"Well, our time is gone. Next time, we'll learn about the last trait that is commonly found in the lives of happy couples—the trait of sharing a lot of time together."

ENRICHMENT ACTIVITIES FOR READERS

1. If you and your mate have been exchanging self-esteem-building behaviors by using the BEST for a period of fourteen days, you can stop the task of marking the checklist. However, esteem-building must continue as a normal part of your daily interaction pattern.

2. Recall at least three past successes you experienced as a child or teenager. Once you and your mate have done this separately, exchange lists.

3. Working as a team with your spouse, recall your success experiences as adults. Think of four each.

Time Together

"Well, this is our final session, and there are two things I want us to do. To begin with, I want us to look at the last trait that is commonly found in the profile of the happy couple—the trait of spending much time together. And then, I think it would be helpful to summarize the key points that you've learned from our counseling sessions. Let's begin by discussing the time together trait.

"Jean, when you came into counseling, one of the complaints about Tom was that he didn't want to spend any time with you. From your viewpoint, all he ever wanted to do was play golf."

"That's right. I felt lonely and rejected for years. I've been so hurt because Tom put his golf game ahead of me. But if it wasn't golf, it would have been something else—restoring his antique car, hunting ducks, or watching TV."

FACTORS THAT INTERFERE WITH COMPANIONSHIP

"I understand. What might be helpful at this point is to explain the three reasons why togetherness dwindles in a marriage. The three factors which rob a couple of their time together include children, careers, and coercion."

Factor 1: Child-Rearing Responsibilities

"When you think back to the history of your relationship, it's clear that the first two years of your marriage were the time of greatest togetherness. You worked full time then, Jean, but since there were no children yet, you and Tom had your evenings and weekends to devote to each other."

"And we had so much fun together then—we put puzzles together, went to the beach on weekends, and ate out at ritzy restaurants. It was just me and Tom and no golf."

"But at the end of the second year, your son, Chris, was born. That event had a major impact on your time together. It caused a shift in focus. Instead of concentrating on pleasing one another and sharing fun times, your attention moved to the task of parenting.

"I don't think most couples stop to consider what happens to their togetherness when they become parents. For example, just think about the fatigue factor. Jean, instead of quitting your job completely, you became a working mother; you had a part-time job plus parenting responsibilities when you got home. And, as you have described Chris, he wasn't an easy child to raise. You had your hands full with a hard-to-manage child. Working and mothering were extremely exhausting, and it robbed you of time with Tom. Why just being a mother is a demanding job by itself, but there you were trying to succeed at both energy-draining tasks. And it's been that way for most of your eighteen years of marriage."

"When you explain it like that, Dr. Martin, I guess I can't blame our lack of togetherness just on Tom's golf."

"Exactly, Jean. The parenting role—especially its time demands—must be appreciated; it cuts right into a couple's companionship. Please, don't get me wrong—children don't cause a marriage to fail. But if we're not careful, we can let children and the parenting role divert our best attention away from our most important role, which is to strengthen the husband-wife relationship. You see, the parenting role can't be first place; it must be secondary. Your best efforts have to focus on the two of you. But like so many couples, I'm afraid you lost that perspective."

Factor 2: Career-Climbing

"The second factor that interfered with your time together is what I call the career-climbing factor, and this especially relates to you, Tom. Soon after marriage, your focus began to shift from Jean to your work. Unknown to you, that shift was programmed into you by society. In our culture, until recently, boys were raised much differently than little girls. As boys grew up, they were socialized to think about the world of work. They were encouraged first to orient themselves toward being a success in an occupation. Repeatedly, they were asked, 'What do you want to be when you grow up?' In subtle ways,

Tom, you were influenced to believe that getting a job and making money were more important than having a good marriage.

"Furthermore, there is something else about the nature of men that can interfere with companionship: It's easy for men to become goal-oriented and achievement-minded, real performance machines. Unfortunately, a man's goal is seldom one of becoming a great husband; the dominating factor in his mind is to reach career and money goals. These are often more important than reaching relationship goals. Having a successful marriage is secondary.

"But little girls were socialized in a different way. They played with dolls and were shaped to think that marriage, children, and relationships were more important than jobs. So when a woman who was socialized in this way becomes an adult, her key source of self-esteem comes from relationships with people, especially her husband. Jean, you were molded to become 'Super Mom' and Tom, you were led to become 'Super Worker.' As a result, those different forces can create separateness rather than togetherness in marriage."

Factor 3: Coercion/Negative Pressure Tactics

"There's a third reason why your time together eroded, and that has to do with negative pressure tactics. During Stage 1, your marriage began to breakdown: Pleasing behaviors—the actions which bonded you together in the first place—began to decrease, and displeasing, annoying behaviors—which you overlooked in courtship—began to increase. Naturally, you wanted to restore the P's and eliminate the D's. But you lacked the skills to solve these problems in positive ways and resorted to coercive tactics like criticism and the silent treatment to change your mate. The result was these negative change methods alienated you and forced you apart."

"That was sure true for me, Dr. Martin. When Jean would get on me about something and start being critical, I'd cut out fast to the golf course, go duck hunting, or work on my car. I'd do anything to avoid those bad confrontations."

"It's normal, Tom, to want to escape a mate's hostility by becoming involved in activities outside the family. It is very hard to stay in any environment when you sense anger increasing."

"And when Tom would do his disappearing act or give me the silent treatment for three days, my hurt and anger really got out of hand," added Jean. "I didn't want to have anything to do with him at that point."

"I understand, Jean. It was a vicious cycle: noticing annoying behaviors in your mate, feeling hurt and angry, wanting change but having no skills, using coercive change tactics, reacting to coercion with escape or silence, increased feelings of hurt and hostility, alienation, and no companionship. Obviously, this cycle only served to put a great wall between you. This coercion element, plus the fact that you were preoccupied with children and career seriously disrupted your time together. But now, since your mate is giving you more P's—like approval, attention, and affection—and fewer N's, you're beginning to see your mate once again as an object of pleasure and enjoyment. It's easier now to want to be with one another. As the quality of your interaction has improved, the quantity of companionship activities has increased."

"Dr. Martin, I think there's another reason we're spending more time together—the 'Friendship' category of the BEST has given us a great menu of companionship activities to choose from. Sometimes it's hard for me to think up new ideas about what to do with Jean. But now, we look for something on the list that we both see as fun and do it."

"I'm glad to hear that you're taking advantage of the Friendship list in the BEST; it's a good source of fun activities. And it's especially good to hear that you are choosing companionship events together. Team planning avoids a situation in which one spouse is the lone planner while the other is merely a passive participant."

TOGETHERNESS: A COMMON TRAIT
OF HAPPY COUPLES

"Now that we've discussed the three conditions that block time together, I want to show you how happy and unhappy couples differ in their companionship activities. In 1979 at the University of Kentucky, researchers Linda Barnett and Michael Nietzel found a definite link between marital happiness and the amount of time couples spend together. Couples who reported much happiness shared many activities together while unhappy couples had little companionship. But these two researchers also discovered that the whole issue of time is an important consideration in marriage. Here's their research story."

Dr. Martin handed Tom and Jean a graph and said, "This graph shows just how different couples are in the matter of time. What interesting things do you see?"

"I know what Tom spots right away," said Jean half-jokingly. "He sees the fact that couples in good marriages have more sex than couples in bad marriages."

"Well," said Tom, smiling, "it does support what I've been saying all these years about more sex being good for us. The graph shows it plainly—happy couples have more sex."

"I'm really surprised that the sex differences are so great between the two groups—the happy ones have sex four times each week, but those in the unhappy group have sex just once. But I'm sure that happy marriages aren't caused just by having more sex."

"You're right on that, Jean. It's tempting to look at this graph and conclude that just jumping in bed more often will automatically make a good marriage; it's more complex than that. Here's how I explain the difference in sex rates: Happy couples have several good things going for them. They exchange many caring behaviors, communicate

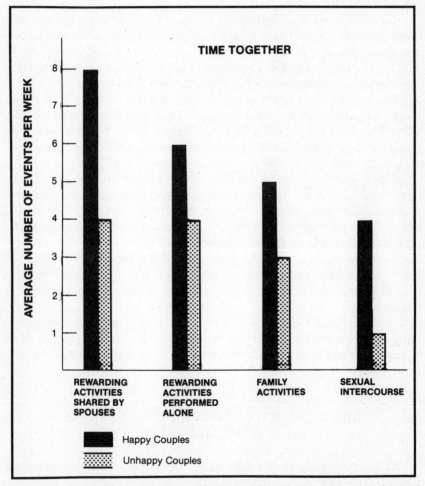

Figure 11. Number of activities reported over a four week period by 11 happy couples and 11 unhappy couples. This study also found that happy couples share more time with other couples than do unhappy couples. Based on L. R. Barnett and M. T. Nietzel, "Relationship of Instrumental and Affectional Behaviors and Self-Esteem to Marital Satisfaction in Distressed and Nondistressed Couples," *Journal of Consulting and Clinical Psychology* 47 (1979): 946-957.

pleasantly, and use few pressure tactics. As a result, they become good friends and good lovers, too. On the other hand, unhappy couples act in ways outside the bedroom which make the bedroom a pretty cold place. They show few caring behaviors, they talk negatively, and they punish one another. Good sex is just hard to have when these conditions exist. You end up seeing each other as enemies, not friends. Naturally, it's difficult to have sex with someone you don't like."

"Are you saying that lack of sex is a sign that something's wrong in the relationship?" asked Jean.

"Right. When sexual frequency is low, it's probably a symptom that other parts of the marriage aren't too healthy. Okay, what else strikes you about the graph?"

"Dr. Martin, the graph shows that happy couples are high in both togetherness and aloneness. How can that be?" asked Jean.

"Yes, it does seem like a contradiction. That finding tells us something very useful about what makes a good marriage—it needs balance. That is, a couple must find much time for each other, and they must also find personal time for themselves as individuals."

"You mean I don't have to give up my golf game?"

"Right, Tom. You need time for doing your own thing, and Jean needs to take time for some separateness, also. Too much togetherness and too little togetherness are both bad for a marriage. A marriage has to allow partners room to breathe. If you're with each other all the time, you can come to feel smothered."

"I'm happy to see what the graph says about family activities," said Jean. "I've always urged Tom to take more time for events that included all members of our family, and the graph supports what I've been saying."

"You're right on that, Jean. When the two groups are compared, happy couples have higher rates of family time as well as higher rates in companionship, independence, and sex. The summary is, togetherness counts."

BRINGING THE COUNSELING SESSIONS
TO A CLOSE

"In the remaining time we have, let's look back on our counseling sessions and summarize the key ideas that you've learned along the way. Tell me what's been important for you."

"Dr. Martin, when I think back to our first counseling session, I realize I must have been pretty obnoxious, especially the way I blamed Tom for everything that had gone wrong. It was very hard for me to let loose of that thinking and start cooperating with him."

"I have to admit the same thing," said Tom. "At the beginning of our counseling, you told us that it takes two people to make a marriage bad. But in my mind, I fought that explanation hard. I was convinced that our problems were caused by only one person—and that person wasn't me."

"If it helps any, you both should realize that it is common for unhappy couples to blame and distort reality. I have to confront and correct all my couples about the same problem—faulty attributions. Most of the couples I see come in with a long list of complaints against each other; it's like they are in a competitive struggle to show who's been worse in the relationship. The fact is, they've made a wrong explanation of why their marriage failed and mistakenly attribute their unhappiness to their partner. Many have blind spots and can't see their own role in the development of marriage problems. But once a couple understands how they have each influenced the marriage and can take a cooperative attitude of 'we are in this together,' the relationship can move ahead. I hope you can both understand now why I had to scold you about the blame problem."

"I must confess, Dr. Martin, that I had that blaming attitude for about three sessions; it didn't disappear right away. But what helped me break through that problem was when Tom and I started to use the BEST. For the first time in many months, I became aware that Tom did care for me. I could see that he showed he cared in specific behaviors. That melted my attitude of blaming and made me want to return caring behaviors to him. The BEST has been a lifesaver to our marriage."

"I'm glad to hear that, Jean. If there's any special power or magic in the BEST it's because it helps a couple focus on the positives. As I have explained, positive, pleasing, caring behavior is what attracted and bonded you together in the first place. The BEST simply helped you to re-experience those good behaviors, and when you're on the receiving end of caring actions, it's almost impossible to hang on to a blaming belief pattern."

"The BEST was a good experience for me, too. I think a lot of my anger toward Jean was because she overlooked my good behaviors. That stirred up hidden resentment. But then Jean started to see and count my good behaviors, and when she would tell me what I did to make her happy, it made me happy, too. I redoubled my efforts to please her more."

"Right, Tom. What you were experiencing was the law of positive reinforcement or positive feedback. That law says that when people notice and respond to your good actions, it creates a new energy to do that same behavior again, only better. In marriages, and society in general, we're far too eager to find and report the faults of another—

which only robs our motivation. We're not very knowledgable about this powerful law, and therefore, not very skilled at giving praise. But it's essential that we take advantage of this law. We must reward effort and reinforce the loving, caring behaviors that are delivered to us from our mate.

"You see, the purpose of the BEST is to help couples become aware of all that is positive in their relationship. It's to help them give and receive love and then talk about it. That is, it creates a dialogue where you describe each other's behaviors which show love, esteem, care, and understanding. That kind of dialogue is a forgotten or unlearned interpersonal art."

"Having Tom show more caring behavior toward me is important, but I'm just as happy about the fact that we're learning how to solve problems. When we first started counseling, I wanted to get right into those problems because they were causing so much tension between us; I sure didn't like it when you told us we'd have to wait. But now I can see that the caring behaviors had to come before our problem-solving. It was so strange—when I felt cared for, I began to relax about all the problems we faced. They didn't seem quite so urgent or overwhelming."

"I understand what you're saying, Jean. It's hard to be a good problem-solving partner if you don't feel cared for," responded Dr. Martin.

"Learning how to solve problems has been important for me, also. I think we're getting better at expressing our feelings without hurting each other. The list of communication behaviors that you gave us and helped us to use on our problems has been real helpful. I just hope I can remember to use the twenty-five positive behaviors and avoid the twenty-five Killer messages when Jean and I have future problems. I can sure see how the Killers cause more conflict."

"Right, Tom. When a couple's style of interaction and problem-solving is destructive, it can make the original problems worse or create new ones. I'm glad that you're becoming aware that a failure in communication will often lead to a failure in marriage. And that is also true of the behavior change methods that a couple uses. If they are negative, it will cause great harm to the relationship."

"I'm glad you taught us the six ways to get behavior changes. Tom and I didn't realize it, but we've been using the wrong ways of working for a change—I've been criticizing, and Tom's been using the silent treatment on me. But those only caused more pain for us."

"Training in behavior change methods is an important area, Jean, and the reason is that marriage is a place where day-to-day annoyances will accumulate; when that happens, partners will inevitably want to change one another. The problem is that we try to change people by negative procedures. The research is clear about this: When couples employ behavior change strategies that are predominately negative, unhappiness results. Criticism, threats, nagging, making your mate feel guilty, silence, and yelling will cause a relationship to suffer. But when a behavior change strategy is mostly positive, the partners will be happy. Seeking changes with the BEST, applying positive reinforcement, making PSR's, touching and telling, writing contracts, and using the twenty-five problem-solving Helpers are the best way to get change and keep your relationship happy, too. Okay, what else stands out in your mind about your counseling experience?"

"Dr. Martin, I've really valued your insight about our self-esteem backgrounds. In some ways, it was painful to look back on those negative influences in my early life; I'd like to block those years out of my mind forever. But that backward glance has given me some self-understanding. I realize now that I didn't have a very secure self-image when I got married, and I'm mindful of how necessary Tom is in helping me rebuild some good feelings about myself.

"And he's been doing such a good job of that lately. A few days ago, we had guests for dinner, and after the meal, Tom showed off my tole painting projects. Then this morning, before he left for work, he gave me a big hug and told me how much he loves my brown eyes and freckles. But the best thing was when Tom rummaged through the boxes in the basement, found my old PTA award, and hung it on the kitchen wall. All of these things really boosted my sense of personal worth. And when I feel good about myself, I become very responsive to him."

"But Jean's been on my side, too, Dr. Martin. She's been laughing at my corny jokes, bragging to the kids about me, and on Monday, she congratulated me because I fixed a leaky faucet. And the best compliment she paid me was when she said I was a good sex partner. When Jean reminds me of my efforts and successes, my confidence really grows; I feel like leaping tall buildings for her!"

As Tom said this, he reached out to grasp Jean's hand. She smiled and responded warmly. It was a tender moment as the couple realized how much they needed each other. They were beginning to recognize the important psychological resource they had married.

"It's great to hear and see what's going on between you. It points out in a real way what I've tried to explain—a strong self-esteem is necessary for a strong marriage. I'm so pleased to hear that you're both communicating positive information to each other. You may not realize it, but you've learned a fundamental marriage skill—the skill of searching for, recognizing, and telling your mate about his/her good points. Giving positive feedback is a powerful way to improve self-esteem. And when you have a good self-concept, it's easier to have a good marriage.

"Well, time's almost gone. Let's wrap things up. As I told you at the start, the counseling program I've been using with you is based on some new research. Most people are unaware that behavior scientists have been searching for solutions to marital unhappiness since 1949. However, the most practical revelations didn't occur until 1975 through 1985. During that time, these family scholars studied happy couples to see what behaviors or interaction patterns were commonplace in their lives. Unhappy couples were also studied. By comparing the behaviors of the two groups, a profile emerged—the researchers were able to pinpoint five characteristics which set happy couples apart from troubled ones. For the last time, here are the key differences which separate good and bad marriages: Happy, compared to unhappy, couples exchange more pleasing and fewer displeasing behaviors; they use more positive behavior change strategies; they rely on more positive communication behaviors to solve problems; they have higher levels of self-esteem; and they spend more time together.

"Detecting the profile differences between happy and unhappy couples was a major breakthrough because up to that point, we didn't know why some marriages had more problems than others or why some marriages succeeded and others failed. Now that we have this new information, it was very clear what ought to be done—teach couples the five happy-couple traits. And it works! The most heartening aspect of the research is the fact that unhappy couples can be changed—they can be happier. That's been my goal for you.

"From my perspective, I feel you've both made excellent progress. For one thing, you have made some important thinking changes— you stopped blaming, started cooperating, and have come to see that marriage rebuilding is a process for two people, not just one. Another thing is that you have learned some vital marriage skills that you didn't have when you got married: partner-pleasing skills, behavior change skills, problem-solving skills, and esteem-building skills. Plus, you are beginning to spend more time together. It takes all of these—the attitude/thinking changes and the behavior/skill changes to make a marriage grow.

"But how you see yourselves is more important than how I see you. The bottom line is, are you happier? Let's find out. Here's another form of the 'Happiness Test' just like the one you took at session one. That test was a pre-test, and it told us what your level of happiness was at that time. Since then, you have had some opportunities to learn new ideas and practice new skills aimed at improving your happiness. Now I want you to take a post-test to see what changes have happened in your level of marital satisfaction."

Tom and Jean worked on the test eagerly and handed the finished forms to Dr. Martin. He quickly scored the tests and compared the results against the couple's pre-test. He smiled broadly and said, "I've got good news for you. Your happiness score has changed dramatically in a positive direction. Congratulations!"

Tom and Jean received the good news with delight. They hugged each other and shook Dr. Martin's hand, thanking him for his help. Dr. Martin walked the couple to the door and invited them to return for a follow-up session three months away. He watched them walk arm-in-arm toward their car and toward a happier future.

ENRICHMENT ACTIVITIES FOR READERS

Dr. Martin gave Tom and Jean two "happiness tests"—one at the beginning of their counseling and another at the end of counseling. Sandwiched in between the tests were education, training, and skill development. Happily for Tom and Jean, their second test showed significant improvement in their marital adjustment.

If you have been following along with Tom and Jean, you may have taken the Happiness Test as a pre-test and received your score. You may now want to take the Happiness Test for the second time to see your own growth. Send your tests to me for scoring, and I will return the results to you (See p. 175 for instructions). A word of caution: The second test cannot be scored unless there have been at least five weeks between test one and test two. The five-week period should give you time to read about each counseling session, complete the Enrichment Activities, and apply the skills and insights to your relationship.

APPENDIX A

Happiness Test

(Dyadic Adjustment Test)

1. To determine if your level of marital happiness or adjustment has changed as a result of reading and completing the Enrichment Activities, you may want to take the Happiness Test. This test should be taken two times—once at the beginning of the book and as you finish the book. The time period between testing should be about five to six weeks. This will allow you time to complete all Enrichment Activities and apply the "Happy-Couple traits." You may make four copies of the test on pp. 176–177 or four copies of the tear-away Dyadic Adjustment Scale provided in *The Traits of a Happy Couple Study Guide*.

2. For a professional evaluation of your tests you may send them along with a check or money order to the following address:

Dr. Larry L. Halter
Behavior Sciences of Oregon
4522 SE 86 Court
Portland, Oregon 97266

3. Fees for scoring and interpreting the tests:

Pre-test $10.00 per couple.
Post-test $10.00 per couple.

DYADIC ADJUSTMENT SCALE

Most persons have disagreements in their relationships. Please indicate below the approximate extent of agreement or disagreement between you and your partner for each item on the following list. Check the appropriate boxes: ☐ Husband ☐ Wife ☐ Pre-test ☐ Post-test

	Always agree	Almost always agree	Occasionally disagree	Frequently disagree	Almost always disagree	Always disagree
1. Handling family finances	5	4	3	2	1	0
2. Matters of recreation	5	4	3	2	1	0
3. Religious matters	5	4	3	2	1	0
4. Demonstrations of affection	5	4	3	2	1	0
5. Friends	5	4	3	2	1	0
6. Sex relations	5	4	3	2	1	0
7. Conventionality (correct or proper behavior)	5	4	3	2	1	0
8. Philosophy of life	5	4	3	2	1	0
9. Ways of dealing with parents or in-laws	5	4	3	2	1	0
10. Aims, goals, and things believed important	5	4	3	2	1	0
11. Amount of time spent together	5	4	3	2	1	0
12. Making major decisions	5	4	3	2	1	0
13. Household tasks	5	4	3	2	1	0
14. Leisure-time interests and activities	5	4	3	2	1	0
15. Career decisions	5	4	3	2	1	0

	All the time	Most of the time	More often than not	Occasionally	Rarely	Never
16. How often do you discuss or have you considered divorce, separation, or terminating your relationship?	0	1	2	3	4	5
17. How often do you or your mate leave the house after a fight?	0	1	2	3	4	5
18. In general, how often do you think that things between you and your partner are going well?	5	4	3	2	1	0
19. Do you confide in your mate?	5	4	3	2	1	0
20. Do you ever regret that you married (or lived together)?	0	1	2	3	4	5
21. How often do you and your partner quarrel?	0	1	2	3	4	5
22. How often do you and your mate "get on each other's nerves"?	0	1	2	3	4	5

	Every day	Almost Every day	Occasionally	Rarely	Never
23. Do you kiss your mate?	4	3	2	1	0

24. Do you and your mate engage in outside interests together?

	All of them	Most of them	Some of them	Very few of them	None of them
	4	3	2	1	0

How often would you say the following occur between you and your mate:

	Never	Less than once a month	Once or twice a month	Once or twice a week	Once a day	More often
25. Have a stimulating exchange of ideas	0	1	2	3	4	5
26. Laugh together	0	1	2	3	4	5
27. Calmly discuss something	0	1	2	3	4	5
28. Work together on a project	0	1	2	3	4	5

These are some things about which couples sometimes agree and sometimes disagree. Indicate if either item below caused differences of opinions or were problems in your relationship during the past few weeks. (Check yes or no.)

	Yes	No	
29.	0	1	Being too tired for sex
30.	0	1	Not showing love

31. The dots on the following line represent different degrees of happiness in your relationship. The point, "happy," represents the degree of happiness of most relationships. Please circle the dot that best describes the degree of happiness, all things considered, of your relationship.

0	1	2	3	4	5	6
•	•	•	•	•	•	•
Extremely unhappy	Fairly unhappy	A little unhappy	Happy	Very happy	Extremely happy	Perfect

32. Which of the following statements best describes how you feel about the future of your relationship:

5 I want desperately for my relationship to succeed and would go to almost any lengths to see that it does.

4 I want very much for my relationship to succeed and will do all that I can to see that it does.

3 I want very much for my relationship to succeed and will do my fair share to see that it does.

2 It would be nice if my relationship succeeded, and I can't do much more than I am doing now to help it succeed.

1 It would be nice if it succeeded, but I refuse to do any more than I am doing now to keep the relationship going.

0 My relationship can never succeed, and there is no more than I can do to keep the relationship going.

Note: From "The Dyadic Adjustment Scale" by Graham B. Spanier, Journal of Marriage and the Family 38 (February 1976): 27–28. Copyright 1976 by the National Council on Family Relations, 1910 West County Road, Suite 147, St. Paul MN 55113. Reprinted with permission.

APPENDIX B

BEST

1. One checklist for the BEST (Behavior Exchange Skills Technique) is found on pages 179–210. You are encouraged to make two copies of the checklist—one for you and one for your mate. A tear-away copy is also available in the separate study guide. The checklists are to be used for fourteen straight days.

2. Couples sometimes like to continue using the BEST beyond the fourteen-day period. BEST materials can be purchased for $10.00 for a two-week supply. Materials can be ordered by sending a check or money order to the following address:

> Dr. Larry L. Halter
> Behavior Sciences of Oregon
> 4522 SE 86 Court
> Portland, Oregon 97266
> Phone: (503) 227-2022

BEST CHECKLIST
Daily Behavior Exchange Record---Week 1

CARE

1. We exchanged back-scratching.		S	M	T	W	T	F	S
	Positive							
	Negative							
	Wanted							

2. Partner gave me a hug.								
	Positive							
	Negative							
	Wanted							

3. Partner greeted me with hug and/or kiss when I came home.								
	Positive							
	Negative							
	Wanted							

4. Partner gave me a kiss.								
	Positive							
	Negative							
	Wanted							

5. Partner put his/her arm around me in public or at home.								
	Positive							
	Negative							
	Wanted							

6. Partner massaged my head, neck, feet, etc.								
	Positive							
	Negative							
	Wanted							

7. Partner reached out to hold my hand.								
	Positive							
	Negative							
	Wanted							

8. Partner gave me an "I love you" touch, (nonsexual pinch, pat, squeeze, etc.).								
	Positive							
	Negative							
	Wanted							

9. Partner rubbed my back until I fell asleep.								
	Positive							
	Negative							
	Wanted							

10. Partner...								
	Positive							
	Negative							
	Wanted							

11. Partner...								
	Positive							
	Negative							
	Wanted							

12. Partner...		S	M	T	W	T	F	S
	Positive							
	Negative							
	Wanted							

Care Totals:

	S	M	T	W	T	F	S
Positives							
Negatives							

COMMUNICATION

1. We talked about an event we shared--- (movie, church, etc.).		S	M	T	W	T	F	S
	Positive							
	Negative							
	Wanted							

2. We reminisced about a happy time in our relationship.								
	Positive							
	Negative							
	Wanted							

3. We laughed about something.								
	Positive							
	Negative							
	Wanted							

4. We talked about events that happened in our day.								
	Positive							
	Negative							
	Wanted							

5. We talked about a special topic (education, politics, religion, etc.).								
	Positive							
	Negative							
	Wanted							

6. We solved a problem.								
	Positive							
	Negative							
	Wanted							

7. Partner told me what was bothering him/her so I wouldn't worry.								
	Positive							
	Negative							
	Wanted							

8. Partner agreed with me on something.								
	Positive							
	Negative							
	Wanted							

BEST-WK1-P1

Communication (Cont.)

9. Partner asked about my feelings or thoughts on a certain subject.		S	M	T	W	T	F	S
	Positive							
	Negative							
	Wanted							

10. Partner showed interest while I explained a problem.								
	Positive							
	Negative							
	Wanted							

11. Partner helped plan an event (picnic, family outing, etc.).								
	Positive							
	Negative							
	Wanted							

12. Partner initiated a peace offer or made a reconciliation gesture.								
	Positive							
	Negative							
	Wanted							

13. We got into an argument.								
	Positive							
	Negative							
	Wanted							

14. We disagreed on something.								
	Positive							
	Negative							
	Wanted							

15. Partner clammed up or sulked (had a problem but refused to communicate).								
	Positive							
	Negative							
	Wanted							

16. Partner interrupted me before I was finished talking.								
	Positive							
	Negative							
	Wanted							

17. Partner made a decision without consulting me.								
	Positive							
	Negative							
	Wanted							

18. Partner...								
	Positive							
	Negative							
	Wanted							

19. Partner...								
	Positive							
	Negative							
	Wanted							

20. Partner...								
	Positive							
	Negative							
	Wanted							

21. Partner...		S	M	T	W	T	F	S
	Positive							
	Negative							
	Wanted							

Communication Totals:

	S	M	T	W	T	F	S
Positives							
Negatives							

INTERPERSONAL SKILLS/EMPATHY

1. Partner held me when I felt anxious or stressed.		S	M	T	W	T	F	S
	Positive							
	Negative							
	Wanted							

2. Partner waved goodbye or walked to the car when I left.								
	Positive							
	Negative							
	Wanted							

3. Partner gave me extra care when I was tired or ill.								
	Positive							
	Negative							
	Wanted							

4. Partner sensed I was sad and encouraged me.								
	Positive							
	Negative							
	Wanted							

5. Partner showed empathy (understood my feelings or took my perspective).								
	Positive							
	Negative							
	Wanted							

6. Partner made a good meal (breakfast, lunch, dinner) for me.								
	Positive							
	Negative							
	Wanted							

7. Partner made one of my favorite foods or desserts.								
	Positive							
	Negative							
	Wanted							

8. Partner complied cheerfully with my request.								
	Positive							
	Negative							
	Wanted							

9. Partner helped me do something when I asked for help.								
	Positive							
	Negative							
	Wanted							

Empathy (Cont.)

		S	M	T	W	T	F	S
10. Partner helped me do something without being asked.	Positive							
	Negative							
	Wanted							
11. Partner gave me an "I love you" note or an Appreciation Note.	Positive							
	Negative							
	Wanted							
12. Partner said "thanks" for something I did.	Positive							
	Negative							
	Wanted							
13. Partner asked me for forgiveness.	Positive							
	Negative							
	Wanted							
14. Partner admitted a fault, apologized, or said he/she was sorry.	Positive							
	Negative							
	Wanted							
15. Partner forgave me for a wrong action.	Positive							
	Negative							
	Wanted							
16. Partner criticized me in a positive or tactful way.	Positive							
	Negative							
	Wanted							
17. Partner asked me what kind of day I had.	Positive							
	Negative							
	Wanted							
18. Partner stayed with me---giving moral support---as I did a project or activity.	Positive							
	Negative							
	Wanted							
19. Partner called to say "hello" and/or ask about my day.	Positive							
	Negative							
	Wanted							
20. Partner showed kindness to my friends or relatives.	Positive							
	Negative							
	Wanted							
21. Partner gave me a beauty treatment (shampooed my hair gave facial, manicure, etc.).	Positive							
	Negative							
	Wanted							

		S	M	T	W	T	F	S
22. Partner reminded me of a good memory in our relationship.	Positive							
	Negative							
	Wanted							
23. Partner brought me breakfast in bed.	Positive							
	Negative							
	Wanted							
24. Partner bought me a gift or goodie from bakery or store.	Positive							
	Negative							
	Wanted							
25. Partner did one of "my" jobs because I was too tired or ill.	Positive							
	Negative							
	Wanted							
26. Partner surprised me by doing one of "my" jobs.	Positive							
	Negative							
	Wanted							
27. Partner helped me deal with a setback or disappointment.	Positive							
	Negative							
	Wanted							
28. Partner let me unload some misery without giving advice.	Positive							
	Negative							
	Wanted							
29. Partner joined me at bedtime rather than watch TV, read a book, etc.	Positive							
	Negative							
	Wanted							
30. Partner asked, "What can I do to make you happier?"	Positive							
	Negative							
	Wanted							
31. Partner asked, "What can I do to help you be less stressed?"	Positive							
	Negative							
	Wanted							
32. Partner made no effort to cheer me when I expressed a need.	Positive							
	Negative							
	Wanted							
33. Partner came home late or didn't call to say he/she would be late.	Positive							
	Negative							
	Wanted							

Empathy(Cont.)		S	M	T	W	T	F	S
34. Partner wouldn't accept my apology.	Positive							
	Negative							
	Wanted							
35. Partner grumbled when I asked for help.	Positive							
	Negative							
	Wanted							
36. Partner scolded or lectured instead of listening to me.	Positive							
	Negative							
	Wanted							
37. Partner embarrassed me by talking about me to others.	Positive							
	Negative							
	Wanted							
38. Partner put his/her leisure activity or work ahead of being with me.	Positive							
	Negative							
	Wanted							
39. Partner...	Positive							
	Negative							
	Wanted							
40. Partner...	Positive							
	Negative							
	Wanted							

Empathy Totals:

	S	M	T	W	T	F	S
Positives							
Negatives							

SEX

		S	M	T	W	T	F	S
1. We had sexual intercourse.	Positive							
	Negative							
	Wanted							
2. We tried new sexual techniques or positions.	Positive							
	Negative							
	Wanted							
3. We hugged, kissed, and/or petted.	Positive							
	Negative							
	Wanted							

		S	M	T	W	T	F	S
4. Partner said he/she needed me sexually today.	Positive							
	Negative							
	Wanted							
5. Partner set mood for love-making (music, candles, sexy words or clothes, etc.).	Positive							
	Negative							
	Wanted							
6. Partner helped me experience orgasm.	Positive							
	Negative							
	Wanted							
7. Partner complimented me about my body.	Positive							
	Negative							
	Wanted							
8. Partner told me he/she enjoyed making love with me.	Positive							
	Negative							
	Wanted							
9. Partner responded positively to my sexual advances.	Positive							
	Negative							
	Wanted							
10. Partner initiated sexual play.	Positive							
	Negative							
	Wanted							
11. Partner let me know exactly what pleased him/her sexually.	Positive							
	Negative							
	Wanted							
12. Partner asked, "How can I be a better sexual mate?"	Positive							
	Negative							
	Wanted							
13. Partner rejected my sexual approaches.	Positive							
	Negative							
	Wanted							
14. Partner hurried into intercourse without romance or foreplay.	Positive							
	Negative							
	Wanted							
15. Partner did not communicate during sexual activities.	Positive							
	Negative							
	Wanted							

Sex (Cont.)

16. Partner pressured me to engage in sexual behaviors I dislike.		S	M	T	W	T	F	S
	Positive							
	Negative							
	Wanted							

17. Partner left me sexually unsatisfied.								
	Positive							
	Negative							
	Wanted							

18. Partner...								
	Positive							
	Negative							
	Wanted							

19. Partner...								
	Positive							
	Negative							
	Wanted							

Sex Totals:

	S	M	T	W	T	F	S
Positives							
Negatives							

PARENTING

1. We played games with the children.		S	M	T	W	T	F	S
	Positive							
	Negative							
	Wanted							

2. We took the children on a family event (camping, vacation, parade, etc.).								
	Positive							
	Negative							
	Wanted							

3. We discussed child's misbehavior and then disciplined together.								
	Positive							
	Negative							
	Wanted							

4. Partner supported (backed me up) when I disciplined children.								
	Positive							
	Negative							
	Wanted							

5. Partner disciplined child firmly but without harshness or over-reaction.								
	Positive							
	Negative							
	Wanted							

6. Partner supported child (tried to understand child's problem, conflict, frustration, or crisis).								
	Positive							
	Negative							
	Wanted							

7. Partner hugged child and/or showed love, affection, acceptance, humor.		S	M	T	W	T	F	S
	Positive							
	Negative							
	Wanted							

8. Partner praised child (for school work, doing chores obedience, etc.).								
	Positive							
	Negative							
	Wanted							

9. Partner said or did something that helped child develop a positive self-esteem.								
	Positive							
	Negative							
	Wanted							

10. Partner spent time with child (read a story, helped with school work, played a game, etc.).								
	Positive							
	Negative							
	Wanted							

11. Partner gave children chores and/or supervised them.								
	Positive							
	Negative							
	Wanted							

12. Partner changed diapers on baby.								
	Positive							
	Negative							
	Wanted							

13. Partner fed children.								
	Positive							
	Negative							
	Wanted							

14. Partner bathed and/or put children to bed.								
	Positive							
	Negative							
	Wanted							

15. Partner cared for child throughout the night.								
	Positive							
	Negative							
	Wanted							

16. Partner taught child an important lesson (on safety, values, money, etc.).								
	Positive							
	Negative							
	Wanted							

17. Partner disagreed with me about child's problem but told me privately.								
	Positive							
	Negative							
	Wanted							

18. Partner contradicted or opposed my discipline in front of child.								
	Positive							
	Negative							
	Wanted							

Parenting (Cont.)

		S	M	T	W	T	F	S
19. Partner showed faulty discipline (didn't exert control when he/she should have).	Positive							
	Negative							
	Wanted							
20. Partner showed faulty discipline (severe physical and/or verbal punishment).	Positive							
	Negative							
	Wanted							
21. Partner showed faulty discipline (was inconsistent in enforcing rules).	Positive							
	Negative							
	Wanted							
22. Partner rejected, ignored, or showed indifference to child.	Positive							
	Negative							
	Wanted							
23. Partner showed poor communication (was too busy to listen to child).	Positive							
	Negative							
	Wanted							
24. Partner over-protected child.	Positive							
	Negative							
	Wanted							
25. Partner was overly permissive (indulged or spoiled child).	Positive							
	Negative							
	Wanted							
26. Partner placed unrealistic demands on child to be perfect.	Positive							
	Negative							
	Wanted							
27. Partner...	Positive							
	Negative							
	Wanted							
28. Partner...	Positive							
	Negative							
	Wanted							
29. Partner...	Positive							
	Negative							
	Wanted							

Parenting Totals:

	S	M	T	W	T	F	S
Positives							
Negatives							

FRIENDSHIP

		S	M	T	W	T	F	S
1. We did a sport together (jogging, swimming, tennis, golf, exercises, etc.).	Positive							
	Negative							
	Wanted							
2. We walked together, took a ride in the car, or rode our bikes.	Positive							
	Negative							
	Wanted							
3. We played a card game or board game (Trivial Pursuit, checkers, etc.).	Positive							
	Negative							
	Wanted							
4. We worked on a home improvement project.	Positive							
	Negative							
	Wanted							
5. We worked in the garden or flower beds together.	Positive							
	Negative							
	Wanted							
6. We watched a TV program.	Positive							
	Negative							
	Wanted							
7. We went to a game (football, basketball, baseball, etc.).	Positive							
	Negative							
	Wanted							
8. We shopped (for new clothes, antiques, furniture, etc.).	Positive							
	Negative							
	Wanted							
9. We went to church or a religious event.	Positive							
	Negative							
	Wanted							
10. We prayed together at home.	Positive							
	Negative							
	Wanted							
11. We went hunting, boating, camping, or fishing.	Positive							
	Negative							
	Wanted							

Friendship (Cont.)

		S	M	T	W	T	F	S
12. We ate at a restaurant and/or went dancing.	Positive							
	Negative							
	Wanted							
13. We went out for an ice cream or coffee date.	Positive							
	Negative							
	Wanted							
14. We had a romantic dinner at home for just the two of us.	Positive							
	Negative							
	Wanted							
15. We went to the library and checked out books.	Positive							
	Negative							
	Wanted							
16. We worked on a school or community project.	Positive							
	Negative							
	Wanted							
17. We went to a movie (museum, concert, play, etc.).	Positive							
	Negative							
	Wanted							
18. We worked on a hobby (photography, recipe collecting, etc.).	Positive							
	Negative							
	Wanted							
19. We told jokes and laughed together.	Positive							
	Negative							
	Wanted							
20. We baked or cooked together.	Positive							
	Negative							
	Wanted							
21. We listened to music or sang together.	Positive							
	Negative							
	Wanted							
22. We read together.	Positive							
	Negative							
	Wanted							
23. We took a bath or shower together.	Positive							
	Negative							
	Wanted							

		S	M	T	W	T	F	S
24. We had friends over to visit or for dinner.	Positive							
	Negative							
	Wanted							
25. We visited with relatives.	Positive							
	Negative							
	Wanted							
26. We went to a party.	Positive							
	Negative							
	Wanted							
27. We...	Positive							
	Negative							
	Wanted							
28. We...	Positive							
	Negative							
	Wanted							

Friendship Totals:

Positives [ ][ ][ ][ ][ ][ ]

Negatives [ ][ ][ ][ ][ ][ ]

INDEPENDENCE

		S	M	T	W	T	F	S
1. We agreed to spend more time together and less time in separate activities.	Positive							
	Negative							
	Wanted							
2. We scheduled and/or spent time doing activities alone.	Positive							
	Negative							
	Wanted							
3. Partner wasn't jealous when I spent time with friends.	Positive							
	Negative							
	Wanted							
4. Partner encouraged me to pursue or continue doing a separate activity.	Positive							
	Negative							
	Wanted							
5. Partner went to an event alone (sport, concert, movie, party, etc.).	Positive							
	Negative							
	Wanted							

Independence (Cont.)

		S	M	T	W	T	F	S
6. Partner didn't invite me to an event I wanted to share.	Positive							
	Negative							
	Wanted							
7. Partner was annoyed because I wanted to spend time alone.	Positive							
	Negative							
	Wanted							
8. Partner was annoyed because I spent time alone on a project.	Positive							
	Negative							
	Wanted							
9. Partner was annoyed because I spent time with someone else.	Positive							
	Negative							
	Wanted							
10. Partner...	Positive							
	Negative							
	Wanted							
11. Partner...	Positive							
	Negative							
	Wanted							

Independence Totals:

	S	M	T	W	T	F	S
Positives							
Negatives							

SELF-ESTEEM

		S	M	T	W	T	F	S
1. Partner said, "I'm glad I married you."	Positive							
	Negative							
	Wanted							
2. Partner said I was better than other spouses in a certain way.	Positive							
	Negative							
	Wanted							
3. Partner bragged about me to the children.	Positive							
	Negative							
	Wanted							
4. Partner showed he/she respected my role of Mother, Father, etc.	Positive							
	Negative							
	Wanted							

		S	M	T	W	T	F	S
5. Partner showed interest in my hobby (craft, etc.).	Positive							
	Negative							
	Wanted							
6. Partner took special interest in me by asking relevant questions.	Positive							
	Negative							
	Wanted							
7. Partner said I was a good ___ (cook, Mom, Dad, provider, etc.).	Positive							
	Negative							
	Wanted							
8. Partner made me feel needed.	Positive							
	Negative							
	Wanted							
9. Partner said I was physically attractive/handsome.	Positive							
	Negative							
	Wanted							
10. Partner said he/she missed me today.	Positive							
	Negative							
	Wanted							
11. Partner showed I come first before kids, career, etc.	Positive							
	Negative							
	Wanted							
12. Partner congratulated me on something I accomplished today.	Positive							
	Negative							
	Wanted							
13. Partner reminded me of one of my past successes.	Positive							
	Negative							
	Wanted							
14. Partner showed off my accomplishment (craft, award, trophy, etc.) for others to see.	Positive							
	Negative							
	Wanted							
15. Partner said I was his/her best friend.	Positive							
	Negative							
	Wanted							
16. Partner said he/she loves something about my body (eyes, freckles, etc.).	Positive							
	Negative							
	Wanted							

Item		S	M	T	W	T	F	S
17. Partner said I showed intelligence or wisdom in something I said or did.	Positive							
	Negative							
	Wanted							
18. Partner said he/she admired a special quality, skill, or trait in me.	Positive							
	Negative							
	Wanted							
19. Partner comforted me or wasn't upset when I made a mistake.	Positive							
	Negative							
	Wanted							
20. Partner encouraged me to develop my talents or interests.	Positive							
	Negative							
	Wanted							
21. Partner praised me publicly in front of other adults.	Positive							
	Negative							
	Wanted							
22. Partner compared me favorably to someone else.	Positive							
	Negative							
	Wanted							
23. Partner expressed confidence in my ability to do something.	Positive							
	Negative							
	Wanted							
24. Partner smiled or winked at me.	Positive							
	Negative							
	Wanted							
25. Partner said he/she loved me.	Positive							
	Negative							
	Wanted							
26. Partner expressed how glad he/she was to see me.	Positive							
	Negative							
	Wanted							
27. Partner laughed when I told a joke or funny story.	Positive							
	Negative							
	Wanted							
28. Partner answered my question with respect or patience.	Positive							
	Negative							
	Wanted							

Item		S	M	T	W	T	F	S
29. Partner said I was a good sexual mate.	Positive							
	Negative							
	Wanted							
30. Partner asked my opinion about something (decision, etc.).	Positive							
	Negative							
	Wanted							
31. Partner told children about my faults or weaknesses.	Positive							
	Negative							
	Wanted							
32. Partner criticized me in front of other adults.	Positive							
	Negative							
	Wanted							
33. Partner said my body was unattractive (fat, ugly, etc.).	Positive							
	Negative							
	Wanted							
34. Partner criticized me for saying or doing something stupid.	Positive							
	Negative							
	Wanted							
35. Partner brought up one of my past failures.	Positive							
	Negative							
	Wanted							
36. Partner talked about our marriage problems to others.	Positive							
	Negative							
	Wanted							
37. Partner expected me to fail at something.	Positive							
	Negative							
	Wanted							
38. Partner wasn't interested when I talked about something (my day, hobby, golf, etc.).	Positive							
	Negative							
	Wanted							
39. Partner ignored me or said he/she was too busy when I needed attention.	Positive							
	Negative							
	Wanted							
40. Partner...	Positive							
	Negative							
	Wanted							

Self-esteem (Cont.)

41. Partner...

	S	M	T	W	T	F	S
Positive							
Negative							
Wanted							

Self-esteem Totals:

Positives								

Negatives								

HOUSEHOLD RESPONSIBILITIES

1. We cleaned house together.

	S	M	T	W	T	F	S
Positive							
Negative							
Wanted							

2. We shopped for groceries.

	S	M	T	W	T	F	S
Positive							
Negative							
Wanted							

3. Partner was punctual by having meal ready on time.

	S	M	T	W	T	F	S
Positive							
Negative							
Wanted							

4. Partner cleaned off table after meal and/or washed dishes.

	S	M	T	W	T	F	S
Positive							
Negative							
Wanted							

5. Partner took care of clothes (washed, ironed, mended, etc.).

	S	M	T	W	T	F	S
Positive							
Negative							
Wanted							

6. Partner cleaned house (vacuumed, mopped, etc.).

	S	M	T	W	T	F	S
Positive							
Negative							
Wanted							

7. Partner made bathroom clean and neat.

	S	M	T	W	T	F	S
Positive							
Negative							
Wanted							

8. Partner took charge of solving a problem (with creditor, phone or utility company, etc.).

	S	M	T	W	T	F	S
Positive							
Negative							
Wanted							

9. Partner handled needed car repairs or upkeep.

	S	M	T	W	T	F	S
Positive							
Negative							
Wanted							

10. Partner made repairs on house (fixed faucet, window, toilet, etc.).

	S	M	T	W	T	F	S
Positive							
Negative							
Wanted							

11. Partner did upkeep on house (painted, cleaned gutters, etc.).

	S	M	T	W	T	F	S
Positive							
Negative							
Wanted							

12. Partner arranged for household repairs or maintenance to be done.

	S	M	T	W	T	F	S
Positive							
Negative							
Wanted							

13. Partner worked in yard (cut grass, pruned shrubs, raked leaves, etc.).

	S	M	T	W	T	F	S
Positive							
Negative							
Wanted							

14. Partner took out garbage.

	S	M	T	W	T	F	S
Positive							
Negative							
Wanted							

15. Partner left dirty dishes in sink or on counter.

	S	M	T	W	T	F	S
Positive							
Negative							
Wanted							

16. Partner wouldn't help do household jobs when I asked.

	S	M	T	W	T	F	S
Positive							
Negative							
Wanted							

17. Partner left a job unfinished.

	S	M	T	W	T	F	S
Positive							
Negative							
Wanted							

18. Partner forgot to put gas and/or oil in car.

	S	M	T	W	T	F	S
Positive							
Negative							
Wanted							

19. Partner neglected something (yard work, car repairs, etc.).

	S	M	T	W	T	F	S
Positive							
Negative							
Wanted							

20. Partner forgot to turn off appliance when leaving the house.

	S	M	T	W	T	F	S
Positive							
Negative							
Wanted							

21. Partner...

	S	M	T	W	T	F	S
Positive							
Negative							
Wanted							

Household (Cont.)		S	M	T	W	T	F	S
22. Partner...	Positive							
	Negative							
	Wanted							

Household Responsibility Totals:

Positives [ ][ ][ ][ ][ ][ ][ ]

Negatives [ ][ ][ ][ ][ ][ ][ ]

MONEY MANAGEMENT

		S	M	T	W	T	F	S
1. We agreed on an important purchase.	Positive							
	Negative							
	Wanted							
2. We worked on finances (budgeting, planning, sharing our money concerns, etc.).	Positive							
	Negative							
	Wanted							
3. We worked together to balance the checkbook.	Positive							
	Negative							
	Wanted							
4. Partner paid bills when due.	Positive							
	Negative							
	Wanted							
5. Partner gave me money to spend as I wished.	Positive							
	Negative							
	Wanted							
6. Partner helped me decide about a purchase.	Positive							
	Negative							
	Wanted							
7. Partner saved money (savings account, piggy bank, vacation fund, etc.).	Positive							
	Negative							
	Wanted							
8. Partner made checkbook error (forgot to record check, balance not up-to-date, etc.).	Positive							
	Negative							
	Wanted							
9. Partner spent beyond the budget.	Positive							
	Negative							
	Wanted							

		S	M	T	W	T	F	S
10. Partner didn't consult me before making an important purchase.	Positive							
	Negative							
	Wanted							
11. Partner was unorganized with our finances (lost or misplaced records).	Positive							
	Negative							
	Wanted							
12. Partner borrowed money from friends, relatives or lending agency.	Positive							
	Negative							
	Wanted							
13. Partner neglected to pay bills on time.	Positive							
	Negative							
	Wanted							
14. Partner didn't compare prices at different stores before buying.	Positive							
	Negative							
	Wanted							
15. Partner said no to something I wanted to buy.	Positive							
	Negative							
	Wanted							
16. Partner charged something on the credit card.	Positive							
	Negative							
	Wanted							
17. Partner didn't use food coupons to save money.	Positive							
	Negative							
	Wanted							
18. Partner...	Positive							
	Negative							
	Wanted							
19. Partner...	Positive							
	Negative							
	Wanted							
20. Partner...	Positive							
	Negative							
	Wanted							

Money Management Totals:

Positives [ ][ ][ ][ ][ ][ ][ ]

Negatives [ ][ ][ ][ ][ ][ ][ ]

PERSONAL HABITS

	S	M	T	W	T	F	S
1. Partner didn't get mad or defensive when I gave negative feedback. Positive							
Negative							
Wanted							
2. Partner showed a sense of humor. Positive							
Negative							
Wanted							
3. Partner was punctual (to dinner, meeting with me, etc.). Positive							
Negative							
Wanted							
4. Partner said he/she respected my opinion even though different from his/hers. Positive							
Negative							
Wanted							
5. Partner took an optimistic outlook about a bad situation. Positive							
Negative							
Wanted							
6. Partner hung his/her clothes in closet rather than leaving on chair or floor. Positive							
Negative							
Wanted							
7. Partner dressed neatly. Positive							
Negative							
Wanted							
8. Partner cared for his/her personal hygiene (shaved, bathed, etc.). Positive							
Negative							
Wanted							
9. Partner talked on phone too long. Positive							
Negative							
Wanted							
10. Partner smoked. Positive							
Negative							
Wanted							
11. Partner made a mess and neglected to clean it up. Positive							
Negative							
Wanted							

	S	M	T	W	T	F	S
12. Partner didn't pick up clothes. Positive							
Negative							
Wanted							
13. Partner cheated on diet. Positive							
Negative							
Wanted							
14. Partner used annoying table manners (belched, slurped, etc.). Positive							
Negative							
Wanted							
15. Partner goofed (left toilet seat up or hogged the hot water). Positive							
Negative							
Wanted							
16. Partner left bathroom messy (dirty sink or bathtub, etc.). Positive							
Negative							
Wanted							
17. Partner stayed in bathroom too long. Positive							
Negative							
Wanted							
18. Partner nagged. Positive							
Negative							
Wanted							
19. Partner neglected his/her personal hygiene (unbathed, unshaved, etc.). Positive							
Negative							
Wanted							
20. Partner tossed and rolled in bed. Positive							
Negative							
Wanted							
21. Partner omitted a courtesy ("thank you," carrying groceries, etc.). Positive							
Negative							
Wanted							
22. Partner misplaced important item (keys, checkbook, drivers license, etc.). Positive							
Negative							
Wanted							
23. Partner acted helpless. Positive							
Negative							
Wanted							

Personal Habits (Cont.)

		S	M	T	W	T	F	S
24. Partner left belongings around house (papers, school, work, etc.).	Positive							
	Negative							
	Wanted							
25. Partner watched too much TV.	Positive							
	Negative							
	Wanted							
26. Partner used a bad driving habit (didn't signal, excessive speed, etc.).	Positive							
	Negative							
	Wanted							
27. Partner showed a bad temper or explosive outburst.	Positive							
	Negative							
	Wanted							
28. Partner wouldn't bend his/her rigid time schedule to fit me or children.	Positive							
	Negative							
	Wanted							
29. Partner...	Positive							
	Negative							
	Wanted							
30. Partner...	Positive							
	Negative							
	Wanted							

Personal Habits Totals:

Positives [ ][ ][ ][ ][ ][ ]

Negatives [ ][ ][ ][ ][ ][ ]

JOB/SCHOOL

		S	M	T	W	T	F	S
1. We celebrated payday (went out to eat, had special dinner, etc.).	Positive							
	Negative							
	Wanted							
2. We celebrated a success at work (pay raise, promotion, etc.).	Positive							
	Negative							
	Wanted							
3. We celebrated a success at school (completed paper, good grade, etc.).	Positive							
	Negative							
	Wanted							

		S	M	T	W	T	F	S
4. Partner showed ability to keep work from interfering with home life.	Positive							
	Negative							
	Wanted							
5. Partner helped me with school or job-related work I brought home.	Positive							
	Negative							
	Wanted							
6. Partner was interested in my school work or job (asked relevant questions, listened, etc.).	Positive							
	Negative							
	Wanted							
7. Partner expressed approval of my accomplishment at work or school.	Positive							
	Negative							
	Wanted							
8. Partner showed motivation in finding a job or in trying to find a better job.	Positive							
	Negative							
	Wanted							
9. Partner consulted me about a work or school decision.	Positive							
	Negative							
	Wanted							
10. Partner stayed upset about work or school long after coming home.	Positive							
	Negative							
	Wanted							
11. Partner talked excessively about his/her work or school.	Positive							
	Negative							
	Wanted							
12. Partner showed no motivation to find job.	Positive							
	Negative							
	Wanted							
13. Partner wasn't interested in my work or school life.	Positive							
	Negative							
	Wanted							
14. Partner...	Positive							
	Negative							
	Wanted							

Job/School Totals:

Positives [ ][ ][ ][ ][ ][ ]

Negatives [ ][ ][ ][ ][ ][ ]

PROBLEM-SOLVING

		S M T W T F S			S M T W T F S
1. Partner described problem in brief, specific, positive and friendly manner.	Positive Negative Wanted		13. Partner said that both our needs should be met by the solution.	Positive Negative Wanted	
2. Partner listened and accurately summarized what I said.	Positive Negative Wanted		14. Partner was willing to put agreement into writing.	Positive Negative Wanted	
3. Partner accepted some responsibility for problem.	Positive Negative Wanted		15. Partner compromised (agreed to change if I agreed to change).	Positive Negative Wanted	
4. Partner complied cheerfully with my request.	Positive Negative Wanted		16. Partner proposed a solution to problem.	Positive Negative Wanted	
5. Partner approved (praised, complimented) something I said or did.	Positive Negative Wanted		17. Partner gave me full attention while we talked.	Positive Negative Wanted	
6. Partner agreed with me on something.	Positive Negative Wanted		18. Partner showed ability to stay on one problem before moving to next one.	Positive Negative Wanted	
7. Partner agreed more often than disagreed as we worked on the problem.	Positive Negative Wanted		19. Partner used the "Positive Specific Request" rule.	Positive Negative Wanted	
8. Partner sought information by asking relevant question(s).	Positive Negative Wanted		20. Partner gave support (asked, "How can I help you meet your goals or reduce stress?").	Positive Negative Wanted	
9. Partner made accurate or factual statement about me or problem.	Positive Negative Wanted		21. Partner touched me affectionately while we problem-solved.	Positive Negative Wanted	
10. Partner engaged in positive mind-reading.	Positive Negative Wanted		22. Partner showed positive nonverbal behavior (smile, head nod, etc.).	Positive Negative Wanted	
11. Partner shared talk-time equally with me.	Positive Negative Wanted		23. Partner was patient (didn't react negatively when I came on too harshly).	Positive Negative Wanted	
12. Partner said "we" both need to change instead of making me the fault or problem.	Positive Negative Wanted		24. Partner was vague, too long, and/or too emotional in describing problem.	Positive Negative Wanted	

BEST-WK1-P14

Problem Solving (Cont.)		S	M	T	W	T	F	S			S	M	T	W	T	F	S
25. Partner cross-complained instead of listening to my problem.	Positive								37. Partner made a counter-proposal.	Positive							
	Negative									Negative							
	Wanted									Wanted							
26. Partner interrupted me.	Positive								38. Partner refused to budge from a position.	Positive							
	Negative									Negative							
	Wanted									Wanted							
27. Partner denied responsibility for any part of the problem.	Positive								39. Partner refused to search for different options.	Positive							
	Negative									Negative							
	Wanted									Wanted							
28. Partner refused to comply with my request.	Positive								40. Partner continued to talk about problem rather than look for solutions.	Positive							
	Negative									Negative							
	Wanted									Wanted							
29. Partner criticized something I said or did.	Positive								41. Partner divided his/her attention (read paper, watched TV, etc.).	Positive							
	Negative									Negative							
	Wanted									Wanted							
30. Partner disagreed with me.	Positive								42. Partner jumped from problem to problem without first getting a solution.	Positive							
	Negative									Negative							
	Wanted									Wanted							
31. Partner disagreed more often than agreed as we worked on problem.	Positive								43. Partner made a negative vague demand.	Positive							
	Negative									Negative							
	Wanted									Wanted							
32. Partner assumed (jumped to conclusion) without first checking it out.	Positive								44. Partner refused to offer support or help when I requested it.	Positive							
	Negative									Negative							
	Wanted									Wanted							
33. Partner exaggerated (used words like "always" or "never").	Positive								45. Partner showed negative nonverbal behavior (angry voice, frown, etc.).	Positive							
	Negative									Negative							
	Wanted									Wanted							
34. Partner engaged in negative mind-reading.	Positive								46. Partner...	Positive							
	Negative									Negative							
	Wanted									Wanted							
35. Partner monopolized talk time.	Positive								47. Partner...	Positive							
	Negative									Negative							
	Wanted									Wanted							
36. Partner blamed me for problem and/or said I had to make all the changes.	Positive																
	Negative																
	Wanted																

Problem Solving Totals:

Positives □□□□□□

Negatives □□□□□□

BEHAVIOR EXCHANGE SKILLS TECHNIQUE SUMMARY---WEEK 1

RATING SCALE

Marital Happiness Rating

0 1 2 3 4 5 6 7 8 9 10

Very Unhappy   Neither Happy nor Unhappy   Very Happy

	S	M	T	W	T	F	S

Observation made by   Husband ☐   Wife ☐

POSITIVES DIVIDED BY NEGATIVES

	S	M	T	W	T	F	S
P:N Ratio (Categories A-L)							
P:N Ratio (Problem-Solving)							

		S	M	T	W	T	F	S
A. CARE	Positives							
	Negatives							
B. COMMUNICATION	Positives							
	Negatives							
C. EMPATHY	Positives							
	Negatives							
D. SEX	Positives							
	Negatives							
E. PARENTING	Positives							
	Negatives							
F. FRIENDSHIP	Positives							
	Negatives							
G. INDEPENDENCE	Positives							
	Negatives							
H. SELF-ESTEEM	Positives							
	Negatives							
I. HOUSEHOLD TASKS	Positives							
	Negatives							
J. MONEY	Positives							
	Negatives							
K. PERSONAL HABITS	Positives							
	Negatives							
L. JOB/SCHOOL	Positives							
	Negatives							
CATEGORY A-L DAILY TOTALS	Positives							
	Negatives							
PROBLEM-SOLVING TOTALS	Positives							
	Negatives							

BEST-WK1-P16

BEST CHECKLIST
Daily Behavior Exchange Record---Week 2

CARE

1. We exchanged back-scratching.		S	M	T	W	T	F	S
	Positive							
	Negative					'		
	Wanted							

2. Partner gave me a hug.								
	Positive							
	Negative							
	Wanted							

3. Partner greeted me with hug and/or kiss when I came home.								
	Positive							
	Negative							
	Wanted							

4. Partner gave me a kiss.								
	Positive							
	Negative							
	Wanted							

5. Partner put his/her arm around me in public or at home.								
	Positive							
	Negative							
	Wanted							

6. Partner massaged my head, neck, feet, etc.								
	Positive							
	Negative							
	Wanted							

7. Partner reached out to hold my hand.								
	Positive							
	Negative							
	Wanted							

8. Partner gave me an "I love you" touch, (nonsexual pinch, pat, squeeze, etc.).								
	Positive							
	Negative							
	Wanted							

9. Partner rubbed my back until I fell asleep.								
	Positive							
	Negative							
	Wanted							

10. Partner...								
	Positive							
	Negative							
	Wanted							

11. Partner...								
	Positive							
	Negative							
	Wanted							

12. Partner...		S	M	T	W	T	F	S
	Positive							
	Negative							
	Wanted							

Care Totals:

Positives							

Negatives							

COMMUNICATION

1. We talked about an event we shared--- (movie, church, etc.).		S	M	T	W	T	F	S
	Positive							
	Negative							
	Wanted							

2. We reminisced about a happy time in our relationship.								
	Positive							
	Negative							
	Wanted							

3. We laughed about something.								
	Positive							
	Negative							
	Wanted							

4. We talked about events that happened in our day.								
	Positive							
	Negative							
	Wanted							

5. We talked about a special topic (education, politics, religion, etc.).								
	Positive							
	Negative							
	Wanted							

6. We solved a problem.								
	Positive							
	Negative							
	Wanted							

7. Partner told me what was bothering him/her so I wouldn't worry.								
	Positive							
	Negative							
	Wanted							

8. Partner agreed with me on something.								
	Positive							
	Negative							
	Wanted							

Communication (Cont.)   S M T W T F S

9. Partner asked about my feelings or thoughts on a certain subject.
Positive							
Negative							
Wanted							

10. Partner showed interest while I explained a problem.
Positive							
Negative							
Wanted							

11. Partner helped plan an event (picnic, family outing, etc.).
Positive							
Negative							
Wanted							

12. Partner initiated a peace offer or made a reconciliation gesture.
Positive							
Negative							
Wanted							

13. We got into an argument.
Positive							
Negative							
Wanted							

14. We disagreed on something.
Positive							
Negative							
Wanted							

15. Partner clammed up or sulked (had a problem but refused to communicate).
Positive							
Negative							
Wanted							

16. Partner interrupted me before I was finished talking.
Positive							
Negative							
Wanted							

17. Partner made a decision without consulting me.
Positive							
Negative							
Wanted							

18. Partner...
Positive							
Negative							
Wanted							

19. Partner...
Positive							
Negative							
Wanted							

20. Partner...
Positive							
Negative							
Wanted							

---

21. Partner...   S M T W T F S
Positive							
Negative							
Wanted							

Communication Totals:

Positives | | | | | | | |

Negatives | | | | | | | |

INTERPERSONAL SKILLS/EMPATHY   S M T W T F S

1. Partner held me when I felt anxious or stressed.
Positive							
Negative							
Wanted							

2. Partner waved goodbye or walked to the car when I left.
Positive							
Negative							
Wanted							

3. Partner gave me extra care when I was tired or ill.
Positive							
Negative							
Wanted							

4. Partner sensed I was sad and encouraged me.
Positive							
Negative							
Wanted							

5. Partner showed empathy (understood my feelings or took my perspective).
Positive							
Negative							
Wanted							

6. Partner made a good meal (breakfast, lunch, dinner) for me.
Positive							
Negative							
Wanted							

7. Partner made one of my favorite foods or desserts.
Positive							
Negative							
Wanted							

8. Partner complied cheerfully with my request.
Positive							
Negative							
Wanted							

9. Partner helped me do something when I asked for help.
Positive							
Negative							
Wanted							

Empathy (Cont.)

		S	M	T	W	T	F	S			S	M	T	W	T	F	S
10. Partner helped me do something without being asked.	Positive								22. Partner reminded me of a good memory in our relationship.	Positive							
	Negative									Negative							
	Wanted									Wanted							
11. Partner gave me an "I love you" note or an Appreciation Note.	Positive								23. Partner brought me breakfast in bed.	Positive							
	Negative									Negative							
	Wanted									Wanted							
12. Partner said "thanks" for something I did.	Positive								24. Partner bought me a gift or goodie from bakery or store.	Positive							
	Negative									Negative							
	Wanted									Wanted							
13. Partner asked me for forgiveness.	Positive								25. Partner did one of "my" jobs because I was too tired or ill.	Positive							
	Negative									Negative							
	Wanted									Wanted							
14. Partner admitted a fault, apologized, or said he/she was sorry.	Positive								26. Partner surprised me by doing one of "my" jobs.	Positive							
	Negative									Negative							
	Wanted									Wanted							
15. Partner forgave me for a wrong action.	Positive								27. Partner helped me deal with a setback or disappointment.	Positive							
	Negative									Negative							
	Wanted									Wanted							
16. Partner criticized me in a positive or tactful way.	Positive								28. Partner let me unload some misery without giving advice.	Positive							
	Negative									Negative							
	Wanted									Wanted							
17. Partner asked me what kind of day I had.	Positive								29. Partner joined me at bedtime rather than watch TV, read a book, etc.	Positive							
	Negative									Negative							
	Wanted									Wanted							
18. Partner stayed with me---giving moral support---as I did a project or activity.	Positive								30. Partner asked, "What can I do to make you happier?"	Positive							
	Negative									Negative							
	Wanted									Wanted							
19. Partner called to say "hello" and/or ask about my day.	Positive								31. Partner asked, "What can I do to help you be less stressed?"	Positive							
	Negative									Negative							
	Wanted									Wanted							
20. Partner showed kindness to my friends or relatives.	Positive								32. Partner made no effort to cheer me when I expressed a need.	Positive							
	Negative									Negative							
	Wanted									Wanted							
21. Partner gave me a beauty treatment (shampooed my hair gave facial, manicure, etc.).	Positive								33. Partner came home late or didn't call to say he/she would be late.	Positive							
	Negative									Negative							
	Wanted									Wanted							

34. Partner wouldn't accept my apology.
- Positive
- Negative
- Wanted

35. Partner grumbled when I asked for help.
- Positive
- Negative
- Wanted

36. Partner scolded or lectured instead of listening to me.
- Positive
- Negative
- Wanted

37. Partner embarrassed me by talking about me to others.
- Positive
- Negative
- Wanted

38. Partner put his/her leisure activity or work ahead of being with me.
- Positive
- Negative
- Wanted

39. Partner...
- Positive
- Negative
- Wanted

40. Partner...
- Positive
- Negative
- Wanted

Empathy Totals:

Positives

Negatives

SEX

S M T W T F S

1. We had sexual intercourse.
- Positive
- Negative
- Wanted

2. We tried new sexual techniques or positions.
- Positive
- Negative
- Wanted

3. We hugged, kissed, and/or petted.
- Positive
- Negative
- Wanted

S M T W T F S

4. Partner said he/she needed me sexually today.
- Positive
- Negative
- Wanted

5. Partner set mood for love-making (music, candles, sexy words or clothes, etc.).
- Positive
- Negative
- Wanted

6. Partner helped me experience orgasm.
- Positive
- Negative
- Wanted

7. Partner complimented me about my body.
- Positive
- Negative
- Wanted

8. Partner told me he/she enjoyed making love with me.
- Positive
- Negative
- Wanted

9. Partner responded positively to my sexual advances.
- Positive
- Negative
- Wanted

10. Partner initiated sexual play.
- Positive
- Negative
- Wanted

11. Partner let me know exactly what pleased him/her sexually.
- Positive
- Negative
- Wanted

12. Partner asked, "How can I be a better sexual mate?"
- Positive
- Negative
- Wanted

13. Partner rejected my sexual approaches.
- Positive
- Negative
- Wanted

14. Partner hurried into intercourse without romance or foreplay.
- Positive
- Negative
- Wanted

15. Partner did not communicate during sexual activities.
- Positive
- Negative
- Wanted

		S	M	T	W	T	F	S
16. Partner pressured me to engage in sexual behaviors I dislike.	Positive							
	Negative							
	Wanted							
17. Partner left me sexually unsatisfied.	Positive							
	Negative							
	Wanted							
18. Partner...	Positive							
	Negative							
	Wanted							
19. Partner...	Positive							
	Negative							
	Wanted							

Sex Totals:

Positives ☐☐☐☐☐☐

Negatives ☐☐☐☐☐☐

PARENTING

		S	M	T	W	T	F	S
1. We played games with the children.	Positive							
	Negative							
	Wanted							
2. We took the children on a family event (camping, vacation, parade, etc.).	Positive							
	Negative							
	Wanted							
3. We discussed child's misbehavior and then disciplined together.	Positive							
	Negative							
	Wanted							
4. Partner supported (backed me up) when I disciplined children.	Positive							
	Negative							
	Wanted							
5. Partner disciplined child firmly but without harshness or over-reaction.	Positive							
	Negative							
	Wanted							
6. Partner supported child (tried to understand child's problem, conflict, frustration, or crisis).	Positive							
	Negative							
	Wanted							

		S	M	T	W	T	F	S
7. Partner hugged child and/or showed love, affection, acceptance, humor.	Positive							
	Negative							
	Wanted							
8. Partner praised child (for school work, doing chores obedience, etc.).	Positive							
	Negative							
	Wanted							
9. Partner said or did something that helped child develop a positive self-esteem.	Positive							
	Negative							
	Wanted							
10. Partner spent time with child (read a story, helped with school work, played a game, etc.).	Positive							
	Negative							
	Wanted							
11. Partner gave children chores and/or supervised them.	Positive							
	Negative							
	Wanted							
12. Partner changed diapers on baby.	Positive							
	Negative							
	Wanted							
13. Partner fed children.	Positive							
	Negative							
	Wanted							
14. Partner bathed and/or put children to bed.	Positive							
	Negative							
	Wanted							
15. Partner cared for child throughout the night.	Positive							
	Negative							
	Wanted							
16. Partner taught child an important lesson (on safety, values, money, etc.).	Positive							
	Negative							
	Wanted							
17. Partner disagreed with me about child's problem but told me privately.	Positive							
	Negative							
	Wanted							
18. Partner contradicted or opposed my discipline in front of child.	Positive							
	Negative							
	Wanted							

Parenting (Cont.)

S M T W T F S

19. Partner showed faulty discipline (didn't exert control when he/she should have).
- Positive
- Negative
- Wanted

20. Partner showed faulty discipline (severe physical and/or verbal punishment).
- Positive
- Negative
- Wanted

21. Partner showed faulty discipline (was inconsistent in enforcing rules).
- Positive
- Negative
- Wanted

22. Partner rejected, ignored, or showed indifference to child.
- Positive
- Negative
- Wanted

23. Partner showed poor communication (was too busy to listen to child).
- Positive
- Negative
- Wanted

24. Partner over-protected child.
- Positive
- Negative
- Wanted

25. Partner was overly permissive (indulged or spoiled child).
- Positive
- Negative
- Wanted

26. Partner placed unrealistic demands on child to be perfect.
- Positive
- Negative
- Wanted

27. Partner...
- Positive
- Negative
- Wanted

28. Partner...
- Positive
- Negative
- Wanted

29. Partner...
- Positive
- Negative
- Wanted

Parenting Totals:
Positives
Negatives

FRIENDSHIP

S M T W T F S

1. We did a sport together (jogging, swimming, tennis, golf, exercises, etc.).
- Positive
- Negative
- Wanted

2. We walked together, took a ride in the car, or rode our bikes.
- Positive
- Negative
- Wanted

3. We played a card game or board game (Trivial Pursuit, checkers, etc.).
- Positive
- Negative
- Wanted

4. We worked on a home improvement project.
- Positive
- Negative
- Wanted

5. We worked in the garden or flower beds together.
- Positive
- Negative
- Wanted

6. We watched a TV program.
- Positive
- Negative
- Wanted

7. We went to a game (football, basketball, baseball, etc.).
- Positive
- Negative
- Wanted

8. We shopped (for new clothes, antiques, furniture, etc.).
- Positive
- Negative
- Wanted

9. We went to church or a religious event.
- Positive
- Negative
- Wanted

10. We prayed together at home.
- Positive
- Negative
- Wanted

11. We went hunting, boating, camping, or fishing.
- Positive
- Negative
- Wanted

Friendship (Cont.)

		S	M	T	W	T	F	S
12. We ate at a restaurant and/or went dancing.	Positive							
	Negative							
	Wanted							
13. We went out for an ice cream or coffee date.	Positive							
	Negative							
	Wanted							
14. We had a romantic dinner at home for just the two of us.	Positive							
	Negative							
	Wanted							
15. We went to the library and checked out books.	Positive							
	Negative							
	Wanted							
16. We worked on a school or community project.	Positive							
	Negative							
	Wanted							
17. We went to a movie (museum, concert, play, etc.).	Positive							
	Negative							
	Wanted							
18. We worked on a hobby (photography, recipe collecting, etc.).	Positive							
	Negative							
	Wanted							
19. We told jokes and laughed together.	Positive							
	Negative							
	Wanted							
20. We baked or cooked together.	Positive							
	Negative							
	Wanted							
21. We listened to music or sang together.	Positive							
	Negative							
	Wanted							
22. We read together.	Positive							
	Negative							
	Wanted							
23. We took a bath or shower together.	Positive							
	Negative							
	Wanted							

		S	M	T	W	T	F	S
24. We had friends over to visit or for dinner.	Positive							
	Negative							
	Wanted							
25. We visited with relatives.	Positive							
	Negative							
	Wanted							
26. We went to a party.	Positive							
	Negative							
	Wanted							
27. We...	Positive							
	Negative							
	Wanted							
28. We...	Positive							
	Negative							
	Wanted							

Friendship Totals:

Positives						
Negatives						

INDEPENDENCE

		S	M	T	W	T	F	S
1. We agreed to spend more time together and less time in separate activities.	Positive							
	Negative							
	Wanted							
2. We scheduled and/or spent time doing activities alone.	Positive							
	Negative							
	Wanted							
3. Partner wasn't jealous when I spent time with friends.	Positive							
	Negative							
	Wanted							
4. Partner encouraged me to pursue or continue doing a separate activity.	Positive							
	Negative							
	Wanted							
5. Partner went to an event alone (sport, concert, movie, party, etc.).	Positive							
	Negative							
	Wanted							

Independence (Cont.)

		S	M	T	W	T	F	S
6. Partner didn't invite me to an event I wanted to share.	Positive							
	Negative							
	Wanted							
7. Partner was annoyed because I wanted to spend time alone.	Positive							
	Negative							
	Wanted							
8. Partner was annoyed because I spent time alone on a project.	Positive							
	Negative							
	Wanted							
9. Partner was annoyed because I spent time with someone else.	Positive							
	Negative							
	Wanted							
10. Partner...	Positive							
	Negative							
	Wanted							
11. Partner...	Positive							
	Negative							
	Wanted							

Independence Totals:

Positives

Negatives

SELF-ESTEEM

		S	M	T	W	T	F	S
1. Partner said, "I'm glad I married you."	Positive							
	Negative							
	Wanted							
2. Partner said I was better than other spouses in a certain way.	Positive							
	Negative							
	Wanted							
3. Partner bragged about me to the children.	Positive							
	Negative							
	Wanted							
4. Partner showed he/she respected my role of Mother, Father, etc.	Positive							
	Negative							
	Wanted							

		S	M	T	W	T	F	S
5. Partner showed interest in my hobby (craft, etc.).	Positive							
	Negative							
	Wanted							
6. Partner took special interest in me by asking relevant questions.	Positive							
	Negative							
	Wanted							
7. Partner said I was a good _____ (cook, Mom, Dad, provider, etc.).	Positive							
	Negative							
	Wanted							
8. Partner made me feel needed.	Positive							
	Negative							
	Wanted							
9. Partner said I was physically attractive/ handsome.	Positive							
	Negative							
	Wanted							
10. Partner said he/she missed me today.	Positive							
	Negative							
	Wanted							
11. Partner showed I come first before kids, career, etc.	Positive							
	Negative							
	Wanted							
12. Partner congratulated me on something I accomplished today.	Positive							
	Negative							
	Wanted							
13. Partner reminded me of one of my past successes.	Positive							
	Negative							
	Wanted							
14. Partner showed off my accomplishment (craft, award, trophy, etc.) for others to see.	Positive							
	Negative							
	Wanted							
15. Partner said I was his/her best friend.	Positive							
	Negative							
	Wanted							
16. Partner said he/she loves something about my body (eyes, freckles, etc.).	Positive							
	Negative							
	Wanted							

Self-esteem (Cont.)

17. Partner said I showed intelligence or wisdom in something I said or did.		S	M	T	W	T	F	S
	Positive							
	Negative							
	Wanted							

18. Partner said he/she admired a special quality, skill, or trait in me.								
	Positive							
	Negative							
	Wanted							

19. Partner comforted me or wasn't upset when I made a mistake.								
	Positive							
	Negative							
	Wanted							

20. Partner encouraged me to develop my talents or interests.								
	Positive							
	Negative							
	Wanted							

21. Partner praised me publicly in front of other adults.								
	Positive							
	Negative							
	Wanted							

22. Partner compared me favorably to someone else.								
	Positive							
	Negative							
	Wanted							

23. Partner expressed confidence in my ability to do something.								
	Positive							
	Negative							
	Wanted							

24. Partner smiled or winked at me.								
	Positive							
	Negative							
	Wanted							

25. Partner said he/she loved me.								
	Positive							
	Negative							
	Wanted							

26. Partner expressed how glad he/she was to see me.								
	Positive							
	Negative							
	Wanted							

27. Partner laughed when I told a joke or funny story.								
	Positive							
	Negative							
	Wanted							

28. Partner answered my question with respect or patience.								
	Positive							
	Negative							
	Wanted							

29. Partner said I was a good sexual mate.		S	M	T	W	T	F	S
	Positive							
	Negative							
	Wanted							

30. Partner asked my opinion about something (decision, etc.).								
	Positive							
	Negative							
	Wanted							

31. Partner told children about my faults or weaknesses.								
	Positive							
	Negative							
	Wanted							

32. Partner criticized me in front of other adults.								
	Positive							
	Negative							
	Wanted							

33. Partner said my body was unattractive (fat, ugly, etc.).								
	Positive							
	Negative							
	Wanted							

34. Partner criticized me for saying or doing something stupid.								
	Positive							
	Negative							
	Wanted							

35. Partner brought up one of my past failures.								
	Positive							
	Negative							
	Wanted							

36. Partner talked about our marriage problems to others.								
	Positive							
	Negative							
	Wanted							

37. Partner expected me to fail at something.								
	Positive							
	Negative							
	Wanted							

38. Partner wasn't interested when I talked about something (my day, hobby, golf, etc.).								
	Positive							
	Negative							
	Wanted							

39. Partner ignored me or said he/she was too busy when I needed attention.								
	Positive							
	Negative							
	Wanted							

40. Partner...								
	Positive							
	Negative							
	Wanted							

41. Partner...		S	M	T	W	T	F	S
	Positive							
	Negative							
	Wanted							

Self-esteem Totals:

Positives ⬚⬚⬚⬚⬚⬚⬚

Negatives ⬚⬚⬚⬚⬚⬚⬚

HOUSEHOLD RESPONSIBILITIES

		S	M	T	W	T	F	S
1. We cleaned house together.	Positive							
	Negative							
	Wanted							
2. We shopped for groceries.	Positive							
	Negative							
	Wanted							
3. Partner was punctual by having meal ready on time.	Positive							
	Negative							
	Wanted							
4. Partner cleaned off table after meal and/or washed dishes.	Positive							
	Negative							
	Wanted							
5. Partner took care of clothes (washed, ironed, mended, etc.).	Positive							
	Negative							
	Wanted							
6. Partner cleaned house (vacuumed, mopped, etc.).	Positive							
	Negative							
	Wanted							
7. Partner made bathroom clean and neat.	Positive							
	Negative							
	Wanted							
8. Partner took charge of solving a problem (with creditor, phone or utility company, etc.).	Positive							
	Negative							
	Wanted							
9. Partner handled needed car repairs or upkeep.	Positive							
	Negative							
	Wanted							

		S	M	T	W	T	F	S
10. Partner made repairs on house (fixed faucet, window, toilet, etc.).	Positive							
	Negative							
	Wanted							
11. Partner did upkeep on house (painted, cleaned gutters, etc.).	Positive							
	Negative							
	Wanted							
12. Partner arranged for household repairs or maintenance to be done.	Positive							
	Negative							
	Wanted							
13. Partner worked in yard (cut grass, pruned shrubs, raked leaves, etc.).	Positive							
	Negative							
	Wanted							
14. Partner took out garbage.	Positive							
	Negative							
	Wanted							
15. Partner left dirty dishes in sink or on counter.	Positive							
	Negative							
	Wanted							
16. Partner wouldn't help do household jobs when I asked.	Positive							
	Negative							
	Wanted							
17. Partner left a job unfinished.	Positive							
	Negative							
	Wanted							
18. Partner forgot to put gas and/or oil in car.	Positive							
	Negative							
	Wanted							
19. Partner neglected something (yard work, car repairs, etc.).	Positive							
	Negative							
	Wanted							
20. Partner forgot to turn off appliance when leaving the house.	Positive							
	Negative							
	Wanted							
21. Partner...	Positive							
	Negative							
	Wanted							

Household (Cont.)		S	M	T	W	T	F	S
22. Partner...	Positive							
	Negative							
	Wanted							

Household Responsibility Totals:

Positives

Negatives

MONEY MANAGEMENT

		S	M	T	W	T	F	S
1. We agreed on an important purchase.	Positive							
	Negative							
	Wanted							
2. We worked on finances (budgeting, planning, sharing our money concerns, etc.).	Positive							
	Negative							
	Wanted							
3. We worked together to balance the checkbook.	Positive							
	Negative							
	Wanted							
4. Partner paid bills when due.	Positive							
	Negative							
	Wanted							
5. Partner gave me money to spend as I wished.	Positive							
	Negative							
	Wanted							
6. Partner helped me decide about a purchase.	Positive							
	Negative							
	Wanted							
7. Partner saved money (savings account, piggy bank, vacation fund, etc.).	Positive							
	Negative							
	Wanted							
8. Partner made checkbook error (forgot to record check, balance not up-to-date, etc.).	Positive							
	Negative							
	Wanted							
9. Partner spent beyond the budget.	Positive							
	Negative							
	Wanted							

		S	M	T	W	T	F	S
10. Partner didn't consult me before making an important purchase.	Positive							
	Negative							
	Wanted							
11. Partner was unorganized with our finances (lost or misplaced records).	Positive							
	Negative							
	Wanted							
12. Partner borrowed money from friends, relatives or lending agency.	Positive							
	Negative							
	Wanted							
13. Partner neglected to pay bills on time.	Positive							
	Negative							
	Wanted							
14. Partner didn't compare prices at different stores before buying.	Positive							
	Negative							
	Wanted							
15. Partner said no to something I wanted to buy.	Positive							
	Negative							
	Wanted							
16. Partner charged something on the credit card.	Positive							
	Negative							
	Wanted							
17. Partner didn't use food coupons to save money.	Positive							
	Negative							
	Wanted							
18. Partner...	Positive							
	Negative							
	Wanted							
19. Partner...	Positive							
	Negative							
	Wanted							
20. Partner...	Positive							
	Negative							
	Wanted							

Money Management Totals:

Positives

Negatives

PERSONAL HABITS

#	Item	Category	S	M	T	W	T	F	S
1	Partner didn't get mad or defensive when I gave negative feedback.	Positive							
		Negative							
		Wanted							
2	Partner showed a sense of humor.	Positive							
		Negative							
		Wanted							
3	Partner was punctual (to dinner, meeting with me, etc.).	Positive							
		Negative							
		Wanted							
4	Partner said he/she respected my opinion even though different from his/hers.	Positive							
		Negative							
		Wanted							
5	Partner took an optimistic outlook about a bad situation.	Positive							
		Negative							
		Wanted							
6	Partner hung his/her clothes in closet rather than leaving on chair or floor.	Positive							
		Negative							
		Wanted							
7	Partner dressed neatly.	Positive							
		Negative							
		Wanted							
8	Partner cared for his/her personal hygiene (shaved, bathed, etc.).	Positive							
		Negative							
		Wanted							
9	Partner talked on phone too long.	Positive							
		Negative							
		Wanted							
10	Partner smoked.	Positive							
		Negative							
		Wanted							
11	Partner made a mess and neglected to clean it up.	Positive							
		Negative							
		Wanted							
12	Partner didn't pick up clothes.	Positive							
		Negative							
		Wanted							
13	Partner cheated on diet.	Positive							
		Negative							
		Wanted							
14	Partner used annoying table manners (belched, slurped, etc.).	Positive							
		Negative							
		Wanted							
15	Partner goofed (left toilet seat up or hogged the hot water).	Positive							
		Negative							
		Wanted							
16	Partner left bathroom messy (dirty sink or bathtub, etc.).	Positive							
		Negative							
		Wanted							
17	Partner stayed in bathroom too long.	Positive							
		Negative							
		Wanted							
18	Partner nagged.	Positive							
		Negative							
		Wanted							
19	Partner neglected his/her personal hygiene (unbathed, unshaved, etc.).	Positive							
		Negative							
		Wanted							
20	Partner tossed and rolled in bed.	Positive							
		Negative							
		Wanted							
21	Partner omitted a courtesy ("thank you," carrying groceries, etc.).	Positive							
		Negative							
		Wanted							
22	Partner misplaced important item (keys, checkbook, drivers license, etc.).	Positive							
		Negative							
		Wanted							
23	Partner acted helpless.	Positive							
		Negative							
		Wanted							

Personal Habits (Cont.)

Item	Type	S	M	T	W	T	F	S
24. Partner left belongings around house (papers, school, work, etc.).	Positive							
	Negative							
	Wanted							
25. Partner watched too much TV.	Positive							
	Negative							
	Wanted							
26. Partner used a bad driving habit (didn't signal, excessive speed, etc.).	Positive							
	Negative							
	Wanted							
27. Partner showed a bad temper or explosive outburst.	Positive							
	Negative							
	Wanted							
28. Partner wouldn't bend his/her rigid time schedule to fit me or children.	Positive							
	Negative							
	Wanted							
29. Partner...	Positive							
	Negative							
	Wanted							
30. Partner...	Positive							
	Negative							
	Wanted							

Personal Habits Totals:

Positives

Negatives

JOB/SCHOOL

Item	Type	S	M	T	W	T	F	S
1. We celebrated payday (went out to eat, had special dinner, etc.).	Positive							
	Negative							
	Wanted							
2. We celebrated a success at work (pay raise, promotion, etc.).	Positive							
	Negative							
	Wanted							
3. We celebrated a success at school (completed paper, good grade, etc.).	Positive							
	Negative							
	Wanted							

Item	Type	S	M	T	W	T	F	S
4. Partner showed ability to keep work from interfering with home life.	Positive							
	Negative							
	Wanted							
5. Partner helped me with school or job-related work I brought home.	Positive							
	Negative							
	Wanted							
6. Partner was interested in my school work or job (asked relevant questions, listened, etc.).	Positive							
	Negative							
	Wanted							
7. Partner expressed approval of my accomplishment at work or school.	Positive							
	Negative							
	Wanted							
8. Partner showed motivation in finding a job or in trying to find a better job.	Positive							
	Negative							
	Wanted							
9. Partner consulted me about a work or school decision.	Positive							
	Negative							
	Wanted							
10. Partner stayed upset about work or school long after coming home.	Positive							
	Negative							
	Wanted							
11. Partner talked excessively about his/her work or school.	Positive							
	Negative							
	Wanted							
12. Partner showed no motivation to find job.	Positive							
	Negative							
	Wanted							
13. Partner wasn't interested in my work or school life.	Positive							
	Negative							
	Wanted							
14. Partner...	Positive							
	Negative							
	Wanted							

Job/School Totals:

Positives

Negatives

PROBLEM-SOLVING

1. Partner described problem in brief, specific, positive and friendly manner.		S	M	T	W	T	F	S
	Positive							
	Negative							
	Wanted							

2. Partner listened and accurately summarized what I said.								
	Positive							
	Negative							
	Wanted							

3. Partner accepted some responsibility for problem.								
	Positive							
	Negative							
	Wanted							

4. Partner complied cheerfully with my request.								
	Positive							
	Negative							
	Wanted							

5. Partner approved (praised, complimented) something I said or did.								
	Positive							
	Negative							
	Wanted							

6. Partner agreed with me on something.								
	Positive							
	Negative							
	Wanted							

7. Partner agreed more often than disagreed as we worked on the problem.								
	Positive							
	Negative							
	Wanted							

8. Partner sought information by asking relevant question(s).								
	Positive							
	Negative							
	Wanted							

9. Partner made accurate or factual statement about me or problem.								
	Positive							
	Negative							
	Wanted							

10. Partner engaged in positive mind-reading.								
	Positive							
	Negative							
	Wanted							

11. Partner shared talk-time equally with me.								
	Positive							
	Negative							
	Wanted							

12. Partner said "we" both need to change instead of making me the fault or problem.								
	Positive							
	Negative							
	Wanted							

13. Partner said that both our needs should be met by the solution.		S	M	T	W	T	F	S
	Positive							
	Negative							
	Wanted							

14. Partner was willing to put agreement into writing.								
	Positive							
	Negative							
	Wanted							

15. Partner compromised (agreed to change if I agreed to change).								
	Positive							
	Negative							
	Wanted							

16. Partner proposed a solution to problem.								
	Positive							
	Negative							
	Wanted							

17. Partner gave me full attention while we talked.								
	Positive							
	Negative							
	Wanted							

18. Partner showed ability to stay on one problem before moving to next one.								
	Positive							
	Negative							
	Wanted							

19. Partner used the "Positive Specific Request" rule.								
	Positive							
	Negative							
	Wanted							

20. Partner gave support (asked, "How can I help you meet your goals or reduce stress?").								
	Positive							
	Negative							
	Wanted							

21. Partner touched me affectionately while we problem-solved.								
	Positive							
	Negative							
	Wanted							

22. Partner showed positive nonverbal behavior (smile, head nod, etc.).								
	Positive							
	Negative							
	Wanted							

23. Partner was patient (didn't react negatively when I came on too harshly).								
	Positive							
	Negative							
	Wanted							

24. Partner was vague, too long, and/or too emotional in describing problem.								
	Positive							
	Negative							
	Wanted							

Problem Solving (Cont.)		S	M	T	W	T	F	S				S	M	T	W	T	F	S
25. Partner cross-complained instead of listening to my problem.	Positive								37. Partner made a counter-proposal.	Positive								
	Negative									Negative								
	Wanted									Wanted								
26. Partner interrupted me.	Positive								38. Partner refused to budge from a position.	Positive								
	Negative									Negative								
	Wanted									Wanted								
27. Partner denied responsibility for any part of the problem.	Positive								39. Partner refused to search for different options.	Positive								
	Negative									Negative								
	Wanted									Wanted								
28. Partner refused to comply with my request.	Positive								40. Partner continued to talk about problem rather than look for solutions.	Positive								
	Negative									Negative								
	Wanted									Wanted								
29. Partner criticized something I said or did.	Positive								41. Partner divided his/her attention (read paper, watched TV, etc.).	Positive								
	Negative									Negative								
	Wanted									Wanted								
30. Partner disagreed with me.	Positive								42. Partner jumped from problem to problem without first getting a solution.	Positive								
	Negative									Negative								
	Wanted									Wanted								
31. Partner disagreed more often than agreed as we worked on problem.	Positive								43. Partner made a negative vague demand.	Positive								
	Negative									Negative								
	Wanted									Wanted								
32. Partner assumed (jumped to conclusion) without first checking it out.	Positive								44. Partner refused to offer support or help when I requested it.	Positive								
	Negative									Negative								
	Wanted									Wanted								
33. Partner exaggerated (used words like "always" or "never").	Positive								45. Partner showed negative nonverbal behavior (angry voice, frown, etc.).	Positive								
	Negative									Negative								
	Wanted									Wanted								
34. Partner engaged in negative mind-reading.	Positive								46. Partner...	Positive								
	Negative									Negative								
	Wanted									Wanted								
35. Partner monopolized talk time.	Positive								47. Partner...	Positive								
	Negative									Negative								
	Wanted									Wanted								
36. Partner blamed me for problem and/or said I had to make all the changes.	Positive																	
	Negative																	
	Wanted																	

Problem Solving Totals:

Positives

Negatives

BEHAVIOR EXCHANGE SKILLS TECHNIQUE SUMMARY---WEEK 2

RATING SCALE →

Marital Happiness Rating

0	1	2	3	4	5	6	7	8	9	10

Very Unhappy   Neither Happy nor Unhappy   Very Happy

S	M	T	W	T	F	S

Observation made by Husband ☐ Wife ☐

POSITIVES DIVIDED BY NEGATIVES →

P:N Ratio (Categories A-L)
P:N Ratio (Problem-Solving)

S	M	T	W	T	F	S

			S	M	T	W	T	F	S
A.	CARE	Positives							
		Negatives							
B.	COMMUNICATION	Positives							
		Negatives							
C.	EMPATHY	Positives							
		Negatives							
D.	SEX	Positives							
		Negatives							
E.	PARENTING	Positives							
		Negatives							
F.	FRIENDSHIP	Positives							
		Negatives							
G.	INDEPENDENCE	Positives							
		Negatives							
H.	SELF-ESTEEM	Positives							
		Negatives							
I.	HOUSEHOLD TASKS	Positives							
		Negatives							
J.	MONEY	Positives							
		Negatives							
K.	PERSONAL HABITS	Positives							
		Negatives							
L.	JOB/SCHOOL	Positives							
		Negatives							

CATEGORY A-L DAILY TOTALS →

Positives
Negatives

PROBLEM-SOLVING TOTALS →

Positives
Negatives

APPENDIX C

Communication Scoring System

In Session 9 (p. 142), we explained that communication between husband and wife can be measured to see what Helpers and Killers are happening during problem-solving. If you would like to have a problem-solving session scored, send a self-addressed, stamped envelope to the following address and directions will be sent to you:

COMMUNICATION SCORING SYSTEM
Dr. Larry L. Halter
Behavior Sciences of Oregon
4522 SE 86 Court
Portland, Oregon 97266
Phone: (503) 227-2022

APPENDIX D

Definitions of Communication Behaviors

Problem-Solving Helpers

1. POSITIVE PROBLEM DESCRIPTION: Short sentences defining a relationship problem. These sentences combine the X-Y-Z Annoyance Rule with the Positive Specific Request Rule: "I feel angry (X) when you don't pay the bills (Y) at the end of the month (Z). I would like you to pay them on a regular basis." Together, these two rules define the problem and seek change. The keys are to be brief, ask for an increase in a behavior, be specific, and ask in a friendly, nondemanding tone of voice.

2. VALIDATION: Sentences which say, "I value you." Validation is expressed by listening, accepting responsibility, compliance, approval, and agreement.

3. ACTIVE LISTENING AND SUMMARIZING: A sentence which rephrases or summarizes your mate's statement.

4. ACCEPTING RESPONSIBILITY: A sentence which says, "I am (or we are) responsible for this problem." These sentences avoid making excuses.

5. COMPLIANCE: Sentence or action that fulfills mate's request.

6. APPROVAL: Sentences that favor spouse's attributes, actions, or statements. Includes compliments or praise ("I like the way you . . .").

7. AGREEMENT: Sentence showing you agree with a statement of fact, opinion, or suggestion made by spouse.

8. HIGH AGREEMENT-TO-DISAGREEMENT RATIO: Using a high number of agreement and a low number of disagreement sentences when problem-solving. This does not mean that mates are in constant agreement. It means that agreement sentences occur more frequently than do disagreements.

9. COMPOSED: Expressing one's own suffering in a calm way.

10. SEEKING INFORMATION: Using questions to get correct information before making a judgment.

11. ACCURATENESS: Sentences that are factual, true, or accurate.

12. POSITIVE MIND-READING: A sentence which infers or assumes a positive attitude on the part of the other mate ("You did my chores so I could relax").

13. TAKING TURNS: Being sensitive to share the talk time equally with mate.

14. COOPERATION; COLLABORATION: Sentences which convey the following: "We need to team up and work together," "This is *our* problem," "We both need to learn some new behaviors," or "We both have to change."

15. NEGOTIATIONS; CONTRACTING: Statements which attempt to find solutions that satisfy both mates or which convey an agreement-making attitude. Includes a willingness to put the solution into a written agreement.

16. COMPROMISE: A sentence offering to mutually exchange behaviors. "I'll agree to write out the bills at the end of the month *if* you agree to stack the bills neatly in the top desk drawer so I won't have to hunt for them."

17. BRAINSTORMING: A process in which the couple creatively lists many solutions to a problem without critiquing them.

18. PROPOSING SOLUTIONS: Constructive sentences aimed at changing the future. Solutions may be positive, in which a behavior is initiated or increased ("I suggest we play more tennis or golf together"). Solutions can also be negative, where a behavior is stopped or decreased ("I suggest we watch less TV"). Or compromise solutions can be offered.

19. PAYING ATTENTION: Focusing undivided attention on your mate and the problem to be solved.

20. TRACKING: Ability to stay on one subject until it is resolved before moving to a different subject.

21. POSITIVE SPECIFIC REQUESTS: PSR's are needed to begin the problem-solving process, but they can also be used at other times. PSR's include three parts: (1) be positive by asking for an increase in behavior, not a decrease; (2) be specific by talking about when, where, and how much; and (3) request changes; don't demand.

22. SOCIAL SUPPORT: Sentences or behaviors that express love, acceptance, approval, appreciation, and affection. Sentences that express unconditional value and worth of another person irrespective of accomplishments. Sentences that express care and empathy: "How can I help you meet your goals?" or "How can I help you deal with demands and stressors?" or "What can I do to make you happier?" Social support or "expressive support" is intended to establish, maintain, or restore a positive relationship with one's mate.

23. POSITIVE PHYSICAL TOUCH: Affectionate touch, hug, kiss, pat, pinch, holding hands.

24. POSITIVE NONVERBAL COMMUNICATION: Nonverbal communication is that part of a message which is not words, but which may accompany words or occur separately from words and includes facial expressions, gestures, posture, tone of voice, volume, etc. Positive nonverbals include

smiles, head nods, laughter, eye contact, winks, gentle voice, touch. It is the skill of talking about a problem and at the same time staying in a positive emotional state.

25. POSITIVE RECIPROCITY: The ability to respond with a positive behavior after receiving a negative behavior from your mate. If wife's antecedent act is nasty, the husband's consequent act is to be nice. Happy couples tend not to return negative behavior when attacked; they are more likely to reciprocate with a positive act.

Communication Killers

1. NEGATIVE PROBLEM DESCRIPTION: A statement of the problem that is too long, too vague, and/or too emotional (harsh, abrasive, hostile tone).

2. CROSS-COMPLAINING: Instead of validating or listening to mate's complaint, you immediately jump in with your own problem.

3. INTERRUPTING: When listener breaks in and disrupts the flow of his/her mate's speech.

4. DENYING RESPONSIBILITY; EXCUSES: Statement which says, "I am (or we are) not responsible for this problem. Excuse is a personal denial of responsibility based on a weak rationale ("The reason I didn't get you a birthday card is that I just couldn't find the right one").

5. NONCOMPLIANCE: Refusal to fulfill mate's request.

6. CRITICISM: Statement of dislike, disapproval, or negative evaluation of a specific behavior or attitude in mate and said with a hostile tone of voice.

7. DISAGREEMENT: Sentence disagreeing with what mate has said ("No, I don't want to go to the Smith's cookout on Saturday").

8. HIGH DISAGREEMENT-TO-AGREEMENT RATIO: Disagreement sentences occur more frequently than do agreement sentences when you are problem-solving.

9. COMPLAINING: Whining or bitter expression of one's own suffering without explicitly blaming the mate ("I'm always the one who has to stay home with the kids"—said in a whining voice).

10. ASSUMPTIONS: Premature conclusions made without first checking out information with one's mate.

11. EXAGGERATION: Sentences which use words like *always* or *never*. Or a sentence which overstates the situation. An overgeneralization.

12. NEGATIVE MIND-READING: Statement attributing negative thoughts, feelings, motives, attitudes, or actions to mate ("You said that just to make me feel guilty"). To assume you know what's going on in your mate's head is unproductive and leads to defensiveness and irrelevant verbal interaction. Negative

Mind-Reading can be prevented with a "checking out" procedure—raising questions to get accurate information.

13. OVERTALK: Behavior of not sharing the air-time equally. Monopolizing.

14. BLAMING: Statement which accuses the other mate of causing the problem.

15. EXCESSIVE COUNTERPROPOSALS: Sentences showing a reluctance to "make a deal." Instead of using sentences aimed at negotiating a mutually satisfying social contract, these sentences convey a contrary attitude.

16. POLARIZED: Sentences indicating a mate is glued into a corner resisting change. These sentences show a refusal to budge from a position and an expectation that the other mate do all the changing.

17. LIMITING OPTIONS: Sentences which attempt to solve the problem with one or two solutions.

18. PROBLEM-ORIENTED: Sentences which continue to describe the problem or focus on past history. A failure to offer positive solutions, negative solutions, or compromise solutions.

19. DIVIDED ATTENTION: Negative nonverbal behaviors that compete with the conversation (reading newspaper, watching TV, etc.).

20. SIDETRACKING: Irrelevant sentences reflecting inability to stick to the point during a problem-solving discussion. Or sentences which jump from problem to problem without first getting resolution. Comments which sidetrack the discussion.

21. NEGATIVE VAGUE DEMANDS: Statements which (1) ask a mate to stop or decrease a behavior; (2) are unclear or confusing; and (3) are delivered in a commanding, ordering tone. Such sentences stoke up antagonisms. "You've got to get rid of that bad attitude now!"

22. PUT-DOWNS; REJECTION: A comment intended to belittle or embarrass the mate. Or a sentence refusing to give help when requested.

23. ALOOFNESS: Body posture reflecting negative attitude. Distance.

24. NEGATIVE NONVERBAL BEHAVIOR: Negative facial cues include frowns; sneers; expressions of fear, anger, disgust. Negative voice cues include voice tones that sound cold, tense, fearful, impatient, whining, sarcastic, blaming, angry, or mocking. Negative body cues and gestures are inattention, finger pointing, and aloofness.

25. NEGATIVE RECIPROCITY: The action in which a mate exchanges coercive behavior. That is, he/she reciprocates (responds in kind) punishment or displeasing behavior. If husband's antecedent act is negative, wife's consequent act is likely to be negative ("An eye for an eye").

REFERENCES

Alexander, J. F. "Defensive and Supportive Communications in Family Systems." *Journal of Marriage and the Family* (November 1973): 613-617.

Avery, A. W., C. A. Ridley, and L. A. Leslie. "Relationship Enhancement with Premarital Dyads: A Six-Month Follow-up." *American Journal of Family Therapy* 8 (Fall 1980): 23-30.

Azrin, N. H., V. A. Besalel, R. Bechtel, A. Michalicek, M. Mancera, D. Carroll, D. Shuford, and J. Cox. "Comparison of Reciprocity and Discussion-Type Counseling for Marital Problems." *The American Journal of Family Therapy* 8 (Winter 1980): 21-28.

Azrin, N. H., B. J. Naster, and R. Jones. "Reciprocity Counseling: A Rapid Learning Based Procedure for Marital Counseling." *Behavior Research and Therapy* 11 (1973): 365-382.

Bandura, A. "Self-Efficacy Mechanism in Human Agency." *American Psychologist* 37 (1982): 122-147.

Bandura, A. *Social Learning Theory.* Englewood Cliffs, NJ: Prentice-Hall, 1977.

Bandura, A. "Self-Efficacy: Toward a Unifying Theory of Behavioral Change." *Psychological Review* 84 (1977): 191-215.

Barnett, L. R., and M. T. Nietzel. "Relationship of Instrumental and Affectional Behaviors and Self-Esteem to Marital Satisfaction in Distressed and Nondistressed Couples." *Journal of Consulting and Clinical Psychology* 47 (1979): 946-957.

Beckfield, D. F., and R. M. McFall. "Development of a Competence Inventory for College Men and Evaluation of Relationships between Competence and Depression." *Journal of Consulting and Clinical Psychology* 50 (1982): 697-705.

Bentler, P. M., and M. D. Newcomb. "Longitudinal Study of Marital Success and Failure." *Journal of Consulting and Clinical Psychology* 46 (1978): 1053-1070.

Billings, A. "Conflict Resolution in Distressed and Nondistressed Married Couples." *Journal of Consulting and Clinical Psychology* 47 (1979): 368–376.

Birchler, G. R. "Improving Communication in Marriage." *Families Today* 1 (1979): 233–247.

Birchler, G. R., and L. J. Webb. "Discriminating Interaction in Behaviors in Happy and Unhappy Marriages." *Journal of Consulting and Clinical Psychology* 45 (1977): 494–495.

Birchler, G. R., R. L. Weiss, and J. P. Vincent. "A Multimethod Analysis of Social Reinforcement Exchange between Maritally Distressed and Nondistressed Spouse and Stranger Dyads." *Journal of Personality and Social Psychology* 31 (1975): 349–360.

Blechman, E. A. "Family Problem-Solving Training." *The American Journal of Family Therapy* 8 (1980): 3–21.

Bornstein, P. H., B. Anton, K. J. Harowski, R. T. Weltzien, T. J. McIntyre, and J. Hocker. "Behavioral-Communications Treatment of Marital Discord: Positive Behaviors." *Behavioral Counseling Quarterly* 1 (1981): 189–201.

Bornstein, P. H., P. J. Bach, J. F. Heider, and J. Ernst. "Clinical Treatment of Marital Dysfunction: A Multiple-Baseline Analysis." *Behavioral Assessment* 3 (1981): 335–343.

Bornstein, P. H., B. J. Balleweg, C. E. Weisser, S. G. Fox, K. L. Kirby, J. C. Andre, C. A. Sturm, G. L. Wilson, and R. W. McLellarn. "Treatment Acceptability of Alternative Marital Therapies: A Comparative Analysis." *Journal of Marital and Family Therapy* 9 (1983): 205–208.

Bornstein, P. H., and M. T. Bornstein. *Marital Therapy: A Behavioral Communications Approach.* New York: Pergamon Press, 1986.

Bornstein, P. H., D. C. Fisher, and B. J. Balleweg. "Problem-Solving in Couples: A Guide for Clinical Research and Applied Practice." *Scandinavian Journal of Behavior Therapy* 11 (1982): 1–13.

Bornstein, P. H., J. S. Hickey, M. J. Schulein, S. G. Fox, and M. J. Scolatti. "Behavioral-Communications Treatment of Marital Interaction: Negative Behaviors." *British Journal of Clinical Psychology* 22 (1983): 41–48.

Bornstein, P. H., and R. Quevillon. "The Effects of Self-Instructional Package on Overactive Boys." *Journal of Applied Behavior Analysis* 9 (1976): 179–188.

Bornstein, P. H., G. L. Wilson, B. J. Balleweg, C. E. Weisser, M. T. Bornstein, J. C. Andre, D. J. Woody, M. M. Smith, S. M. Laughna, R. W. McLellarn, K. L. Kirby, and J. Hocker. "Behavioral Marital Bibliotherapy: An Initial Investigation of Therapeutic Efficacy." *The American Journal of Family Therapy* 12 (1984): 21–28.

Bredehoft, D. J., and R. N. Hey. "An Evaluation Study of Self-Esteem: A Family Affair." *Family Relations* 34 (1985): 411–417.

Burke, R. J., and T. Weir. "Husband-Wife Helping Relationships As Moderators of Experienced Stress: The 'Mental Hygiene' Function in Marriage." In *Family Stress, Coping, and Social Support*, edited by H. I. McCubbin, A. E. Cauble, and J. M. Patterson. Springfield, IL: Charles C. Thomas, 1982.

Caplan, G. "The Family As a Support System." In *Support Systems and Mutual Help: Multidisciplinary Explorations*, edited by G. Caplan and M. Killilea. New York: Grune and Stratton, 1976.

Clarke, C. "Group Procedures for Increasing Positive Feedback between Married Partners." *The Family Coordinator* 19 (1970): 324-328.

Clinebell, H. J., and C. H. Clinebell. *The Intimate Marriage*. New York: Harper & Row, 1970.

Christensen, A., and D. C. Nies. "The Spouse Observation Checklist: Empirical Analysis and Critique." *The American Journal of Family Therapy* 8 (1980): 69-79.

Cooper, J. E., J. Holman, and V. A. Braithwaite. "Self-Esteem and Family Cohesion: The Child's Perspective and Adjustment." *Journal of Marriage and Family* 45 (1983): 153-159.

Curran, D. *Traits of a Healthy Family: Fifteen Traits Commonly Found in Healthy Families by Those Who Work with Them*. Minneapolis, MN: Winston Press, 1983.

Dillow, L. *Creative Counterpart*. New York: Thomas Nelson, 1977.

Doherty, W. J. "Attribution Style and Negative Problem Solving in Marriage." *Family Relations* 31 (1982): 23-27.

Doherty, W. J. "Cognitive Processes in Intimate Conflict: I. Extending Attribution Theory." *American Journal of Family Therapy* 9 (1981): 5-13.

Doherty, W. J. "Cognitive Processes in Intimate Conflict: II. Efficacy and Learned Helplessness." *American Journal of Family Therapy* 9 (1981): 35-44.

Eidelson, R. J., and N. Epstein. "Cognition and Relationship Maladjustment: Development of a Measure of Dysfunctional Relationship Beliefs." *Journal of Consulting and Clinical Psychology* 50 (1982): 715-720.

Epstein, N. "Cognitive Therapy with Couples." *American Journal of Family Therapy* 10 (1982): 5-16.

Epstein, N., and R. J. Eidelson. "Unrealistic Beliefs of Clinical Couples: Their Relationship to Expectations, Goals and Satisfaction." *American Journal of Family Therapy* 9 (1981): 13-22.

Filsinger, E. E., and R. A. Lewis. *Assessing Marriage: New Behavioral Approaches*. Beverly Hills, CA: Sage, 1981.

Fineberg, B. L., and J. Lowman. "Affect and Status Dimensions of Marital Adjustment." *Journal of Marriage and the Family* (February 1975): 155-159.

Floyd, F. J., and H. J. Markman. "Observational Biases in Spouse Observation: Toward a Cognitive-Behavioral Model of Marriage." *Journal of Consulting and Clinical Psychology* 51 (1983): 450–457.

Glick, B. R. and S. J. Gross. "Marital Interaction and Marital Conflict: A Critical Evaluation of Current Research Strategies." *Journal of Marriage and the Family* (August 1975): 505–512.

Gottman, J. M. *Marital Interaction: Experimental Investigations.* New York: Academic Press, 1979.

Gottman, J., H. Markman, and C. Notarius. "The Topography of Marital Conflict: A Sequential Analysis of Verbal and Nonverbal Behavior." *Journal of Marriage and the Family* 39 (1977): 461–477.

Gottman, J., C. Notarius, J. Gonso, and H. Markman. *A Couple's Guide to Communication.* Champaign, IL: Research Press, 1976.

Gottman, J. M., C. Notarius, H. Markman, S. Bank, B. Yoppi, and M. E. Rubin. "Behavior Exchange Theory and Marital Decision Making." *Journal of Personality and Social Psychology* 34 (1976): 14–23.

Gottman, J. M., and A. L. Porterfield. "Communicative Competence in Nonverbal Behavior of Married Couples." *Journal of Marriage and the Family* 43 (1981): 817–824.

Gurman, A. S., and R. M. Knudson, "Behavioral Marriage Therapy: I. A Psychodynamic-Systems Analysis and Critique." *Family Process* 17 (1978): 121–138.

Gurman, A. S., R. M. Knudson, and D. P. Kniskern. "Behavioral Marriage Therapy: III. Take Two Aspirin and Call Us in the Morning." *Family Process* 17 (1978): 165–180.

Harrell, J. and B. Guerney. "Training Married Couples in Conflict Negotiation Skills." In *Treating Relationships*, edited by D. H. Olson. Lake Mills, IA: Graphic Publishing, 1976.

Hickok, J. E., and M. G. Komechak. "Behavioral Modification in Marital Conflict: A Case Report." *Family Process* (1974): 111–119.

Jacobson, N. S. "Behavioral Treatments for Marital Discord: A Critical Appraisal." In *Progress in Behavioral Modification*, edited by M. Hersen, R. Eisler, and P. Miller. New York: Academic Press, 1980.

Jacobson, N. S. "A Component Analysis of Behavioral Marital Therapy: The Relative Effectiveness of Behavior Exchange and Communication/Problem-Solving Training." *Journal of Consulting and Clinical Psychology* 52 (1984): 295–305.

Jacobson, N. S. "Contingency Contracting with Couples: Redundancy and Caution." *Behavior Therapy* 9 (1978): 426–427.

Jacobson, N. S. "Increasing Positive Behaviors in Severely Distressed Adult Relationships: The Effectiveness of Problem-Solving Training." *Behavior Therapy* 10 (1979): 311–326.

Jacobson, N. S. "The Modification of Cognitive Processes in Behavioral Marital Therapy: Integration of Cognitive and Behavioral Intervention Strategies." In *Marital Interaction: Analysis and*

Modification, edited by K. Hahlweg and N. S. Jacobson. New York: Guilford, 1984.

Jacobson, N. S. "Problem Solving and Contingency Contracting in the Treatment of Marital Discord." *Journal of Consulting and Clinical Psychology* 45 (1977): 92–100.

Jacobson, N. S. "A Review of the Research on the Effectiveness of Marital Therapy." In *Marriage and Marital Therapy: Psychoanalytic, Behavioral, and Systems Theory Perspectives*, edited by T. J. Paolino and B. S. McCrady. New York: Brunner/Mazel, 1978.

Jacobson, N. S. "Specific and Nonspecific Factors in the Effectiveness of a Behavioral Approach to the Treatment of Marital Discord." *Journal of Consulting and Clinical Psychology* 46 (1978): 442–452.

Jacobson, N. S. "A Stimulus Control Model of Change in Behavioral Couples' Therapy: Implications for Contingency Contracting." *Journal of Marriage and Family Counseling* 4 (1978): 29–35.

Jacobson, N. S. "Training Couples to Solve Their Marital Problems: A Behavioral Approach to Relationship Discord." *International Journal of Family Counseling*. New York: Brunner/Mazel, 1977.

Jacobson, N. S., and E. A. Anderson. "The Effects of Behavior Rehearsal and Feedback on the Acquisition of Problem-Solving Skills in Distressed and Nondistressed Couples." *Behavior Research and Therapy* 18 (1980): 25–36.

Jacobson, N. S., R. Berley, K. N. Melman, R. Elwood, and C. Phelps. "Failure in Behavioral Marital Therapy." In *Failures in Family Therapy*, edited by S. Coleman. New York: Guilford Press, 1985.

Jacobson, N. S. and W. C. Follette. "Clinical Significance of Improvement Resulting from Two Behavioral Marital Therapy Components." *Behavior Therapy* 16 (1985): 249–262.

Jacobson, N. S., W. C. Follette, and R. W. Elwood. "Outcome Research on Behavioral Marital Therapy: A Methodological and Conceptual Reappraisal." In *Marital Interaction: Analysis and Modification*, edited by K. Hahlweg and N. S. Jacobson. New York: Guilford, 1984.

Jacobson, N. S., W. C. Follette, and D. W. McDonald. "Reactivity to Positive and Negative Behavior in Distressed and Nondistressed Married Couples." *Journal of Consulting and Clinical Psychology* 50 (1982): 706–714.

Jacobson, N. S. and G. Margolin. *Marital Therapy: Strategies Based on Social Learning and Behavior Exchange Principles*. New York: Brunner/Mazel, 1979.

Jacobson, N. S., D. W. McDonald, W. C. Follette, and R. A. Berley. "Attributional Processes in Distressed and Nondistressed Married Couples." *Cognitive Therapy and Research* 9 (1985): 35–50.

Jacobson, N. S., and D. Moore. "Spouses as Observers of the Events in Their Relationship." *Journal of Consulting and Clinical Psychology* 49 (1981): 269–277.

Jacobson, N. S., H. Waldron, and D. Moore. "Towards a Behavioral Profile of Marital Distress." *Journal of Consulting and Clinical Psychology* 48 (1980): 696–703.

Kelly, M. L., W. O. Scott, D. M. Prue, and R. G. Rychtarik. "A Component Analysis of Problem-Solving Skills Training." *Cognitive Therapy and Research* 9 (1985): 429–441.

Margolin, G. "Behavior Exchange in Happy and Unhappy Marriages: A Family Cycle Perspective." *Behavior Therapy* 12 (1981): 329–343.

Margolin, G., A. Christensen, and R. L. Weiss. "Contracts, Cognition, and Change: A Behavioral Approach to Marriage Therapy." *Counseling Psychologist* 5 (1975): 15–26.

Margolin, G., and B. E. Wampold. "Sequential Analysis of Conflict and Accord in Distressed and Nondistressed Marital Partners." *Journal of Consulting and Clinical Psychology* 49 (1981): 554–567.

Margolin, G., and R. L. Weiss. "Communication Training and Assessment: A Case of Behavioral Marital Enrichment." *Behavior Therapy* 9 (1978): 508–520.

Margolin, G., and R. L. Weiss. "A Comparative Evaluation of Therapeutic Components Associated with Behavioral Marital Treatment." *Journal of Consulting and Clinical Psychology* 46 (1978): 1476–1486.

Markman, H. J. "The Application of a Behavioral Model of Marriage in Predicting Relationship Satisfaction of Couples Planning Marriage." *Journal of Consulting and Clinical Psychology* 4 (1979): 743–749.

Markman, H. J. "Prediction of Marital Distress: A 5-year Follow-up." *Journal of Consulting and Clinical Psychology* 49 (1981): 760–762.

Markman, H. J., and F. Floyd. "Possibilities for the Prevention of Marital Discord: A Behavioral Perspective." *American Journal of Family Therapy* 8 (1980): 29–48.

Mason, M. *The Mystery of Marriage.* Portland, OR: Multnomah Press, 1985.

Mehrabian, A. *Nonverbal Communication.* Chicago, IL: Aldine Atherton, 1972.

Meichenbaum, D. H. *Cognitive-Behavior Modification.* New York: Plenum Press, 1977.

Miller, S., E. Nunnally, and D. Wackman. *Alive and Aware.* Minneapolis, MN: Interpersonal Communications Program, 1975.

Murstein, B. I., and G. D. Beck. "Person Perception, Marriage Adjustment, and Social Desirability." *Journal of Consulting and Clinical Psychology* 39 (1972): 396–403.

Nelson, R. O. "Realistic Dependent Measures for Clinical Use." *Journal of Consulting and Clinical Psychology* 49 (1981): 168–182.

Nesselroade, J. R., and S. M. Stigler. "Regression Toward the Mean and the Study of Change." *Psychological Bulletin* 88 (1980): 622–637.

Neuringer, C. and J. L. Michael. *Behavior Modification in Clinical Psychology*. New York: Appleton-Century-Crofts, 1970.

Noller, P. *Nonverbal Communication and Marital Interaction*. New York: Pergamon Press, 1984.

O'Farrell, T. J., and H. S. G. Cutter. "Behavioral Marital Therapy for Male Alcoholics: Clinical Procedures from a Treatment Outcome Study in Progress." *The American Journal of Family Therapy* 12 (1984): 33–46.

O'Leary, K. D., and H. Turkewitz. "A Comparative Outcome Study of Behavioral Marital Therapy and Communication Therapy." *Journal of Marital and Family Therapy* 7 (1981): 159–169.

O'Leary, K. D., and H. Turkewitz. "Methodological Errors in Marital and Child Treatment Research." *Journal of Consulting and Clinical Psychology* 46 (1978): 747–758.

O'Leary, K. D., and H. Turkewitz. "The Treatment of Marital Disorders from a Behavioral Perspective." In *Marriage and Marital Therapy: Psychoanalytic, Behavioral, and Systems Theory Perspectives*, edited by T. J. Paolino and B. S. McCrady. New York: Brunner/Mazel, 1978.

Olson, D. H., ed. *Treating Relationships*. Lake Mills, IA: Graphic Publishing, 1976.

Olson, D. H., H. I. McCubbin, H. L. Barnes, A. S. Larsen, M. J. Muxen, and M. A. Wilson. *Families: What Makes Them Work*. Beverly Hills: Sage, 1983.

Patterson, G. R., H. Hops, and R. L. Weiss. "Interpersonal Skills Training for Couples in Early Stages of Conflict." *Journal of Marriage and the Family* (May 1975): 295–302.

Patterson, G. R., and J. B. Reid. "Reciprocity and Coercion: Two Facets of Social Systems." In *Behavior Modification in Clinical Psychology*, edited by C. Neuringer and J. Michael. New York: Appleton-Century-Crofts, 1970.

Pittman, J. F., S. Bonham, and P. C. McKenry. "Marital Cohesion: A Path Model." *Journal of Marriage and Family* (August 1983): 521–530.

Rappaport, A. F., and J. A. Harrell. "A Behavioral Exchange Model for Marital Counseling." In *Couples in Conflict*, edited by A. S. Gurman and D. G. Rice. New York: Jason Aronsen, 1975.

Raush, H. L., W. A. Barry, R. K. Hertel, and M. A. Swain. *Communication, Conflict and Marriage*. San Francisco: Jossey-Bass, 1974.

Rettig, K. D., and M. M. Bulboz. "Interpersonal Resource Exchanges As Indicators of Quality of Marriage." *Journal of Marriage and the Family* 45 (1983): 497–509.

Robin, A. L. "A Controlled Evaluation of Problem-Solving Communication Training with Parent-Adolescent Conflict." *Behavior Therapy* 12 (1981): 593–609.

Robinson, E. A., and M. G. Price. "Pleasurable Behavior in Marital Interaction: An Observational Study." *Journal of Consulting and Clinical Psychology* 48 (1980): 117–118.

Spanier, G. B. "Measuring Dyadic Adjustment: New Scales for Assessing the Quality of Marriage and Similar Dyads." *Journal of Marriage and the Family* 38 (1976): 15–28.

Spanier, G. B., R. A. Lewis, and C. L. Cole. "Marital Adjustment over the Family Life Cycle: The Issue of Curvilinearity." *Journal of Marriage and the Family* (May 1975): 263–275.

Spinks, S. H., and G. R. Birchler. "Behavioral-Systems Marital Therapy: Dealing with Resistance." *Family Process* 21 (1982): 169–185.

Stewart, J., ed. *Bridges Not Walls: A Book about Interpersonal Communication.* New York: Random House, 1986.

Stuart, R. B. "Behavioral Remedies for Marital Ills: A Guide to the Use of Operant-Interpersonal Techniques." In *Couples in Conflict,* edited by A. S. Gurman and D. G. Rice. New York: Jason Aronson, 1975.

Stuart, R. B. *Helping Couples Change: A Social Learning Approach to Marital Therapy.* New York: Guilford Press, 1980.

Stuart, R. B. "Operant-Interpersonal Treatment for Marital Discord." *Journal of Consulting and Clinical Psychology* 33 (1969): 675–682.

Sullaway, M., and A. Christensen. "Assessment of Dysfunctional Interaction Patterns in Couples." *Journal of Marriage and the Family* (August 1983): 653–660.

Tearnan, B., and J. R. Lutzker. "A Contracting 'Package' in the Treatment of Marital Problems: A Case Study." *The American Journal of Family Therapy* 8 (Spring 1980): 24–31.

Thibaut, J. W., and H. H. Kelley. *The Social Psychology of Groups.* New York: Wiley, 1959.

Thomas, E. J. *Marital Communication and Decision-Making.* New York: The Free Press, 1977.

Turkewitz, H., and K. D. O'Leary. "A Comparative Outcome Study of Behavioral Marital Therapy." *Journal of Marital and Family Therapy* 7 (1981): 159–170.

Vincent, J. P., L. L. Friedman, J. Nugent, and L. Messerly. "Demand Characteristics in Observations of Marital Interaction." *Journal of Consulting and Clinical Psychology* 47 (1979): 557–566.

Vincent, J. P., R. L. Weiss, and G. R. Birchler. "A Behavioral Analysis of Problem-Solving in Distressed and Nondistressed Married and Stranger Dyads." *Behavior Therapy* 6 (1975): 475–487.

Watzlawick, P., J. H. Beavin, and D. D. Jackson. *Pragmatics of Human Communication.* New York: Norton, 1967.

Weiss, R. L. "Cognitive and Behavioral Measures of Marital Interaction." In *Marital Interaction,* edited by K. Hahlweg and N. Jacobson. New York: The Guilford Press, 1984.

Weiss, R. L. "The Conceptualization of Marriage from a Behavioral Perspective." In *Marriage and Marital Therapy: Psychoanalytic, Behavioral, and Systems Perspectives*, edited by T. J. Paolino and B. S. McCrady. New York: Brunner/Mazel, 1978.

Weiss, R. L. "Contracts, Cognition, and Change: A Behavioral Approach to Marriage Therapy." *The Counseling Psychologist* 5 (1975): 15–26.

Weiss, R. L. "Strategic Behavioral Marital Therapy: Toward a Model for Assessment and Intervention." In *Advances in Family Intervention, Assessment and Theory* (Vol. 1), edited by J. P. Vincent. Greenwich, CT: JAI Press, 1980.

Weiss, R. L., G. R. Birchler, and J. P. Vincent. "Contractual Models for Negotiation Training in Marital Dyads." *Journal of Marriage and the Family* 36 (1974): 321–331.

Weiss, R. L., H. Hops, and G. R. Patterson. "A Framework for Conceptualizing Marital Conflict, Technology for Altering It, Some Data for Evaluating It." In *Behavior Change: Methodology, Concepts, and Practice*, edited by L. A. Hamerlynck, L. C. Handy, and E. J. Mash. Champaign, IL: Research Press, 1973.

Weiss, R. L., and G. Margolin. "Assessment of Marital Conflict and Accord." In *Handbook of Behavioral Assessment*, edited by A. R. Ciminero, H. Adams, and K. Calhoun. New York: Wiley, 1977.

White, S. G., and C. Hatcher. "Couple Complementarity and Similarity: A Review of the Literature." *American Journal of Family Therapy* 12 (1984): 15–25.

Widra, J. M. and E. Amidon. "Improving Self-Concept Through Intimacy Group Training." *Small Group Behavior* 18 (1987): 269–279.

Williams, A. M. "The Quantity and Quality of Marital Interaction Related to Marital Satisfaction: A Behavioral Analysis." *Journal of Applied Behavior Analysis* 12 (1979): 665–678.

Wills, T. A., R. L. Weiss, and G. R. Patterson. "A Behavioral Analysis of the Determinants of Marital Satisfaction." *Journal of Consulting and Clinical Psychology* 42 (1974): 802–811.

Witkin, S. L., J. L. Edleson, S. D. Rose, and J. A. Hall. "Group Training in Marital Communication: A Comparative Study." *Journal of Marriage and the Family* 45 (1983): 661–669.

Wood, L. F. and N. S. Jacobson. "Marital Distress." In *Clinical Handbook of Psychological Disorders*, edited by D. H. Barlow. New York: The Guilford Press, 1985.

Wright, J., and C. Fichten. "Denial of Responsibility, Videotape Feedback and Attribution Theory: Relevance for Behavioral Marital Therapy." *Canadian Psychology Review* 17 (1976): 219–230.